The Bodies Beneath

THE BODIES BENEATH

The Flipside of British Film & Television

William Fowler and Vic Pratt

The Bodies Beneath: The Flipside of British Film and Television
by William Fowler and Vic Pratt
Published by Strange Attractor Press 2019
ISBN: 978-1-907222-72-6

Layout by Rachel Sale

Strange Attractor Press
BM SAP, London, WC1N 3XX, UK
www.strangeattractor.co.uk

Distributed by The MIT Press, Cambridge, Massachusetts.
And London, England.

Printed and bound in Estonia by Tallinna Raamatutrükikoda.

CONTENTS

COME OVER TO THE FLIPSIDE

'The off-beat...the uninhibited...the scintillating...the intriguing!'

The Flipside was a regular cinema strand that we developed and programmed at BFI Southbank, London, from 2006 to 2013 that was designed to showcase strange, unusual and unexpected film and television, and it developed into a Blu-ray and DVD brand, BFI Flipside, that runs to this day. Both began with one particular film; a film that, years previously and entirely independently of each other, we had both longed to see, without ever seriously thinking that we would: Arnold Miller and Stanley Long's *Primitive London* (1965).

It was apparently a British 'mondo' film: a homegrown example of a strange and briefly popular genre of pseudo-documentary emanating from Italy in the early 1960s. Mondo films fused a bewildering assortment of documentary bits and pieces with blood, guts and titillation – censors permitting – usually interspersed with a dry and somewhat sanctimonious voice-over commentary. Will had spotted the film amidst the lurid video sleeves depicted in *The Art of the Nasty*, a 1998 book of sleazy VHS releases by Marc Morris and Nigel Wingrove. He'd been fascinated by the sensational sleeve art depicting a statuesque woman in a leopard-skin bikini

‹ **Bare breasts**: Stanley Long chases the chicken shot for *Primitive London* (1965).

erupting from a map of London. A brief synopsis noted that the film had been made by Compton-Cameo Films, an independent precursor to Tigon British Film Productions, and that it boasted rare interviews with mods and rockers. Shot in 1965, on the cusp of the whole Swinging London thing, it had appeared on home video in the early 1980s, before promptly disappearing, again, into the ether. Vic had seen an article about the film, and had even read a review in the pages of that august journal of record, *The Monthly Film Bulletin*. Though it had been dismissed by their reviewer in no uncertain terms, it was hard to believe that any film featuring a leopard girl, a corn removal operation, and the truth about roast chicken dinners could be unworthy of a viewer's attention.

What, then, was the film actually like? And, more importantly, how would we ever see it? *Primitive London*, and umpteen more like it, seemed to have slipped, entirely unmourned, from the film-history radar. It was hardly at the top of the list for cinematheque reappraisals, and the pre-2000 internet revealed little. As luck would have it, fate would soon bring us, and the film, together.

In 2005, Will got a job at the BFI National Archive, where Vic had been employed as a film archivist since 1998. Our mutual excitement led us to check the archive's holdings on the film, and we discovered that 35mm materials were held and, what's more, a VHS viewing tape! We called it up from the vaults, consumed its glories, and began to conspire…

So what was it like? It was just as 'mondo' as *Mondo Cane* (1962) the sleazy Italian semi-documentary that kick-started the genre, but this Blighty-born example seemed to have been shot through an oddly fusty filter of parochial Britishness. Yes, here, as in Italy, everything – shocking, silly, salacious or stupid – looked zingy, vivid, and visually exciting; in this case courtesy of Stanley Long's unfailingly powerful photography. Yet amidst the gloss could be glimpsed the grubbiness. With National Service finally coming to an end, short back and sides were de rigeur: everybody was outwardly so respectable, yet many faces might also have borne the traces of last night's booze-up, skin puffy, pink, capillarised. Everyone wore a smart suit; yet one still had the sense that it could all have fallen apart in a moment.

Mondo was a film movement made for post-war Britain, at a moment when, perhaps, many viewers both feared and longed for some kind – any kind – of 'swinging' action. Sensational change was on the way; or so this film – both hopeful and horrified – suggested. The mods were mad and ate cat food, whilst a spotty teenager, smoking a pipe in a pub, suggested that 'if a man and woman love each other, they are married'. Meanwhile, you get to see what goes on within the chicken slaughterhouse, to the accompaniment of an eerie early electronic cacophony. No Beatles here – by 1965, they were already far too expensive.

Amidst the supposed sensations of things like topless swimsuits – chopped by the censors, inevitably – it shone a light on the things other documentarians would not touch, filling in more gaps – almost making more sense – than other, more highly-regarded examples of cinema. It was a forgotten, subterranean circuit-board for all kinds of components of the cultural experience of the capital. As it showed, there was a clear and direct, if unarticulated, link from all those fancy new Soho restaurants to that battery-chicken abattoir. Yes, this was a cynical film; sensational, undoubtedly; filled with lies, of course; yet didn't it, paradoxically perhaps, somehow speak some honest truths, absent from the other kind of documentary?

We thought so, and were greatly honoured with the opportunity to screen it at exactly the kind of cinema it had never played upon release: the National Film Theatre (now BFI Southbank). We invited Stanley Long to introduce the screening, and he arrived in a smart, chauffeur-driven car; immaculately turned out, for this, his first celebration by 'the establishment', in a sharp black suit, black shirt, and cravat. Reminding us of his integral role in making the film, which is credited on screen as being solely directed by his one-time collaborator Arnold Miller, he came out with various gossipy tit-bits of information. Derek Ford, he noted, had written all the narration. It figured: he often wrote for Compton-Cameo at the time, and the writing's cynical tone didn't fit its credited author, Arnold Miller. But Ford wasn't credited. Why not? Stanley also reminded us that *Primitive London* was merely a stepping stone on the path to far greater successes, including the film that made him his first million, *The Wife Swappers* (1970), which he produced, and co-wrote with Ford, and his money-spinning series of smut comedies, *The Adventures of…* trilogy. But despite remembering *Primitive London* as a minor work (perhaps because he didn't own the copyright) he was delighted to be in the limelight, accompanied on stage after the screening by comedy-legend Barry Cryer who, as a youngster, had played a baffling bit-part in some faked-up coffee-commercial scenes. The indefatigable Mr Cryer entertained the audience, telling them he'd never

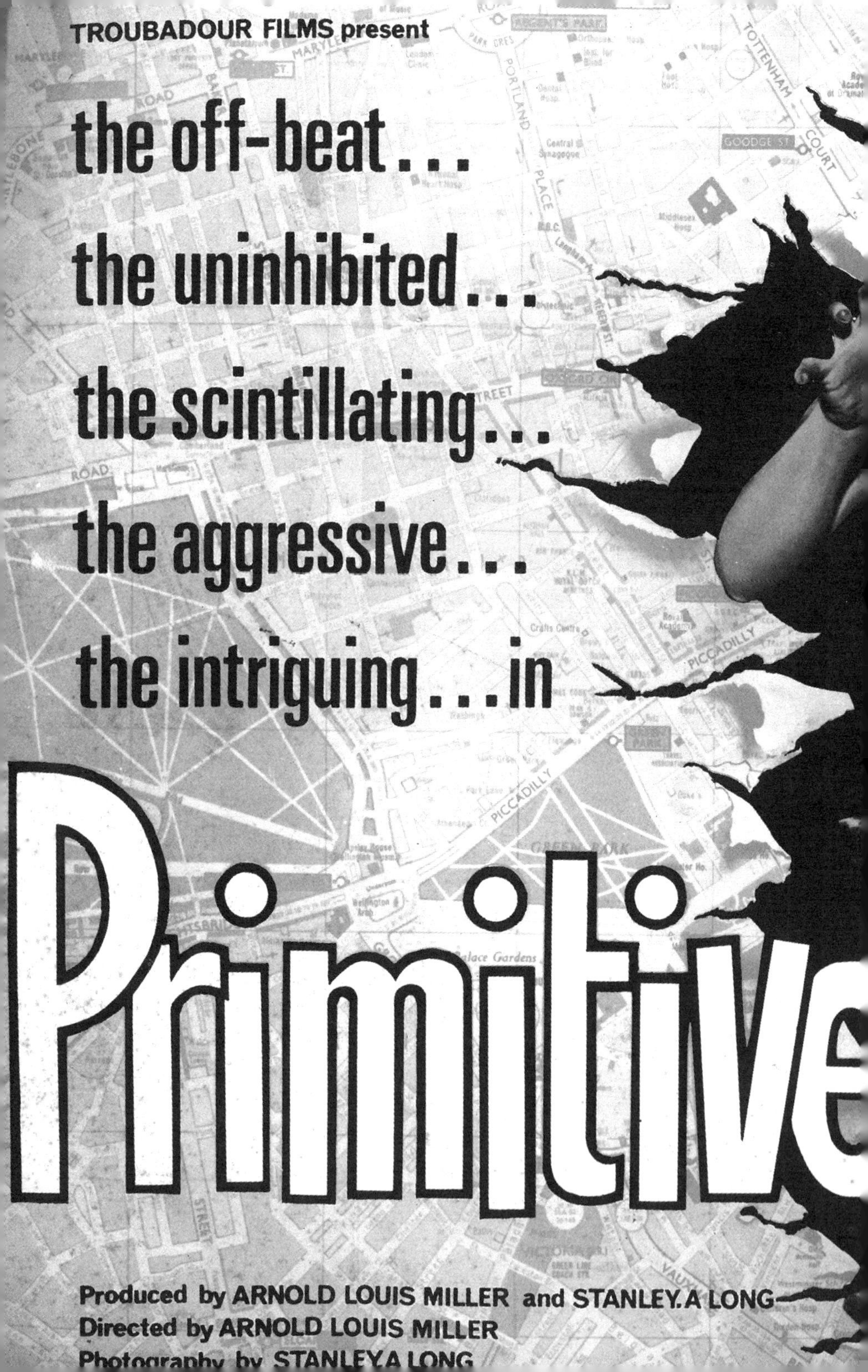
TROUBADOUR FILMS present
the off-beat...
the uninhibited...
the scintillating...
the aggressive...
the intriguing...in
Primitive
Produced by ARNOLD LOUIS MILLER and STANLEY.A LONG
Directed by ARNOLD LOUIS MILLER
Photography by STANLEY.A LONG

London

« **The leopard girl bares her teeth:** original quad poster for *Primitive London* (1965).

seen the film before. At the time, he'd stayed away: his friends had told him it was a porno.

So many forgotten connections on the lost pop-culture circuit board, if you care to look. The aforementioned Derek Ford – a man still-less celebrated than even Long and Miller – had later written and directed a witchcraft 'documentary', *Secret Rites* (1971), which we also recovered from the vaults and screened in our Flipside slot. We'd already learned from John Hamilton's excellent 2005 book *Beasts in the Cellar: The Exploitation Film Career of Tony Tenser* that Ford had been something of a pioneer when it came to the blurring of documentary modes with scripted fictions. The results, perhaps unwittingly, took the films in more edgy, even experimental, directions than some of the docudramas that appeared in ground-breaking British television strands like *Play for Today*. So *Primitive London*, as an early work in this lineage, was – like it or not – unavoidably connected to this more respected successor and, more broadly, to the bigger picture of British film and television history.

British film history is all linked up, in ways you wouldn't expect. One of the shocks and pleasures of that night we screened *Primitive London* was welcoming one of Stanley's guests – the legendary cameraman Jack Cardiff. Cardiff lived near Long and the two were firm friends, despite their very different cinematic pedigrees. They formed part of a loose social circle of celebrities, media-types, musicians, artists, actors and filmmaking folk which also included David Van Day of pop duo Dollar, 60s heart-throb Jess Conrad, pantomime dame-deluxe Christopher Biggins, songstress Anita Harris, and the bloke who played Nick Cotton in the BBC soap opera *EastEnders* (1985-). Together at last, for one night only, were the man who'd shot *A Matter of Life and Death* (1946) for those darlings of British cinema, Powell and Pressburger, and the man who'd shot *The Adventures of a Plumber's Mate* (1978). Both were up to no good at all after the screening, indulging in some slightly outrageous elderly-boyish revelry at Stringfellows.

It was a weird and surreal scenario; as incongruous, in its way, as the intercutting of the scenes of London life in the film we'd just watched. We were invited along, but sat at a separate table with Stanley's chauffeur, who

Dinner date: the authors out on the town in London with Stanley Long in 2007.

seemed keen to impress upon us that he wasn't, in fact, a chauffeur. Beneath the surface, there were always strange truths. *Primitive London*, on this odd night, had again united divergent forces. What did Jack really think of Stanley's film? What did Stanley think of Jack's films? We'll never know. Many would consider it heresy to speak of Cardiff and Long's work in the same breath; but they instinctively sensed a whole series of connections upon which we, as outsiders attempting to construct our own hack version of history, can only speculate.

Of course the films and programmes within these pages, like so many others, were not necessarily deliberately dismissed and (temporarily) lost to time. Many fell into obscurity for other, more pragmatic reasons: in a world of ever more stuff to watch, they may have become lost amidst the whirl of an ever-expanding visual culture that increasingly blurs the lines between new and old, yet remains reliant on methods and means of access, delivery and visibility.

Unless the film artefact under discussion is available for all to see, and a sign post is erected to lead you to it, how can it be found? *Primitive London* disappeared after its first run, not because of adverse criticism but because it had served its function as an ephemeral, sensational near-newsreel and was thus quickly out of date. Like so many independent, non-canonical films, it had not, until now, been loved, looked after, logged, or catalogued, or its memory maintained and represented in the way more critically respected titles have been.

This isn't to suggest that critical canons aren't valuable – but those films' continued representation as the only valid examples of British filmmaking tends to obscure the colossal heap of titles upon which they form only the uppermost pinnacles. Cinema classics – regularly lavished with money, attention, and, holiest of all holies, restoration – will always have the upper-hand; such is the way of things.

Of course, such neglect can generate another kind of aura, a decidedly unholy one: the outsider status of the forgotten, forbidden or neglected 'cult' film.

But what if the film in question doesn't lend itself to a sing-along as readily as *The Rocky Horror Picture Show* (1975)? Some 'cult' films lose their exotic edge when seen in the zingy 4K digital scan of daylight, but, for the most part, to see a film in its intended cut and correct ratio – not panned and scanned, or squashed for television broadcast – is to have a significantly improved viewing experience. An example: Italian director Lucio Fulci's UK-shot *The Black Cat* (1981). A minor film amidst many with the same name, it arguably has much to commend it. For a start, this latter-day reworking of the Poe prototype boasts the glory of a splendid performance by much-missed, oft-neglected, beetle-browed master-thesp Patrick Magee. Maligned and chopped about in the past, this film slipped through the cracks of critical consciousness. But just look what a lavishing of love and attention can do: recent years have seen it sharply reissued and crisply represented on Blu-ray. Suddenly, it seems more significant. Thus revitalised, even filmic footnotes like this one – and footnotes to the footnotes – might start to re-embed themselves within a newly conceived film history – or, dare we suggest, an all-embracing canon.

A handful of remaining home-entertainment labels presiding over a smaller, but still lively market of viewers who still love beautiful objects, are now presenting a far wider range of films, in a wider variety of ways, than anyone could have dreamt possible back in the days of VHS; let alone back when you had to get the Pathescope 9.5mm projector out of the loft. And it would seem that this new era's attention to those films that have been historically less lauded has also had an effect on what would be called a 'cult' film. Have the original 'cult' films, as first celebrated by such pioneering film-writers as Danny Peary back in the 1980s – *The Wicker Man* (1973), *Quadrophenia* (1979), *Withnail and I* (1987) – more recently become part of the 'mainstream' canon? And nowadays, in marketing terms, has the term 'cult' come merely to signify a genre film? We're not attempting to dictate with this book what is 'cult' and what isn't. This book is, though, a part of our own personal mission to figure it all out, in an enjoyable way, in our own minds, rather than allowing traditional cultural guardians or marketing departments to decide for us.

The titles in this book, then, are a selection of those films we're most fascinated by and which we think speak to, or highlight, larger patterns in the lesser-explored territories of British film and television – some of them are even very good *and* unusual. We're generally of the opinion that pretty much everything is worth a look, and it's all part of the bigger picture. You'll find the occasional acknowledged classic included here, shamelessly placed alongside stuff that obviously isn't so great. We're not necessarily trying to argue that high regard for one and low regard for the other is wrong, but we do think that every film or programme we've written about here has something special and exciting about it, and we definitely believe that even the duffest of these selections constitute important aspects of an incompletely-mapped moving-image landscape, which is in need of many more years of extensive survey work.

The liberalisation of censorship laws in the UK over the decades has meant that many once-shocking films have become harder to place contextually in relation to the time of their original release, and it has become harder to understand the furore that once surrounded them. Often, watching such works can be a precarious process of trying to tunnel back to a time when they were considered dangerous, and appreciating them simultaneously as they once were, as they seem now and within the context of what has happened in the world at large between those two points. Let's take a well-known example: the original *Dracula* (1931). Before you can even begin to creep up on this dearly beloved but sometimes creaky chiller you have to displace in your own modern mind multiple generations of sequels, pastiches, clichés, social changes, cynicisms, modernism, post-modernism and other immeasurable cultural shifts…and it is not easy – it may even be impossible. But luckily despite the difficulty there still remains something truly wonderful embedded within this film. The immediate power it once had has obviously been disrupted by all that's come after – and so we need to realign our process of watching it in advance in order to get as much out of it as we can. We're endeavouring to do that with all the films and programmes in this book – and we hope that you will, too.

Our selection begins in the very early days of cinema and concludes in the run up to the 1990 UK Broadcasting Act, which triggered the deregulation of television and the creation of Channel 5 and the UK's first ever satellite television stations, Sky Television PLC and British Satellite Broadcasting. Also, more titles became available on VHS and, by the end of the 1990s, DVD had become a serious concern, further affecting viewing habits. And then of course there came the internet.

What interested us about the earlier phase – ending in the late 1980s, covering approximately ninety-years-worth of moving image creation and exhibition – was the extreme variation and proliferation of production that had been possible within a comparatively narrow media bandwidth. For the most part, until the full-blossoming of home video, viewing structures were heavily controlled due to censorship, the limits of film distribution and the paltry number of television stations – only three until 1981 – all of which determined what was shown, when and how. Yet so much creatively extraordinary and bewildering work was made, much of which still remains beneath the radar. And that's where *The Bodies Beneath* comes in.

The return of the repressed can take weirder and stranger forms than one sometimes expects, and we admit that our choices can be wilfully personal and erratic, reflecting our own eccentricities as archivists, viewers and weirdos. We hope you'll trust us as your guides as we veer deep into obscure cultural hinterlands, and the realms of the awkward and unloved. It's a long meandering journey, and yet the titles we've unearthed so far, after many years of painful spadework, represent just a handful of the artefacts that await rediscovery.

Others lie buried deeper still – there are plenty more bodies beneath.

William Fowler and Vic Pratt

PROLOGUE

By Nicolas Winding Refn

Flipside is Punk Rock.

Their obsessive dedication to searching out obscure films and missing links of British pop cinema brings glorious results.

Their vast diversity of films shows us that British cinema can be many things and since England has one of the most significant film histories, it is important that we not just focus on the obvious but put equal emphasis on the obscure. Bringing life to the forgotten is a noble gesture for true cinephiles.

What I love about Flipside's attitude is that they go against what is traditionally considered 'good taste,' thereby preserving the rich world of film for cinephiles of generations to come. For that single reason, Flipside will go down in history as the ultimate Punk Rock film label.

ACKNOWLEDGEMENTS

In 2009, the monthly Flipside cinema strand we originated expanded to become a Blu-Ray and DVD imprint run by the BFI Video Publishing department. We would like to thank Sam Dunn and Jane Giles who made that happen. The four of us worked in direct collaboration on the concept, and on all the early releases, establishing and shaping the Flipside idea. The 'brand' still continues.

Laura Adams, Nigel Algar, Upekha Bandaranayake, Shona Barrett, James Bell, Eddie Berg, James Blackford, Charlie Bligh, Grant Boult, Jo Botting, Stuart Brown, John Curran, Simon Duffy, Maggi Hurt, John McKnight, Julian Marsh III, Sonia Mullett, John Oliver, Julie Pearce, Marcus Prince, John Ramchandani, Jill Reading, Phil Roberts, Peter Stanley, Ben Stoddart, Trevona Thomson and Douglas Weir all worked with us and have been part of the Flipside – and all other associated events and activities – and we have truly appreciated all their help and good company.

This book has been a long time coming, having been written slowly around other larger events in our lives, and we are grateful to Maya and Stuart Brisley, Gareth Evans, Will Fowler (Snr), Matthew Harle, John Henderson, Kate Lees, Ian Ryan, Sukhdev Sandhu, Virginie Selavy, Michael Winner, Rob Young and Nicolas Winding Refn for all their help, support and encouragement. A special thank you to Mark Pilkington for suggesting the book be written, and to he and his colleague Jamie Sutcliffe at Strange Attractor Press for then patiently waiting many years for it to be completed. Thanks also to Rachel Sale for her splendid work designing this volume.

Many kind people, notably Tony Bicât, Steve Dwoskin, Cosey Fanni Tutti, Derek Hill, Jeff Keen, Stella Keen, Bruce Lacey, Stanley Long, Barry Miles, Stuart Pound, Tony Rayns, Zoe Simon, Peter Whitehead, Michael Whyte and Terry Wilson, spoke to us about cinema and their British-film lives. Thank you all – and anybody we have inadvertently forgotten to acknowledge here – for so generously giving of your time, support and assistance.

Deborah Allison, Jenny Hammerton, Justin Harries, Jane Giles, Travis Miles, Leigh Milsom Fowler, Mark Pilkington and Corinna Reicher took the time to read early versions of *The Bodies Beneath* and gave perceptive, vital feedback that helped steer its final shape. Reading a rough long draft of anything is no small enterprise and we sincerely thank them.

Will would like to say a personal thank you for all love, support and encouragement, now and always, to: Leigh Milsom Fowler, Stephen Fowler and Helen, Nolan, Dominic and Harriet Price. His contributions are dedicated to the memories of Jenifer Fowler and Hugh Fowler.

Vic would like to say a personal thank you to Deborah Allison, for her love, support and encouragement. My part of this volume is dedicated to her. Additionally, I proffer grateful thanks to my splendid chums Jenny, Corinna and Jane. I'd like to thank my Paw, lifelong cineaste Alan Pratt, who got me into films, books and comics in the first place; and to express my gratitude for the encouragement of Alix, Egg, Jac and Steve, not forgetting my book-loving nephew and niece, Ben and Becky. I tip my titfer towards fellow *Lord Tramp* fans Jan and Diana Manthey; and am grateful for the endless encouragement of Jo Botting. Lastly, I'd like to thank artist, writer and all-round good egg Anna O'Brien, who, amidst her other, rather more significant acts of life-saving, helped me shape portions of the text into their earliest drafts, long, long ago.

This whole enterprise was founded on curiosity, friendship and enthusiasm and we would like to say a final thank you to anyone who came to the Flipside screenings or who has shown interest in the DVD and Blu-ray label, as well as to our fellow cinephiles, film freaks, nerds and weirdos everywhere. We hope you understand.

THE TUNNEL OF LOVE

If you bite your stiff upper-lip you might be inclined to confess that the British have always had something of an unusual attitude towards romance, love, sex and marriage; and that this has been reflected in our national cinema. Certainly, there is a reserve about it. Even in the comparatively liberal times in which we live today – when, theoretically at least, we can let it all hang out – many Brits still seem to prefer to keep it all in. Back in the day it appeared at least to be more straightforward. Let's look for a moment towards David Lean's still-resonant archetypal British love story, *Brief Encounter* (1945). In this affecting tale of railway-station liaisons between two middle-class marrieds, the naughty-but-nice couple are far more comfortable chuckling snootily over a below-par cello quartet in a corner café than illicitly getting it on. In fact, their near-dalliance ends almost before it begins with a chaste return to suburban safety with their respective dull but dependable partners. Sighs of relief are breathed all round, and no doubt cucumber sandwiches are served on the lawn.

And if this was a particularly middle-class mythos for the toffee-nosed townies for the avoidance of carnal cinema, out in the regions they had their own hang-ups. The provincial audiences had their on screen love, romance and unmentionables filtered through the historic humour of the saucy

‹ **Eyes on the prize:** *Secrets of Sex* (1970).

seaside postcard. They chuckled over the antics of common-man clowns like wide-grinned George Formby, who hid his expressions of love behind the earthy innuendos of cheeky songs involving window cleaners, flanelette nightshirts, and little sticks of Blackpool rock, brilliantly knocked out on his bawdy little banjulele. Through a string of cheery comedies like *No Limit* (1935) and *Keep Fit* (1937) he played a gormless child-man, hopelessly coy around the ladies, only capable of whacking it out via his instrument; and even though eventually he adopted an unusually adult persona in Ealing's *Turned Out Nice Again* (1941), portraying a married underwear salesman, with a pretty young wife, both of them eager to go upstairs of an evening, he still couched his compassion within the safe-space of his naughty songs. 'You can't go wrong in these,' he chirrups suggestively, at a foundation-wear sales fair, charmingly upstaging the clever-clogs Londoners as usual, but still ensuring it's all neatly stowed away, somewhere behind that enigmatic face-splitting Cheshire-cat grin of his.

A predilection towards libidinal secrecy, doing it very much behind closed doors, preferably in a bed, and most certainly in the missionary position, hasn't just affected our attitudes to the carnal deed; it has also meant that the fuller gamut of sexuality and sexual experience has thus found expression through some unusual and unexpected modes of filmmaking. As homosexuality was criminalised prior to the Sexual Offences Act of 1967, Caribbean actor, later director, Lloyd Reckord was daring indeed to make *Dream A40* in 1965, only properly released in more-liberal 1971, by which time it could be more explicitly appreciated as a low-key film about gay relationships and the authoritarian state. It was set on the road from Fishguard to Wales, but drew on European and American influences by way of Jean Cocteau and Kenneth Anger. It was both parochial and international.

And so too, in his way, was the sixties TV and movie secret agent: James Bond, and the many imitations that came after. Sleeping around with importunity, and moving up and down the social strata with slippery ease, dressing up, adopting disguises, and assuming all manner of alternative personas, he – it was usually a he – was a proto-rock star, representing sexual proclivity and flexibility, in the depressive Cold War period and later. James Bond was the top gun, of course, but there were numerous other spy adventurers too, and they were all at it. Except, that is, for John Drake,

TV's *Danger Man* (1960-62 & 1964-67), played by Patrick McGoohan, an actor who didn't just resist the permissive age but actively and aggressively condemned it, sometimes even taking it out on his female co-stars, some alleged. An angry man, by his own admission as well as by that of others, also charismatic and broodingly handsome, his sexual allure was undeniably a powerful one; but oddly, in those times, perhaps, one that centred on restraint, denial even. His approach and way of being certainly cut against the thrust of that oh-so-swinging decade, complicating what sex and sexuality meant.

Speaking of the 1960s, ad-man and producer Alan Parker said later in the midst of that most reactionary decade, the 1980s: 'whatever the Swinging Sixties are going to be remembered for it won't be the films. The moment you saw a red London bus go through a shot, you knew you were in for a rotten time.' And yet, courtesy of the groovy songs on the radio, and the arrival of the contraceptive pill that freed up carnal desire in whole new ways, the era's cinema did loosen up our views and visions of sex and relationships, and it continues to exert a powerful impact today, in terms of style and sexuality. Rita Tushingham was open to unmarried desire and love in *Girl with Green Eyes* (1964), and Oliver Reed cheerfully did it with countless women in *I'll Never Forget What's 'IsName* (1967), to name just two. The self-medication of post-war depression plus the media quickly brought about what would become known as 'the permissive age'.

It took years for the censor to fully catch-up, however, and Antony Balch's *Secrets of Sex* (1970) – the title says it all, about British cinema, and society – was held in censorial lock-down for months. And it wasn't because of Balch's gay or experimental leanings. For all the coyness that resonates through British cinema of the Lean or Formby variety, and further afield, there was another kind of film, a type of cinema that Balch's movie just about belonged to, and which goes right back to the beginning. The sex film.

Nameless purveyors of erotica were of course some of the earliest to embrace the filmic medium, knocking out semi-saucy shorts whilst keeping just the right side of society's censorial types; one of the earliest existent British examples being *Victorian Lady in Her Boudoir* (1896). The original title is unknown, but one suspects that, in keeping with most Brit-smut to come, this short film may have promised more than it delivered. A young

You can't go wrong in these: George Formby approaches the unmentionable in this sordid scene from *Turned Out Nice Again* (1941).

lady removes her stays in a most suggestive manner, but she doesn't go the whole hog – her chemise remains discreetly in place. Not long after there was the thrusting passion of the more famous *The Kiss in the Tunnel* (1899) – plunging towards pre-Freudian suggestiveness as that red-hot pressure-powered train penetrated that dark, steamy tunnel. It must have had those burly be-whiskered chaps at the 'smoking concert' almost choking on their cigars – they may even have missed its pioneering early use of parallel editing. Humour and sauce were quickly fused. *Merry Moments in France* (1908) combined slapstick comedy with a dancing girl flashing her ankles in a dervish-like dance.

But enough sniggering at the back, boys. Serious sex education films followed shortly afterwards. The 1920s saw such fascinating stuff released as docudrama *The Uncharted Sea* (1928), in which a naïve country boy is tormented by a gold-digging girl, robs money from the work cash-box, and ends up catching an STD from a prostitute.

The Irresponsibles (1929) followed the following year: a public information film advising on the threat of venereal disease and its possible effects if not treated, centering upon an unwise young woman walking along a road who allows herself to be picked up by a motorcyclist.

Meanwhile, across the Atlantic, spicy short comedies, starring dapper chaps like Charley Chase, hinted at a more liberated era of post-flapper and pre-Hays code sexuality. Here at home cheery cheapie British B-pictures followed their lead with marvellous movie material like *Strip! Strip! Hooray!!!* aka *Fun With the Sunbathers* (1932), which took place at a location that looked a lot like that real-life resort Spielplatz – the home-counties haven for healthy naturists. The only thing was that – for the censor's sake – the jazz-baby residents frolicking beside this particular pool kept their bathing suits well and truly on. As the cinematic world moved towards a more demure era, marvellous pioneering female director Mary Field preferred to conceal sexual asides in animal-world allegory, as evidenced in this section's *The Mystery of Marriage* (1932), and in her other works, including the splendidly named *Mixed Bathing* (1936). Nudity did eventually sneak in to British cinema, though, by unusual means. In the supposedly straight-laced 1940s, *Action in Slow Motion* (1943) daringly depicted a young woman completely starkers, frolicking about on the beach. But it is important to note that this was strictly for the eyes of serious art students. A stern warning card at the beginning of this adults-only episode noted that exhibitors faced prosecution and even prison should the film ever be used for titillating purposes.

Sometime in the 1950s, the evil floodgates of cinematic nudity on screen were officially opened when an American documentary shot in a nudist camp slipped past the censors. Fully certificated feature-length British nudist film *Nudist Paradise* (1958), shot at Spielplatz, was something of a breakthrough, and immediately British exploitation filmmakers jumped aboard the bare-bosom bandwagon. Later on, in the True Stories section of this book, we will meet one of the first serious visitors to the resort, crusading journo Dan Farson, visiting for his *Out of Step* (1957) programme. Shortly afterwards, and with more exploitative intent, Soho-based 8mm home-movie striptease short supplier and kitsch colour cat calendar publisher George Harrison Marks shot *Naked as Nature Intended* (1961), perhaps the only travelogue to feature a coachload of torrid tourists on a quaint 1950s holiday excursion inexplicably deciding to go topless for beach-ball antics in the first suitably remote seaside spot they come to.

D. H. Lawrence's controversial 1928 novel *Lady Chatterley's Lover* made it on to British bookstalls in unexpurgated paperback for the first time in 1960. It wasn't long after that cinema became rather more revealing – and by the time of *Hugs and Kisses* (1967) viewers were treated to their first officially authorised glimpses of pubic hair. The times they were a-changing. Anything went! Crikey! By the beginning of the next decade American imports like *Deep Throat* (1972) and French fancies like *Emmanuelle* (1974) were heralding what was known Stateside as the 'Golden Age of Porn' and raising the bar on what you could see in mainstream cinema. Homegrown British sex cinema still smacked of a certain embarrassment, though, and our own erotic exemplars were cut from a different cloth. Or a chamois leather, in the case of Robin Askwith's Timmy Lea, star of the hugely successful but critically derided *Confessions of a Window Cleaner* (1974). Timmy was more likely to be caught with his trousers around his ankles than standing proud. And if there's a lingering soap sud of deja vu, maybe that's to do with the fact that Formby was singing saucy songs about window cleaning back in the 1930s.

Jubilee year saw porn-mag glamour-queen Mary Millington top-billed in *Come Play With Me* (1977), the longest continuously running film ever to be shown at a British cinema, according to the *Guinness Book of World Records*. Assuming you have a copy to hand (and who doesn't?), and after you've made your usual checks on the current record for the longest beard of bees, why not look it up? It was a wondrous run of 201 weeks at the Moulin Cinema, Great Windmill Street, Soho, from April 1977 to March 1981.

Silly sleaze aside, what about the counter-cultural, independent films of the same era, trying to take into account feminism, and bodily transgressions, and surrealism – these have rarely troubled the history books either. Could it be that experimenta and exploitation – disparate poles that they are – both have some intangible something about them that conflict somehow with how we want to document British film and cinema history?

A few years later, of course, with the advent of home video, and then the insidious internalised intrusion of the internet, the need to creep out to the cinema for your illicit thrills was no more. Now, in our new nihilistic online nirvana, we can now all stream endless uncensored filth straight into our living rooms. Happy days, eh?

So, first let's begin by rewinding to an era when you would attempt to bare all whilst revealing nothing…and bear witness as love and sex undergo Mary Field's skew-whiff scrutiny…

The Mystery of Marriage

UK Film | 1932 | black and white | sound | 32mins
Director Mary Field
Screenplay Mary Field
Production Company British Instructional Films

Though her hefty contribution to film history still remains largely unsung, Mary Field's reputation is growing. An accomplished figure in British filmmaking, producing and directing numerous educational films for use in the study of science in the 1920s and 1930s, she later went on to play an integral role (with philanthropic Lord Rank, cornerstone of the sprawling Rank Organisation) in the setting up of the Children's Film Foundation. This long-lived non-profit organisation, which had its heyday in the 1950s, was responsible for the production of wholesome, high-quality cinema entertainment for the young. But the films she made before all this are odder than the thoroughly wholesome credits on her film-CV might suggest.

Slowly but surely, as scholars dig around in the unturned earth of British film history, Field's odd oeuvre is being gradually re-explored and celebrated. A pioneering filmmaker in a largely male dominated field, it is already established that her films are historically important. What is less often acknowledged, however, is just how strikingly strange some of her films are. Clearly always keen to invest what might have been dry projects with something extra, Field's directorial style is often splendidly bizarre, her approach intriguingly unpredictable. Working as a writer and director for hire, her films are made odder still thanks to their subject matter. They provide a

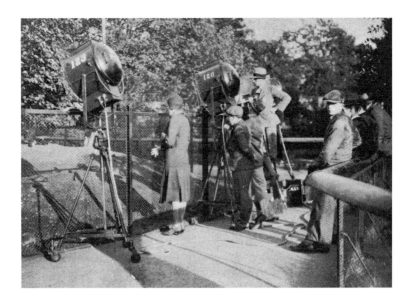

Nature studies: the British Instructional Pictures film unit shooting on location.

tiny window into the complexities of an educational system so distant and remote from the modern curriculum that it is almost impossible to believe.

Initially trained as a teacher and historian, by 1926 Mary had joined the staff at British Instructional Films. The following year saw her collaborate with eccentric natural history filmmaker Percy Smith on the innovative *Secrets of Nature* series, groundbreaking in its use of stop motion photography. Percy and Mary's films were unusual, experimental, fascinating and are a wonder to watch today; but at the time they were viewed with a skeptical eye by some critics and educationalists, who didn't think Smith and Field took their subjects seriously enough.

Magic Myxies (1931) – Smith and Field's cheery time-lapse study of a slime fungus – was enlivened by a chirpy jovial commentary, and dramatic music at relevant points in the action (occasionally somewhat akin to the exciting *Dick Barton* theme music). Jolly though it all was, the critics over at the *Monthly Film Bulletin* were not amused. They didn't enjoy the frivolous approach to the subject matter; and, what's more, according to them, scientific errors had crept in to the script, too. Shocking indeed, but no matter: it remains a lovely looking film. Never was slime so beautifully shot.

Undeterred, growing in confidence, and inspired by her collaborations with Smith, Field plowed deeper into what was becoming both a distinctive and peculiar filmic furrow. Field's strange talent had free rein in her early masterpiece, *The Mystery of Marriage* (1932). This was an attempt to explain, compare and contrast the mating rituals of animals, plants and humans for students, without ever mentioning the unsavoury subject of sex, which just wasn't done in Britain in 1932, all in just a little over half an hour.

It was an ambitious undertaking, and one that Field may perhaps have realised was probably beyond the educational powers even of British Instructional Films; so, it seems, she had fun with the idea and made the most of her opportunity to write, direct, and hire actors to provide visual comparisons between humans and what the narration describes as 'lower forms of life'. Beautiful close-ups of mould, flowers, hunting spiders, sticklebacks, birds, and other creatures are coyly intercut with odd little scenes of human behaviour that supposedly reflect the reproductive exploits of these other orders of living things.

The results may not teach you much about the messy details of life, but are nonetheless splendidly memorable, occasionally haunting, and shot through with just the slightest hint of acute melancholy. There is an air of tragedy as a close-up of a praying mantis flexing its legs across its body – 'a gay bachelor,' the narration notes – is juxtaposed with a shot of an angular, insect-like man with a jutting chin brushing his hair back across his head and jerkily shooting his cuffs.

There is a twinge of sadness, and opportunities lost, in what the upbeat, plummy voiced narrator describes as the 'pretended coyness' of a spider tempted by her mate's offer of a 'juicy fly wrapped in silk' juxtaposed with a rather downbeat scene in a smoky pub, where a seedy-looking gruff voiced gent asks a somewhat crumpled young lady in faded finery 'what's yours?' 'Well, I don't know,' is her riposte; before she is eventually tempted with a half pint of stout plonked down upon a grubby saloon-bar table, and as cigs smoulder away sadly in the ashtray. Neither party in this courtship ritual could be described as an oil painting. 'This is as good an offer as she can hope to get in these difficult times,' notes Field's dry script. The scene fades – one imagines what might happen next: you might even surmise the pair embark upon a doubtless stilted, awkward conversational preamble to an empty sex act.

The film is littered with tragic-comic sequences that strike one as vaguely akin to lost vignettes from one of Patrick Hamilton's wryly tragic novels of London life. Another haunting scene is shot at a snack bar – what was once known as a 'tea wagon'. This scene demonstrates rivalry in the mating process. A flirty girl arrives with her beau – but it is not long before she's making eyes at another young man (presumably pausing for a quick mug of Bovril). It's touch and go for a moment – but when her boyfriend makes a slightly threatening gesture, the rival is seen off and slinks back into the night. 'Amongst civilised human beings, the affair ends tamely' chirrups the narrator. What strikes you about it all is the cold air of sadness in the whole scene.

Indeed, Field doesn't seem to have much time for the reproductive processes she has been commissioned to depict. The narration speaks of 'the feminine perversity in choosing queer male objects for admiration' as a shapely, well-proportioned girl steps out with a short man, waddling along in his spectacles. 'Ain't nature grand?' the commentator quips drily.

It is not only the male of the species that Field smirks at, however. The 'bitter rivalry' of praying mantises is explained through imagery of two haughty-looking society ladies getting dressed in their finery for an evening out. As they emerge from their respective boudoirs, one of them sneers cattily from the side of her mouth 'that dress *still* looks charming.'

The film is bookended with an odd framing sequence, featuring a young couple out for a romantic stroll, the concluding section of which seems ever more lonely and cynical once you've watched and absorbed the main body of the film. At the beginning of the film, birds tweet, bees buzz; and the now-ancient soundtrack hisses and grinds. A girl gathers flowers and a man – her beau – wanders along a country path. She hides from him. United at last, she asks him how they can be sure they are right for each other. Her boyfriend, all neat 'tache and Brylcreem, is sure of the answer, which comes across like a renegade line from a Beckett play. 'Because we are,' is his clipped response. Then he begs 'Oh, Stella, do marry me…I've had a rise this year – and next year I'll have another.' Birds warble prettily in the background. The soundtrack creaks on. 'We'll buy a little house…and you can choose the furniture…' He pauses, before delivering the clincher: '…and we'll get a car!' How hollow it seems somehow, as these lines, recorded indoors on some soulless soundstage, eternities ago, reverberate out of this bewildering edu-drama.

A many splendored thing, supposedly: *The Mystery of Marriage* (1932).

The scene is set. The narrator cheerily pipes up:

Marriage, mating and the age-old mystery of the universe. The secret of the attraction that draws one individual to another [shots of birds, flowers, trees]... *it can be discovered even amongst the lower forms of life. Now, take mould,* [cut to close up of tendrils of bacteria] *that curious growing plant that goes about decaying things...*

...and that's just the beginning.

About half an hour later, the film concludes. The framing sequence ends with that same couple, walking the same lane; but now they are pushing a pram. It would appear that they have fulfilled their biological imperative – though we, the audience, have only had the vaguest hints towards the reproductive process, and none at all as to why anyone would actually bother. A quick caress behind a haystack is all we have seen. No wonder; as the young couple stare bleak-eyed at another pair romancing where once they did, the man intones flatly: 'it's a mystery…this marriage business…'

Not all of Field's diverse educational output is as strikingly odd or as reflective of a dry sharp wit as *The Mystery of Marriage*, and the actual educational success of her methods is certainly open to debate. But it's beautifully odd stuff. Even the most mundane of her works bear the marks of a filmmaker who wanted to stretch herself and challenge her audience.

One further, albeit more minor, example of Field's strange talent at work would be the splendid educational film *Hereford Pedigree Cattle* (1937). The subject matter itself is odd enough to modern eyes. School syllabuses change, of course, but even given an acute awareness of the extreme, ever-widening distance yawning back from now to then, it still seems hard to contemplate a time where young men were being taught in class to assess the qualities of bullocks. Yet that seems to be the subject matter of this film; though, it is never explicitly specified, and Field's film maintains a presumably accidental but hauntingly enigmatic quality regarding the central subject matter. But even if we accept that studying the shape of livestock was once a pertinent element of the nation's schooling (difficult) it is harder still to see how Field's film could have been used as a teaching aid.

Despite its brief running time, amidst the Zen-like calm of an idyllic rural hamlet (Field was always good at creating a near-hypnotic sense of peace and stillness when shooting the countryside), boys in janitors' coats solemnly pace around a field assessing bulls, mysteriously ranking them in order of 'quality', while a 'gentleman farmer' who never takes his hand from his pocket, and in fact seems vaguely embarrassed throughout, discusses farm life from the side of his mouth. All of this is shot in a proto-verité style, and occasionally from unusual angles. The strange film ends as abruptly as it began. Were we supposed to learn something? If so, what have we learned? Perhaps we have learned that farming – like marriage – is a mystery.

Of course, given the nature of the kind of work she did, too little of her material is available on DVD. It probably won't be on television any time soon. Luckily, a few examples, thankfully including *The Mystery of Marriage*, are currently available on DVD. Much of Mary's work may be destined forever to remain mysterious, but if you get the chance to watch a Mary Field film – any of them – you should. Share the mystery. *VP*

Fast-forward now through the cataclysmic change of World War Two to take a look at a bashful Britain on the brink of the permissive era, from the thoroughly male perspective of Patrick McGoohan, a supposedly sexy small-screen star, rigidly reluctant to expose the sensitivity within…

Danger Man

UK TV | 1960-1962 & 1964-1967 | colour and black and white | Episodes 25mins & 50mins
Creator Ralph Smart
Directors Include Don Chaffey, Clive Donner, Charles Crichton, Seth Holt, Patrick McGoohan
Writers Include Brian Clemens, Ralph Smart, Philip Broadley
Producers Include Ralph Smart, Sidney Cole
Production Company ITC
Cast Includes Patrick McGoohan, Bernard Bresslaw, Earl Cameron, Judy Geeson, Joan Greenwood, Susan Hampshire, Burt Kwouk, Moira Lister, Jane Merrow, Warren Mitchell, Nicola Paget, Sylvia Syms

The James Bond movies combined a 1950s, post-war international gent persona with a bright, brash, pop psychedelic aesthetic. Bond was big. And so too was the man offered the secret agent 007 part before Sean Connery. Patrick McGoohan, an Irish actor, had cut quite a dash over the course of a series of Rank thrillers, radiating powerful charisma and taut, contained physical force. Spotted in 1958 by ITC's Lew Grade and Ralph Smart, he was offered *Danger Man* and quickly became a star. There was a problem with the James Bond offer though; womanizing was abhorrent to him. He turned down the role on precisely those grounds. The same thing then happened again. *The Saint* (1962-1969), ITV's sexy spy; would he like it? Patrick McGoohan: 'I refused because I thought – and still think – that the character's a rogue. A rat. The Saint called for a promiscuous character. I wouldn't like to play a part like that.' He appeared to be a man very much out of step.

He was a man of considerable principles and had had to overcome both a chronic shyness and an interest in the priesthood before treading the boards

at all. He started at the Sheffield Rep, and then moved to other theatres and TV, and then landed a contract at the Rank film studio. Apparently, an executive saw him in test footage standing next to Dirk Bogarde and promptly offered him a starting salary of £4,000 – a considerable sum in the 1950s. Whatever was going on inside, his charisma was palpable.

His contract with Rank had forced to him accept roguish roles which frankly he abhorred. However, they did suit him well – with his slightly shifty good looks and smouldering personality. When it came to the television series *Danger Man*, he insisted on certain clauses: the fistfights should vary in shape and delivery, John Drake (the spy, *Danger Man*) would use his brain before a gun, and, much to the horror of the men in charge, no kissing. One executive retorted 'a celibate spy? Why don't we go the whole way and hire a monk?'

The sixties were a time of change: sex was pushed to the forefront and social barriers were crumbling. Not, though, it seemed for Patrick McGoohan. Despite his star rising over the course of the increasingly decadent decade, with his lead roles in *Danger Man* and then *The Prisoner* (1967-68), he seemed to get increasingly uptight as the years went by. 'I think it would do Cathy incalculable harm if her schoolmates were able to come to her and say "that was a nice bit of fluff I saw your old man necking with on TV last night,"' he said, and would repeat, again and again, about his daughter or daughters. His anger at the permissive society went beyond progressive parental concern, however. Famously resisting scripted flirtations, he chose to turn love scenes on their head and notably shouted his lines at his 'love interest' in *The Prisoner* episode *Dance of the Dead* (transmitted 26/11/1967), exuding pronounced antipathy, even aggression.

For all his popularity, his approach was an unusual one. His portrayals were often a curious subversion of genre expectations. It was all part of the allure. The pleasures of *Danger Man* came from simply watching McGoohan, projecting repression and yet exuding charisma. Don Chaffey, a frequent director of the show (and many of the best episodes of *The Prisoner*), understood this and, as in the episode *Such Men Are Dangerous* (21/01/1965), constructed the action carefully but otherwise just watched McGoohan, stalking him with his camera whilst he set-up spying devices

‹ **A man undercover:** Patrick McGoohan in *Danger Man* (1960-1962 & 1964-1967).

or navigated unusual terrain, whole long stretches of time passing with no dialogue at all. 'Look into those bright blue eyes and die' said *Danger Man* casting director Rose Tobias-Shaw to *Cosmopolitan* as McGoohan accumulated a sizeable female fan base. Patrick McGoohan is 'the most attractive man on television,' wrote Mrs Patricia Burrows to the *TV Times*.

Something of a puritan, McGoohan appeared to at least like John Drake. He's 'an interesting character. Admittedly, he hasn't got as many facets at Hamlet, but I find the part stimulating. I hope it has reasonable sort of influence in that we don't perpetrate evil.' And he honed the part, establishing his own rules about how Drake might act and what he might do. To that end: 'I never carry a gun. They're noisy, and they hurt people. Besides, I manage very well without,' he said in *To Our Best Friend* (09/12/1965). And instead he drew on his boxing talents nurtured at Radcliffe College, Leicestershire. McGoohan stared directly ahead with total focus and concentration as the fists flew. He often appeared to avoid the gaze of his fellow actors, making him seem either shifty or distracted. (The chronic shyness never truly lifted.) It all seemed to feed into McGoohan's rewriting of the spy drama rules. Jean-Luc Godard famously said 'all you need is a girl and a gun', implying that after that anything can happen – and yet McGoohan didn't just avoid these well-trodden genre paths, he actively resisted them.

Danger Man was certainly a unique show and evolved as it went along. Season one saw him as an American agent working for NATO – it was made to sell to the American market – investigating cases of international intrigue. It then stopped, and after a two-year gap returned, but in a different guise. Suddenly Drake was English, perhaps picking up on the cool Britannia vibe promoted by *The Avengers* (1961-1969) and *The Saint*, and now he reported to M9 and the British government. Episodes now ran to fifty minutes, rather than the previous twenty-five, and were often downbeat, even cynical in tone.

Increasingly stylized, the second series also saw the introduction of a new pre-title sequence. A thug-like McGoohan plodded menacingly towards the camera whilst a circling harpsichord refrain repeated with

Immediate withdrawal, or departure deferred: *Danger Man* paperback cover. ›

CONSUL BOOKS 3/6

DANGER MAN

Departure
Deferred

W. Howard Baker

**An original novel based on the great TV series
starring PATRICK McGOOHAN as Agent John Drake**

increasing intensity, before a punchy brass section blasted the notes back up again, as if punching the viewer in the face. It concluded with a freeze-frame of McGoohan staring intently at the camera. It was powerful stuff.

The show was stylishly shot on 35mm film, massive in the UK and sold all around the world, appearing as *Secret Agent* in the USA. McGoohan was Britain's highest paid actor at its peak, taking home £2,000 a week. The first new episodes struggled to find a shape, however, as the cast and crew tussled with the extended format, plus the lead's unusual approach. A temporary reprieve came with *Don't Nail Him Yet* (22/12/1964), Drake assuming the role of a meek schoolteacher in an attempt to befriend a nervous informer. The strange, refracted identity shift suddenly introduced a new depth to the role, and subsequently the series as a whole. Danger meant earning someone's confidence through a shared shyness now, not by confronting a gang leader, or by pretending to be a journalist, as was often the case. McGoohan's back stoops and he looks furtively around, appearing fragile and lonely. He seems vulnerable but curiously manipulative too, prepared to dupe someone by appealing to their personal insecurities. The episode also visits sad, lonely London locations: a quiet out-of-the-way pub, a bookshop, further underlining the grey melancholia of the capital city in the middle of the decade.

It took a while for the show to revisit this unusual vein of writing. But when it did, McGoohan's versatility and acting abilities shone ever more brightly as he, in turn, modified his identify, body posture and voice according to the demands of each undercover assignment. Decades later Peter Falk reflected 'I have never played a scene with another actor who commanded my attention the way Pat did.' Orson Welles said he was 'one of the big actors of his generation'. The only writers who appeared to appreciate the detail of his talents in the early 1960s, however, were *Danger Man* creator and script editor Ralph Smart, and Philip Broadley, a regular contributor. Slowly they began to focus more and more on McGoohan, just him, going undercover, in a strange scenario, living the life of another character – not chasing the coattails of an overly complicated storyline.

In Ralph Smart's brilliant *No Marks For Servility* (08/12/1964), Drake dons the coattails of a butler and listens to a gang of covert undercover criminals as they mastermind a kidnapping. The story centres on Drake's

One flash of light but no smoking pistol: Patrick McGoohan ignites uncertain passions in *Danger Man* (1960-1962 & 1964-1967).

relationship with the boss, the loud, arrogant Gregori (Howard Marion-Crawford). Convinced there is more to his obsequious manner than meets the eye, the moustachioed bully shouts at Drake incessantly, pushing him and aggressively complaining, time-after-time, about bad service. Drake, looking forever sharp and as cool as ice, resists and plays an eternal straight-bat. 'As you say, sir.' But the stalemate can't last. Pushed to breaking point, having completed job after job, Drake/McGoohan finally, and briefly, erupts. He shatters a whiskey glass with his bare hands.

At its best *Danger Man* is great stuff, and far from just prehistory to *The Prisoner*, the latter always assuming preeminence and considerably more interest. Certainly, *The Prisoner* is more intricately unusual. It combined a Kafkaesque reflection on power and identity with a striking psychedelic aesthetic, in a way perfectly tipping the world from the drop out flower power of 1967 to the violent comedown of '68. The last episode saw people being slaughtered by machine gun to the sound of *All You Need is Love*.

But *Danger Man* had its own identity too, even if it was uneven and depended on the scriptwriter (the same was also true of *The Prisoner*). It belonged to the grey sixties and tellingly only lasted two further episodes once colour was introduced at the beginning of season 4. The espionage, double-crossing, it all played to the time. Even the use of technology belonged to the era. Large computers and hypnotic tape-recorders and telephone signals all regularly featured. Machines and devices became not so much pathways to the future but means of sewing doubt and confusion, revealing secrets, but also fragmenting and obscuring them. Colonial and governmental authority was shifting and even Drake mistrusts and disobeys his paymasters at M9. It was a time of questions, not answers.

McGoohan returned as an undercover butler, after *No Marks For Servility*, in *The Hunting Party* (27/01/1966), broadcast just over a year later. This time, however, he assumed a more flirtatious relationship with his employer, a Miss Claudia Jordan (Moira Lister). McGoohan looks good in a sharp, crisp suit whilst stylish glasses highlight his strong, pronounced bone structure. He also literally towers over the other actors here, as he often did, being just under 6ft 2. Might the sexual tension break, just this once? No.

Women would occasionally feature as potential sexual interest, but then invariably turned into either traitors or villains, or just friends. With her Anna Karina-style, sharp bob haircut and bold tenacity, the siren-like Nicola Pagett points her finger at Drake in *The Mirror's New* (09/03/1965), and tries to reel him in – in to both her affections and her schemes. He obliges for a while, but then reveals it was all for the job.

'I knew he had an aversion to being associated with any woman on screen,' remembered actress Susan Hampshire, who appeared in episodes *You Are Not in Any Trouble, Are You?* (21/09/1965) and *Are You Going to be More Permanent?* (02/12/1965); 'he wouldn't be in a kissing scene or anything like that.' *The TV Radio Mirror* on-set report from August 1966, meanwhile, observed:

'The shapely brunette threw her arms around Patrick McGoohan's neck and gave a romantic sigh. It should have quickened the pulse of even the stone-hearted, iceberg-cool John Drake… "Mr Drake", she murmured. "How can I ever thank you?"…" Try to think of me as a humble civil servant", said Pat… But the words and the occasion were too much for the girl. Amorously, she drew her co-star close to her and planted a far-from platonic kiss on his lips…In an instant the calm, detached demeanour of Patrick McGoohan erupted into raging fury. "Cut!" he yelled at the cameraman…he wheeled to face the girl. "That wasn't in the script!" he shouted at her. "Nobody gets in a clinch with John Drake – nobody!"'

For all his appeal and female popularity, McGoohan was clearly troubled, by his acting roles, the structures and expectations of film and TV, and by his very being. He became an increasingly agitated and agitational presence on TV, ironically further honing and foregrounding his personal idiosyncrasies and charisma. The agitation spread to the *Danger Man* episodes that he directed. In *The Paper Chase* (31/03/1966) a woman tinkers on a piano while sweaty, tense characters in the foreground spar over a claustrophobic game of poker. McGoohan deliberately places the two sound sources in direct conflict with each other and it's hard to hear what's being said. It's absurd. Later, he escapes from a ruffian by driving off in a child's kit car, emerging from a pile of hay. These were the confrontational stylings from which *The Prisoner* would eventually develop.

Was the agitation and internal conflict in some way connected to his relationship to women and sex? What was that about? It was too anger-fuelled to be just about his family, surely? Was he impotent, gay? He *was* raised Catholic. His aversions to sex became the flipside to the likes of James Bond and *The Saint*, but it also inadvertently highlighted the new permissive age by way of McGoohan's hard, contrary, one might even say, then, reactionary position. His biographer, Rupert Booth, remarked: 'he despised Bond and his attitude to women, his cheapening of life at the end of his Walther PPK'. In this day and age we might ask, whose attitude was the more progressive? McGoohan was, after all, in favour of decriminalising homosexuality.

'Why did you resign?' was repeatedly asked of his character in *The Prisoner*. The same question could have been, and presumably was, posed to McGoohan about *Danger Man*. The questions and these sixties shows stayed with him. When directing episodes of the American detective TV show *Columbo* (1971-2003), he would often include references to *The Prisoner*, also sometimes embellishing his acting turns (he appeared in the show too) with an obsequious, highly mannered 'be seeing you!' The salutation had been a heavily codified staple feature of his old show, and he inserted it – or if not that then some other detail – into many of his subsequent acting roles, which ranged from *Escape from Alcatraz* (1979) to *The Simpsons* (1989-), from *Scanners* (1981) to *Braveheart* (1995). *The Prisoner* ended in 1968 but it was as though he took 'the Village', the home of retired spies, with him, holding it around himself, finding a place for it in all the other parts of his life. And with no *Danger Man* there'd have been no *Prisoner*. The latter only lasted seventeen episodes.

He couldn't escape it and clearly didn't want to. He did, however, seek relief. 'I occasionally like a drink of beer,' he said in 1966. The pass time had escalated – significantly – by the *Scanners* era. 'He said to me, "If I didn't drink I'd be afraid I'd kill someone"', recalled director David Cronenberg. His nervous reply to his star being? 'Keep drinking.' McGoohan was angry. Extreme tension and ill feeling sometimes radiated powerfully from his strange facial contortions and laboured footsteps in both *Danger Man* and *The Prisoner*. It was as though he wore the residual guilt and repression of another age on his shoulders. And in '66 he was clear, at least to the press: 'every boy who sees his heroes on TV wants to grow up like them. Let other actors play the parts of men addicted to kissing and killing. I prefer to set myself higher standards.' Kissing was bad. *WF*

Prior to the passing of the 1967 Sexual Offences Act and the decriminalisation of homosexuality, gay culture was to be found underground, secreted in quiet pubs and clubs, and also in left-field literature...

Dream A40

UK Film | 1965 | black and white | 23mins
Director Lloyd Reckord
Script Lloyd Reckord
Producer Lloyd Reckord
Production Company Reckord Productions
Cast Michael Billington, Nicholas Wright

Books by, amongst others, Denton Welch and Jocelyn Brook, spun highly individualistic tales where gay characters and narratives were not explicitly identified, but the right readers sought them out. Cinema, by way of contrast, was more difficult to infiltrate. In the days before home video, let alone DVD and the internet, cinema was truly a mass medium, designed to be consumed by a mass audience, and films passed several pairs of eyes before making it to the big screen.

Lloyd Reckord's 1965 gay interest film *Dream A40*, however, resisted this unwritten rule and cut against the grain. Low key by later standards, it was still very daring for its time and it is difficult to imagine how such a film would get supported or find an audience.

Taking the form of a sci-fi allegory, it follows two men as they drive from a Swinging London party to an unknown destination, encountering various different sexual dynamics en route. Caught speeding by a police motorcyclist, they are taken to a strange, enormous industrial building where downcast men sit in lengthy rows, quietly staring at the floor. The industrial castle appears like a processing station for a concentration camp. The older man, losing patience, tries to find a way out and eventually manages to purchase their freedom from a lone cashier. On his return, however, he finds chaos, and death – men are strewn on the floor and his dear friend hangs limply in a hangman's noose. His eyes, however, flutter open and the older man presses their lips together, giving him something between the kiss of life and a final passionate embrace. He drags him to the world outside.

Director Lloyd Reckord never formally identified as gay, partly because he was from homosexual-wary Jamaica, but he was sensitive to the reality of UK social politics and noted 'all these horrible things were happening,' referring to the numerous high profile public prosecutions of gay men, and also violence. 'Why should a certain set of people have to live like that with fear and looking over one's shoulder?'

Originally coming to the UK at the suggestion of his playwright brother Barrie Reckord, he had first appeared on stage, almost always playing the part of a black man in a relationship with a white girl. He then moved from the Royal Court Theatre to ABC's *Armchair Theatre*, taking part in the first interracial kisses on British television, in *Hot Summer Night* (transmitted 01/02/1959) and *You in Your Small Corner* (05/06/1962); and then he got into film.

His directorial debut, *Ten Bob in Winter* (1963), addressed class division and difference amongst Black British immigrants. The stylish short told the story of an out of work Jamaican who, having borrowed money from a

DREAM A40

A FILM BY LLOYD RECKORD

friend, and travelling across town, feels compromised and uncomfortable when a darker-skinned, tatty-looking musician asks him for a loan. When a posh friend turns-up, the tension only increases. Using hip, beat-talk narration and swinging jazz from the Joe Harriott Quintet, and often splicing in stock-saving still photography for images, *Ten Bob in Winter* was modest and clearly low-budget, but it made the most of its limitations.

Reckord remained immersed in the nurturing world of the Royal Court Theatre throughout this time. It was there that he found support for *Dream A40* via star of the age, David Hemmings, who had been interested in a leading role, plus finance from an unidentified film and theatre director who was probably Tony Richardson. Through his company, Woodfall, and a deal with Warner Brothers, the filmmaker behind *A Taste of Honey* (1961) and *The Loneliness of the Long Distance Runner* (1962) had been advancing money to Kevin Brownlow and Andrew Mollo for *It Happened Here* (shot between 1956 and 1964) (which featured Reckord as an extra, incidentally), and to James Scott for unfinished feature, *The Sea* (1962). Later coming-out as bi-sexual, Richardson may have wanted to help a film that would put gay issues up on the big screen.

Rude awakening: Nicholas Wright in *Dream A40* (1965).

Reckord found further creative support from underground film: an immersive, risqué world that demonstrated other possibilities. Reaching back into his mind in 1991, he said 'Anger. What was it called? Flaming Angels, with bikers and homosexuality,' conflating Kenneth Anger's *Scorpio Rising* (1963) and Jack Smith's *Flaming Creatures* (1963), both of which had been highly controversial and presented playful yet forthright visions of homosexuality. He probably saw *Scorpio Rising* at its first UK screenings, at the Camberwell School of Art in 1964, when Derek Jarman also first saw it – a tantalising prospect, making it the gay cinema equivalent of when the Sex Pistols played Manchester's Free Trade Hall.

Reckord also drew on overground influences. Jean Cocteau's ground-breaking *Orphée* (1950) signified a change in cinema and was dreamy, groovy and moody, combining inward notions of self-reflection with references to the Nazi occupation of France. *Orphée* had been a very popular, arty post-war film and *Dream A40* transposed elements of its mood and imagery. The shimmering, bonging sound heard when the police motorcyclist arrives in *Dream A40*, for example, was, in function, not unlike the buzz of radio static that featured when the gangster-bikers turn-up in *Orphée*; both indicate a shift to dream space, the dial-of-reality being spun.

Dream A40 is imbued with the existential mood of its time and is, at its heart, about guilt and repression, the nightmare being initially triggered at the point the older man rejects his lover's hand. The piece includes loose swinging jazz but otherwise runs silent; looks, gestures and strange places instead telling its story. Vehicles also symbolize different types of character. The two men, trying to escape illegality, secrecy and guilt, drive a Ford Zephyr, a family style vehicle, whilst the woman who throws them flirtatious glances on the road, speeds along in a flash, streamlined MG sports car. (A sensible headscarf does, however, slightly undermine the sexual imagery.)

Shot street-style, it used the new technologies and techniques developed by Free Cinema and the French New Wave. Like the earlier *Ten Bob in Winter*, it was also grounded in place and location, each environment specifically informing the different parts of the story and, in psychogeographic terms, determining the politics of character interaction. The groovy, decadent party at the beginning, with its swinging loose jazz music and skinny ties, may be the couple's immediate social scene, but their homosexuality is still kept undercover. In fact, the older man appears to have been kissing a woman. The whole film also refuses to resolve itself or conclude. Sure, the two men escape but it's not clear if the younger of the two is still alive or not, or quite what the world has to offer. There's no truly free, open space available to them, except perhaps the road, and only for a time.

It spoke to Reckord's sexual, racial and filmmaking experiences. He was, in some respects, implying that to be gay was to be more of an outsider than it was to be black. The older man, dancing ecstatically, openly kisses a black woman at the party and then, en route, a black woman cavorts and smiles gloriously for a photographer, *Blow-Up* (1966) style, at a petrol station. In the world of the young and counter-cultural, in this film at least, racism was less of an issue. Reckord's film may not have been as verbose, as decadently glamorous as Kenneth Anger's *Scorpio Rising* (1963), but it was still a taboo-busting piece of work.

'Okay so you've made a couple of short films but TV is a different type of thing,' was how Reckord remembered the BBC brush-off. Directing

Choose your masques: bikers in *Dream A40* (1965) (top) and *Orphée* (1950) (bottom).

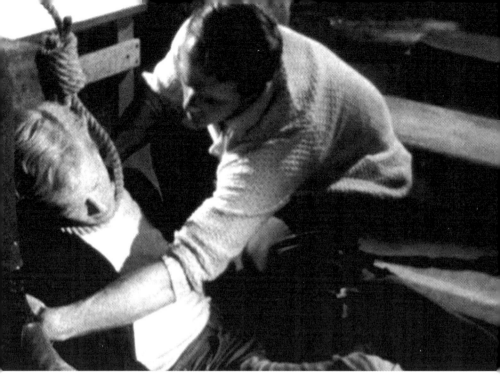

The dream is over: *Dream A40* (1965).

heavy, interlinked cathode ray tube cameras in a television studio is different to shooting 16mm film on location, but there's more to this. Several key British TV talents came from a 16mm shooting background – Ken Russell, Peter Watkins and John Schlesinger – and later returned to cinema. TV and cinema also began to take-up an interesting dialogue, with several TV pieces being shot on celluloid and informed by stylistic developments in the underground and international art cinema. Russell's work was a case in point.

Dream A40 didn't do it for the BBC. It was subtle and carefully constructed, using bold symbolic imagery, if occasionally inadvertently displaying its budgetary limitations. It didn't do it for anyone at early screenings, it seems. It slept, going unseen and undistributed until 1971, when it was picked up first by Barrie Pattison (an Australian who edited the film) through his Arron Project company, and then BFI distribution. It screened at the London Film Festival. Reviews in 1971 noted how out of time and even quaint it seemed, also stressing, unfairly I would argue, its more amateur qualities. The world had certainly moved on, homosexuality being now not only legal but vigorously promoted. Queer culture proclaimed itself increasingly boldly and overtly, even in the face of resistance and sometimes violence. Shame and the hidden gay life as witnessed in *Dream A40* were now out of step, and even jarring for some.

Lloyd Reckord seemed to struggle at every stage and appeared plagued by misfortune and forms of institutional racism. He arrived in the UK at the time of the angry young men – or at least angry young white men – and theatre was on the rise, finding a new identity in a changing post-war world. 'Theatre reflects life,' he said. 'I've seen what English theatre is like and I've seen what English films are like and people like me don't appear in them. Sooner or later people like me would appear,' following the immigration of the Windrush generation and later. But then 'I wanted to be in a profession that needed my talent rather than a young black man to be persecuted or something. I wanted to play Hamlet, like everyone else, but I don't think anyone out there wanted me to play Hamlet.'

For Reckord to make a film about a gay couple was extremely bold. His choice of subjects may not have exactly helped his career, but it was as though he felt compelled to tackle areas close to his heart, and perhaps felt empowered by this strange revolutionary time. He was highly cine-literate and wanted to draw elements of the underground style and themes upward, creating a bold, more visible type of alternative cinema. And he wanted to direct because he wanted to prove himself on the basis of his own personal merits, rather than through his skin colour, or because his scriptwriter brother had got him the part. That aspiration created an interesting tension, however. How far should a bold, individual vision go if a person is essentially touting for work, in his case at the BBC? Putting racism, implicit or explicit, to one side, Reckord mused, with hindsight, on *Dream A40*: 'it wasn't sensational by any means. If it were sensational perhaps that would have done it.'

More broadly there was now a place for black men and women on the screen, reflecting recent Caribbean immigration, but working behind the camera was still a different matter. Aspirant Caucasian film and television makers had less trouble – one of Reckord's white colleagues at the Royal Court Theatre ended up directing *Z Cars* (1962-1978), but for people of colour the old prejudices remained. It was enough to send Reckord back to the Caribbean, where he established and ran the National Theatre Trust, producing, directing and even taking the lead in as many as five plays a year. He left behind a very unusual, very English, gay film. It was neither truly underground nor overground. And maybe that was the problem. But the bigger problem was implicit in the institutional rules that determined who could, and who couldn't, make a film. *WF*

Several salacious, cheeky movies about sex were not just made but exhibited in the UK at the end of the 1960s. They promised flesh and entertainment. Usually they were comedic, the British preferring their liaisons to be shrouded in embarrassment and the ridiculous...

Secrets of Sex aka *Bizarre*

UK Film | 1970 | colour and black and white | 85mins (cut), later 91mins
Director Antony Balch
Script Martin Locke, John Eliot, Maureen Owen, Elliot Stein, Antony Balch
Producer Richard Gordon
Production Company Noteworthy Films
Cast Kenneth Benda, Dorothy Grumbar, Anthony Rowlands, Yvonne Quenet, Sue Bond, Elliott Stein, Valentine Dyall (narrator)

Under-the-counter 8mm pornographer George Harrison Marks upgraded his film stock and appeared in practically every scene of his 35mm feature *The Nine Ages of Nakedness* (1969). He had a tendency to hog the limelight and fancied himself as something of a music hall legend, perhaps considering himself a comedian rather than a purveyor of smut. If so, he was deluded. *The Wife Swappers* (1970) meanwhile presented itself as a serious documentary but could be, ironically, extremely entertaining. Producer Stanley Long, a recurring figure in our canon, combined a mixture of 'professional opinion', talking heads and on-the-street action, all of which were faked.

Sex on screen was profoundly commercially viable, and yet, in its more overt guises, was still considered shocking and risqué. The censors kept an eagle eye on what was happening and the major studios held back, not being quite sure what was acceptable and what was not. They were also mindful of their reputations and wary of spending money on a film that might seem tame by the time it came out, such was the speed of change. The hacks and low-budget filmmakers, by way of contrast, pushed boldly forward, getting films out there quickly and doing whatever was necessary to get them talked about and seen.

Filmmaker Antony Balch was another low-budget entrepreneur to enter the fray. His *Secrets of Sex* was made the same year as the aforementioned *Nine Ages of Nakedness* and *The Wife Swappers,* and like these films it pushed sex to the fore, at least in the advertising. Posters were basic and direct, utilising high contrast photos of women dressed in sparse underwear whilst also plugging *The Heterosexual* (aka *Mademoiselle De Sade*) (1969), the supporting film that made even 'normal' sex sound weird and fruity.

It was a come-on, of course. But whilst sweaty, frothing viewers looking to spoil their lower-garments might have gone home disappointed, Balch's film definitely delivered on the weird and unusual front. The poster wasn't kidding when it said 'Just when you thought you'd seen it all.' *Secrets of Sex* was one of the strangest films to get a general release as the 1960s turned into the 70s. It was weird, uneven – sometimes brilliant, sometimes boring – and like nothing else before or since.

Lured by the promise of naked bodies and general salaciousness, what viewers actual got was a decidedly odd assortment of short stories and skits based around the battle of sexes. Of course, nudity did feature, but when a man dressed as an Egyptian mummy introduced each section, confused ticket holders may have found it hard to build-up a sweat. Particularly when his rich, deep voice, provided by character actor Valentine Dyall, suggested: 'your epoch has brought great confusion to the sex war. Your life is so steeped in fantasy that it ceases to be reality'. His dialogue was formal and ridiculous and a terrific set-up against the seven or so weird stories that flowed over the film's eighty-five minutes on original UK release.

The film set out its stall almost immediately. First there is a story about our new Egyptian mummy friend who explains how his lover's husband locked him in a chest many centuries ago. Then, after speaking to the viewer directly, the mummy intones with his insistent deep voice, 'imagine you are making love to this boy, imagine you are making love to this girl,' and so on. And then

Mummy's the word: *Secrets of Sex* (1970).

'imagine this boy is making love to you, imagine this girl is making love to you.' And at each turn a semi-nude young boy or girl is presented in front of a black background, their eyes staring directly ahead in Warhol-ian fashion. The men stare impassively forward, while the women smile knowingly.

It gets weirder still as the majority of the men strike poses with cocked machine guns. One clothed man sits next to his shiny motorbike, smoking and reading a magazine. He's dressed mod style but it's strongly reminiscent of Kenneth Anger's *Scorpio Rising* (1963), particularly when considered in the larger homoerotic mix of sex, violence and beautiful bodies; all of which reflected Balch's homosexuality.

Finally, the strange, precisely edited spell is broken when, having said many, many times over 'imagine you are making love to this boy, imagine you are making love to this girl', the mummy concludes: 'imagine the consequences', and a bucket of water splashes down on the head of model Sue Bond (who also appears in *The Nine Ages of Nakedness*). Sex is frequently weird and for the most part humiliating in this film: the men turn on the women, pointing their guns at the frankly unimpressed females, who've already had baked beans and cabbages hurled at their semi-naked bodies. Sue Bond responds by pulling out a switchblade.

Like *The Nine Ages of Nakedness* and *The Wife Swappers*, *Secrets of Sex* was constructed in sections, but it was in most other respects very different to these other films. It's definitely lively and Balch's energy and playfulness are written in from the outset, but the relationships and sexual episodes are all quite odd, and more about entrapment and disappointment than anything else; early on, a woman strips slowly to sad church organ music and later a strange man asks a call girl to do her stuff in front of his pet lizard. It's ultimately not very concerned with titillation – which, however, clumsily done, was usually groped towards in some awkward, slightly shame-ridden way in other British exploitation pictures.

By way of contrast, technology and modernity feature prominently. In one story, an aeroplane overhead shimmers in the early morning light as a slight-looking burglar prowls around a house. Hearing a noise, the young mod-guy whose home it is puts down his copy of *The Miracle of the Rose* by gay author Jean Genet and makes his way downstairs. 'Christ, a bird!' he says as he pulls off the woman burglar's flat-cap. They quickly get it on, kissing in the shower, and his radio provides a kind of running commentary: 'of course these luscious tropical growths require a great deal of water and consequently the atmosphere is rather torrid.' Moving to the bed, the guy then puts a telephone inside the woman's pants and a voice emerges from within: 'subscriber, will you please replace your receiver.' 'Do you require assistance?' It's happening, but sexual anxiety is being mediated through technology and the scene moves between the stilted and the vigorous.

Balch drew on a British awkwardness about the carnal deed but his influences and personnel were international. Producer Richard Gordon was American and had a long experience of making horror films going back to the 1950s. He and Balch had met at the Cannes Film Festival and bonded over a shared, obsessive love of Bela Lugosi; Gordon had organized the Lugosi UK Dracula theatre tour that Balch attended when it came to Brighton in 1951. (See this book's entry on *Mother Riley Meets the Vampire*). The two became close friends and quickly concocted both horror movie schemes and plans to adapt the William Burroughs book *Naked Lunch*. Gordon must have really liked Balch as *Secrets of Sex*, with its absurdist, psychedelic humour was quite different to his usual fare. Gordon had considerable movie-making experience and received a prominent credit in the opening titles. He later sold the film in the States and would have been thinking about the American audience all the while during production. Other British sex films, by way of contrast, were resolutely homemade, intended almost solely for the British market.

Thinking about this film, psychologists, amateur or otherwise, might find it hard not to reflect on stories told about Balch's mother by his friend Terry Wilson. She was loving but forceful and Balch felt pressure to shave and look presentable in her presence, even when he was profoundly ill with cancer at the end of the seventies. The relationship was a difficult one and here was a film that billed itself as being about the battle of the sexes, narrated by an Egyptian mummy who had been locked in a chest and buried underground. It's a great image but also one that very strongly evokes a Freudian subconscious finding a voice. Or trying to find a voice – the mummy's mouth and face remain tightly bandaged throughout.

Antony Balch was definitely interested in the inner workings of the mind. He had hooked up with queer artists and writers William Burroughs and Brion Gysin when at the Beat Hotel in Paris in the early 1960s. They remained close friends until Balch's death and made a number of experimental films together. Balch and Burroughs lived in the same building in the posh St James's Court areas off Piccadilly, London and were both active participants in Scientology. Balch was also interested in Burroughs' and Gysin's shamanic work with metaphysics and their films *Towers Open Fire* (1963) and *The Cut-Ups* (1966) explored precisely these concerns. Ideas about psychological and political control were simultaneously presented and exploded through the layering and 'cutting-up' of images into non-linear patterns. Critic Tony Rayns recalled 'they really fucked with people's minds, these movies.'

It's perhaps because of this background that *Secrets of Sex* has been called an avant-garde sex film. Allusions to Burroughs do crop up. A model at the beginning is seen reading his novel *Nova Express* and then the fireworks at the end reference Burroughs' ever present ejaculation imagery – as in *Towers Open Fire*. A term favoured by Burroughs and Scientologists also features in the story about a sadistic photographer. 'Pain inflicted during anesthesia, not consciously experienced, is still recorded by you and can be re-stimulated at a later date. Such recordings are called engrams' says the

Doing the figures: *Secrets of Sex* (1970).

stern, unforgiving woman who then sets-up a photography session in which a male model is strung-up above a medieval torture instrument.

The discussion and description of plants and fauna whilst human sexual activity takes place (as in the woman burglar story but also later when a woman says the souls of her lovers are trapped inside a display of flowers) evokes *Kronhausen Psychomontage No. 1* (1962), a relentlessly filthy experimental film that Balch had contributed camerawork to just a few years earlier. (It is also evocative of the animal imagery of Mary Field's *The Mystery of Marriage* (1932).) Directors Phyllis and Eberhard Kronhausen were sexologists from the USA and Germany respectively and their black and white short edited together nature photography in unusual combinations, with different sounds over the top, leading the viewer on. The sequence of a woman straddling a dog in the park is, shall we say, bold. Elsewhere monkeys bray as wasps and bees penetrate budding flowers. The animalistic side to sex was brought out, both here and in *Secrets of Sex*, though the latter seemed to use similar techniques to create feelings of alienation and absurdity as opposed to anything more physical.

Balch's film was unusual, partially experimental but by the same token clearly conceived with a populist agenda. It plays with form but it doesn't challenge the viewer overtly. If anything, it was a kind of visual imprint of Balch's lively, obsessive cinephile imagination, a kind of brain dump of everything he'd been watching and thinking about the previous ten years. It throws in so many references, parodying silent film, James Bond, slapstick, European horror, and the imagery is colourful, plastic, vivid and psychedelic.

Balch was in fact fixated on popular, commercial success, and he had to be; his film obsession extended to programming two London cinemas, the Jacey Piccadilly and The Times Baker Street. Art house cinema was typified as including some nudity but the directors whose films showed at the Jacey were not discussed or debated in the pages of *Cahiers Du Cinema*. Rather they were true outsiders, making cheap exploitation films that in many cases have even now yet to be evaluated - let alone re-evaluated - in the UK. Balch was a distributor and from the States bought *The Gay Deceivers* (1969), a film about two groovy dudes who go gay as a way of avoiding the draft, and from France, *Don't Deliver Us From Evil* (1971), a tale about two schoolgirls who pledge their lives to Satan. He also often made radical title changes to increase a film's commercial return, or so he hoped. *Le Grand Cérémonial* turned into *The Weird Weirdo* (1969) and *Traitement De Choc* (literal translation: 'Shock Treatment') into *Doctor in the Nude* (1973). His was a cheap and eccentric operation.

Ever the canny salesman, when it came to *Secrets of Sex* he made a point of including a story with a comic strip character from the porn magazine *Mayfair*. Lindy Leigh, originally drawn by Alfred Mazure and here played by model Maria Frost, is sent to investigate a creepy looking Russian agent plagued by attentive women. 'Why am I cursed by this sex allure?' Why indeed? *Mayfair* provided reciprocal marketing and profiled the film in a two-page spread, noting that 'Lindy Leigh typified London's innocent acquiescent dolly to whom nudity was as inevitable as shopping in King's Road.' Incidentally, just shortly before this, the magazine was publishing articles by William Burroughs.

Sex, film and art frequently collided and crossed-over in the late 60s and the intermingling is certainly evident in Balch's movie. In the States it got called *Bizarre* and bold distributor, New Line Cinema, marketed it alongside other new weird movies – sadly now unknown – under the tagline *Pornography or Art?* It was a canny move, milking the increasingly blurred boundaries between different film forms whilst hooking viewers with the promise of both sex and something else. New Line appeared to know their audience; later taking on *Pink Flamingos* (1972) plus other early John Waters films, they introduced college students and other viewers to some of the strangest cinematic fruits around.

The film was to have been called *Bizarre* in the UK too but the British Board of Film Censors snipped-out nine minutes and 'fucked it up', according to Balch speaking in 1971. Its new title, *Secrets of Sex*, was brought in to 'rescue' the film and to sell it to hungry cinemagoers just adjusting to the new mores of the age. He changed other film titles, making European art house movies sound like sexploitation pictures, so why not here too?

The censors rarely knew what to do with the films that Balch either made or submitted for distribution. They considered Ted V. Mikels' blatant tongue-in-cheek movie *The Corpse Grinders* (1971) 'so unrelieved by any lightness of touch, by any wit or slapstick, that we are driven to the conclusion that it was meant as straightforward horror cinema', and overlooked the fact that Balch had filmed himself masturbating in *Towers Open Fire*. But then Balch was really quite a wayward character, confusing (at least British) people with his unusual doubling up of art and sex, and the overly populist and the really quite esoteric. He came from a show business family (his mother had been a dancer and worked at the Windmill Club in Soho) and he enjoyed the thrill of ceremony and the event. As a child he had set-up a cinema in the family home, and charged admission. For him, cinema seemed to exist way beyond what happened on screen and, chiming with the ideas of Burroughs and Gysin, he took neither film nor 'reality' at face value. Which differed quite radically to the then frankly out-of-touch BBFC.

Balch's own view of *Secrets of Sex* was that: 'this is a very uneven film, but three episodes and a single shot, are good.' This is easy to agree with, but repeated viewings highlight its broader, overarching strengths; each section seems to riff on a set of varying ideas and imagery and it's sharp and well put together. Colours are bright, the editing confident and it's better shot than Balch's follow-up *Horror Hospital* (1973) – though that's also great, but for other reasons.

Secrets of Sex revels in the changing attitudes of the time, mocking almost everything in jovial nihilistic fashion whilst traveling far and wide in terms of what sex meant. Free love and the permissive hippies were rarely out of the papers in the 1960s and the latter part of the decade also saw legalization of homosexuality and significant increases in the use of the Pill. 1970 also saw changes in the cinema. From now on only eighteen-year-olds and above would be officially permitted to see an X-rated film; in the past the bar had been set at sixteen. Films got stronger and punters got more for their shilling.

Balch's film is neither just tits nor cynical voyeurism. Which is not to say that it presented some clear overriding message. It's weird and was ultimately an experiment. Could Balch make an actual feature film? And how would he knit all these ideas and different creative personalities and contributors together?

If it did say something then it was that sex is compelling – but hellish. And yet somehow a great lark too. Abnormality is rife and for the most part, we do what we can, whatever that is, whilst staring, perhaps laughing, at the gates of paradise, a world from which we have long since been banished – quotes from Milton's *Paradise Lost* both open and close the film. Balch just threw it all in like a depraved witch stirring-up an evil broth. For all its oddity and playfulness, *Secret of Sex* was also a personal film, at least of sorts.

The director may not have entirely liked the results but the public at the time did. It's bright, lurid and brash and ran for over six months at the Jacey Piccadilly, more than recouping its costs, and later enjoyed a repeat run in an edited version when it was re-released in 1977. Running at thirty minutes, it presumably included only Balch's very favourite bits, and was punchy and to the point. The fact that it could still find an audience nearly ten years later suggests that its weirdness and lack of outright ogling had – and has – ultimately helped it to stand the test of time. The only thing is, the shorter version doesn't seem to exist anywhere. What was in it? How did he cut it? We'd truly love to know. If you know where it is, please get in touch. It must be the best and weirdest thing ever: a piece of messed-up, sexual psychedelia unleashed at the height of punk. *WF*

Life out of the fast lane: *All the Right Noises* (1971).

Underage sex, pretensions of intimacy and closeness, plus a spot of architectural criticism all made for strange bedfellows in...

All the Right Noises

UK Film | 1971 | colour | 91mins
Director Gerry O'Hara
Script Gerry O'Hara
Producers John Quested, Si Litvinoff
Production Company Trigon Productions
Cast Olivia Hussey, Tom Bell, Judy Carne

Films and Filming was one of the few film journals or magazines to write about *All the Right Noises* when it came out in 1971. They conjured tabloid-

style images of wife-swapping and awkward free love, and called it '*Brief Encounter* meets Swinging London'. An intriguing prospect. The film is about an extra-marital affair – the thing that nearly happens in David Lean's *Brief Encounter* (1945) – and its social mores are very different to those of and before the War, but it could hardly be described as bawdy or frivolous.

In fact, it's bleak. Len, the leading character and perpetrator of the affair, doesn't care about his moral position – or lack of it. He's sullen yet brazen, qualities conveyed with great care by Tom Bell, the powerful yet subtle actor best known for his turn in *The L-Shaped Room* (1962). Len's mistress, Val, played by Olivia Hussey, is only fifteen but that doesn't seem to matter much either. He's shocked when he sees her in school uniform, realizing that she's under the age of consent, but relaxes when she says that she'll change into a dress. If she doesn't look underage then, what's the problem? It's similar to when he says his wife won't know he's having an affair because 'as long as you pick up your cues and make the right noises' women don't notice things. Appearances are all that count and while he has gravitas, he's not very easy to identify with. But then none of the characters in *All the Right Noises* encourage our sympathies. Even Len's wife, Joy, appears alienated and ambivalent about life. The film isn't then about a moral dilemma – as in *Brief Encounter* – it's about doing what you want and the hope of getting away with it. It's domestic, yet nihilistic.

It's not overtly sensational though. 20th Century Fox marketed the film with the questions 'Is 15 1/2 too young for a girl? Is one wife enough for one man?' but unlike other British films released in the 1970s that used an underage girl storyline – such as *Twinky* (1970) or *Home Before Midnight* (1979) – the exploitative element, the issue of age, doesn't stay centre stage. Also, there's no heavy-handed increase in sexual tension when the affair is finally consummated. The lifestyles of the main characters are similarly rather ordinary and non-sensational, largely centred on school and domestic duties. This everydayness, and absence of youth culture in Val's case, loosens the film's attachment to the year in which it was produced: 1969.

20th Century Fox delayed the release of *All the Right Noises* for two years; writer and director Gerry O'Hara would hardly have been pleased. It was a

‹ **Bell of the ball:** Tom Bell in *All the Right Noise*s (1971).

personal project, made through his company Trigon, with investment from American producer Si Litvinoff (who also funded Nic Roeg's *Walkabout* (1971)). The curious thing is, if Fox acquired the movie for distribution, surely they knew what they were getting into? O'Hara may have been primarily known as a reliable assistant director, having worked on, amongst others, *The L-Shaped Room* (making the connection with Tom Bell), *Term of Trial* (1962), *Cleopatra* (1963) and *Tom Jones* (1963) but he had directorial credits on his CV too. *Amsterdam Affair* (1968), a thriller, had been well received by the press, if less so at the box office, while *The Pleasure Girls* (1965), another personal project, had scored on both fronts. The latter had been marketed like an exploitation picture (this time by its production company, Trigon) but as with *All the Right Noises*, its tagline only told part of the story – if that: 'They made love their way – ANY WAY!!!'. Focusing on a group of young women who share a house in the beatnik era of Swinging London, *The Pleasure Girls* was as much a kitchen sink drama as a tantalizing look at the mores and sensibilities of a new generation. Yes, the women go out clubbing and hook up with gangsters (including a rather demure Klaus Kinski) but they also confide in each other, go food shopping, don't necessarily rush into sex and are considerate when a male friend comes out as gay. It ticks some of the exploitation boxes but, like *All the Right Noises*, it resisted straightforward characterization and approached societal changes in a thoughtful, open way.

All the Right Noises didn't really lose anything by being released two years later. The haircuts might have seemed a little dated and the dresses too short and bright but the film's jaded cynicism and the indifference of its characters feels right on cue for a decade marked with greyness, uncertainty and decline. Similarly, the decision to use London locations on one hand looks back to the tourist visions of London promoted by Michael Winner (*The Jokers* (1967)) and Michelangelo Antonioni (*Blow-Up* (1966)) but it also looks forward. O'Hara's places are circumspect and idiosyncratic: a park, a pub and a modern tower block. They present a mundane, sometimes grubby version of London familiar to the 1970s.

O'Hara developed an enthusiasm for location shooting through his assistant directorial work, most notably on *Tom Jones* (1963) by Tony Richardson. Appreciating that it could inject greater realism and stronger continuity he shot all of *All the Right Noises* – the pub and flat interior scenes

Statuesque beauties: Tom Bell, Olivia Hussey and Henry Moore's *Three Standing Figures* in *All the Right Noises* (1971).

aside – this way. From Brighton Beach to Battersea Park, we get to see the actors performing in real places, adding to the drama and heightening the tension that surrounds the characters' acts of deceit.

The locales in *All the Right Noises* were often specific and evocative, reflecting and supporting the secretive events that unfold, none more so than the modern block of flats where Len and his family live. The end of World War Two brought both a housing crisis to Britain and, paradoxically, a sense of optimism about how to greet the future and literally rebuild the country. Len and Joy's mid-rise block by the Thames represents this rebuild and so do the new towns and blocks dotted around the country and visible in various British films from the 1960s and later. In *Work Is a Four Letter Word* (1968), *I Start Counting* (1969) and even *The Loneliness Of the Long Distance Runner* (1962) with its prefabs, the alienating and community-fracturing new architecture presents no real respite or welcome escape from the bad memories and stasis of the past, usually represented by an overpopulated and/or physically crumbling house. Like Barry Evans considering his future in the new town of Stevenage in *Here We Go Round the Mulberry Bush* (1968), the protagonists in these films are caught between worlds, unsure of their identities.

The bland, functional flats in *All the Right Noises* stand in stark contrast to the intimacy of Len and Val's relationship. The fact they decide to spend their first night together there – an extra marital affair for Len – suggests that there is little or no local community that might observe or absorb this detail. Val is concerned that she'll be spotted when she leaves but Len reassures her and says 'don't worry, once you're out front you could have come from fifty other flats.' He suggests that any or all the other flats might house an indiscretion but that no one knows or indeed cares. He is right; Val leaves and even passes Len's wife but all to no immediate consequence. The very architecture of the post-war block enables and encourages their affair.

The locations also comment on the liaison. The brief central presentation of the Henry Moore sculpture *Three Standing Figures* in the Battersea Park scene isn't significant in terms of the development of the story, but it's not incidental. It confirms the location – they're near Len's flat – but more than that, it offers ironic commentary on Len and Val's relationship. The BBC transmitted a half-hour documentary entitled *Henry Moore* on 30th April 1951; the next day *Sculptures and Drawings by Henry Moore* (an exhibition organised by the Arts Council) opened at the Tate and two days later again, King George VI opened the Festival of Britain at the new Royal Festival Hall where Moore's *Reclining Figure* had recently been installed. Moore was an important, government-endorsed artist and his family sculptures have a significant place in the parks across the country. In many respects these statues symbolise the state's investment in art but also the post-war investment in the nuclear family. This film seems to be saying the aspiration failed. The flats that Len's family live in were built to house a nuclear family but their functionality and uniformity worked against them.

Len and Val's affair concludes, however, towards the end of the film and life seems to return to normal. In keeping with everyone's tendency to obfuscate, details and evidence are conveniently swept under the carpet. But somehow a tension remains. Events do not just start and stop and actions have consequences. Len has inherited his father's weakness for gambling for instance – a small background detail – but will he end up homeless too? Will there be more affairs? Will his wife leave him? Appearances and events can be ignored to some extent but as with the stories that cling to the buildings in which they happen – unprecedented destruction and an international war – larger narratives remain.

The sense of fragmentation in *All the Right Noises* feels appropriate to the 1970s. The so-called 'permissive society' was settling down but also settling in. The irony is, however, that while it made sociological sense in 1971 (a very different time to the 1945 of *Brief Encounter* or even 'Swinging London'), the film was always going to struggle against the likes of *The Devils*, *Straw Dogs* or *A Clockwork Orange,* all released in that same year. They share the sense of nihilism that *All the Right Noises* has but deliver it at a considerably higher temperature. It's telling that the lesser known *Something to Hide* made in 1971 also begins in a domestic setting but then ramps-up dramatic ambition and delivers a shock ending; Peter Finch is drive to madness and murder after picking-up a teenage hitchhiker played by Linda Hayden. The early 1970s brought a period of change to British society, not least in the film world where the directorship of the British Board of Film Classification changed hands, again in 1971, and stronger films were not just made but also let through – often to considerable controversy. *All the Right Noises* is a very fine film that talks to us about the period in which it was distributed in subtle, nuanced ways. It was, however, totally out of keeping with the filmmaking sensibilities of its era. If it wasn't going to be wet with blood or sex then it needed a Hollywood star and a saccharine sensibility. The film sank and O'Hara had to wait for a Joan Collins vehicle, *The Bitch* (1979), to find commercial success. *WF*

Speaking of commercially successful erotica, it's always been a bit thin on the ground in Blighty. Across the pond, as they were getting down and getting on with shocking 1970s stuff like Deep Throat, *and* Emmanuelle, *our flagging film business was focusing on just as shocking but possibly less erotic stuff, often featuring men running about with their trousers around their ankles…*

Under the Doctor

UK Film | 1976 | colour | 86mins
Director Gerry Poulson
Script Ron Bareham
Producer Ron Bareham
Production Company GPA Films
Cast Barry Evans, Liz Fraser, Hilary Pritchard, Penny Spencer, Jonathan Cecil

Poster boy: Barry Evans in his heyday, a-grinnin' and a-typin' in a late 60s pin-up.

The once-boyish Barry Evans shot *Under the Doctor* straight after his success as the louche lead in Stanley Long's first rip-off of the Confessions comedies, *Adventures of a Taxi Driver* (1976). The thing was, Barry hadn't really wanted to make *Adventures of a Taxi Driver*, still less *Under the Doctor*. Though his career up to the mid-seventies might have suggested otherwise, he still considered himself to be a proper actor, and yearned to appear in serious drama, not sleazy flim-flam. Stanley, meanwhile, had none of the torment of the 'serious' artiste. He thought 'film genius' people he'd worked with – like Polanski – wasted far too much time and film (Stanley ended up shooting the bits Roman forgot to cover for *Repulsion* (1965), uncredited, for Tony Tenser's Compton company). He saw film simply as something you sold, and couldn't understand why anybody would want to make anything excessive, self-indulgent, or that would lose money.

With this in mind, Stanley was fond of relating the sad tale of Evans' repeated attempts to return to the stage as a proper thespian. He said poor Barry had blown the money he'd made in Long's taxi-cab money spinner – even selling back his percentage in the production to canny Mr Long, who didn't argue – using the money he'd made to fund an ambitious and very serious theatre company out in the sticks somewhere, which promptly went under. Not long after, according to Stanley, poor Barry was back, in somebody else's film, stripping off his pants and baring his pasty bum once more.

It's a bit of a shame. Barry's share in *Adventures*, Stanley recounted every time the Evans name cropped up, would have safely seen him through the years to a happy retirement. But alas, it was not to be. And, unfortunately,

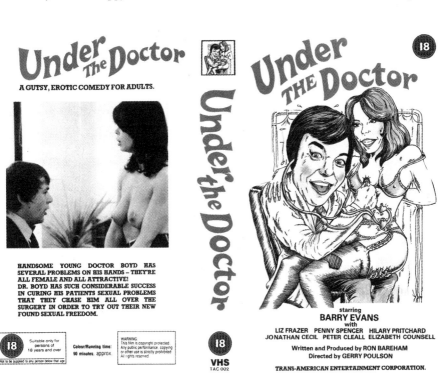

Fixed grin: discount video indignity with this 1990s VHS release of *Under the Doctor* (1975).

Big-screen Bazzer: *Here We Go Round the Mulberry Bush* (1968) movie tie-in paperback (left); *Die Screaming Marianne* (1971) press book (right).

though the money from it must have paid Barry's rent, *Under the Doctor* has none of the well-oiled production value of a Stanley Long film – it is, unfortunately, an especially feeble and flaccid example of that fusty, crusty but thoroughly fascinating genre, the Great British 1970s smut comedy. Just pop your clothes behind the screen there, and let's have a closer look at it.

Barry, of course, had once been a bright young thing of British cinema, back in his 1960s heyday. He'd been the smooth-cheeked teenage heart-throb of Clive Donner's splendid psychedelic coming-of-age comedy *Here We Go Round the Mulberry Bush* (1968), playing the archetypal oversexed teenage tearaway, cycling around the swanky new shopping centre in

Stevenage, enthusiastically exhaling an energetic 'phwoarr!' at every mini-skirted young lovely unlucky enough to catch his oglesome eye, as he rode around on his butcher's boy bicycle. Grown up a bit, but still looking baby-faced, he played the lead in Pete Walker's thriller *Die Screaming Marianne* (1971). After that came an ongoing starring role in the ensemble cast that fronted the hit TV comedy series *Doctor at Large* (ITV 1971). But then things took a slightly downward turn. 1975 had, in fact, according to IMDB, only yielded a bit part in *Crossroads* for ITV; hence cash-strapped Barry's awkward and uneasy submersion in sauce.

Let's not forget, though, that far more respectable players than Barry were taking what they could get, film-wise, in the seedy seventies. While the rank and file of the British film biz were fairly quality conscious when it came to television parts, being worried about being seen again in television repeats, in those days lots of actors took flat fees for films they didn't think much of, assuming that they'd be seen once in a few fleapits and then the offending film would be gone forever. Home video was still pretty much just a glimmer in Mr VHS's eye, don't forget. Hence fickle fate found Barry lurching, semi-naked, around grey, rain-spattered suburban streets for Mr Long, in the guise of a promiscuous taxi driver. But Barry, though an expert at looking boyish (until time took its toll), and a master of going 'phwoar!' and pulling embarrassed faces, was never going to be a super-stud.

Things, it would seem then, were not exactly going to plan for Mr Evans. But you might say that things weren't going to plan for British cinema generally around that time. It was a time of cinema slump. The biggest homegrown hitters of the early seventies were films like *On the Buses* (1971), the first big-screen spin-off from the grisly ITV comedy show about cheeky clippies. Watch it at your peril, but it was packing them in in '71. While the big studios struggled, enterprising independents were filling the gaps. Hence the success of entrepreneurs like Stanley Long and Pete Walker, lesser but determined figures like dogged, doomy Donovan Winter, and a whole bundle of other penny-pinching producers, jumping in with a film or two, eager to grab a slice of the pie and some tax-break Eady funding – a government film funding incentive eventually dismantled by the Thatcher administration.

Under the Doctor is in many ways an archetypal example of British 1970s sex-comedy filmmaking, clearly bearing many distinctive characteristics of the genre. Here's how it fits the bill. Firstly, it was quickly and callously knocked up to make money once, purely by getting people through the cinema doors, to be thoroughly disappointing, then to be discarded by all concerned and forgotten forever. Secondly, it's not at all funny. Quite the reverse, in fact – at points it has the distinct air of tragedy, though that's not to say it is devoid of entertainment value, if you are of a certain disposition. Thirdly, it's not in any way titillating or erotic. Every 'sexy' scene seems somehow demeaning and uncomfortable for all those concerned, male and female, and is generally equally disquieting to watch. Fourthly, it includes some players who could, should and sometimes did appear in better quality productions more suited to their talents elsewhere. Fifthly, it was shot for next to nothing, in order to ensure the best chance for a profit. Sixthly, and lastly, it's very 'bad' indeed – if such value judgments are what you crave. This is a key example of the kind of film that cultural organisations and erudite critics despise, or, more often, simply ignore. It is filled with dubious stereotypes, outmoded and/or inept depictions of gender and sexuality, clumsily done. It would of course have been roundly derided by the BFI in the *Monthly Film Bulletin*.

So, then, what do we do with a film like *Under the Doctor*? Do we dismiss it, dump it? Do we ignore it altogether and simply pretend that British cinema is all about David Lean, Powell and Pressburger? Do we squash it into some indicative statistic or signifier for academic assessment in a peer-reviewed paper? Or do we sit down and watch it, all the way through? Might it be an absorbing watch, in fact? Do we acknowledge, even, that it can *actually* tell us something significant?

It finally resurfaced on VHS home video, in a large format clamshell case, sometime in the 1980s. It was then briefly available from such quality purveyors of fine goods as the AB Superstore, late of Hounslow High Street, shelved amidst scented candles, slug powder, pick and mix sweets, ornamental salt and pepper shakers, and budget paint stripper. Garishly adorned in a sickly yellow sleeve, it was ornamented with a dreadful caricature of Barry in doctor's attire, painfully leering out from a crummy cartoon cover, with a scantily clad woman in the background.

Only a masochist, surely, would press play; only a madman could expect to achieve the nirvana of even half-baked arousal. It begins cheerfully enough with a jaunty – almost heartfelt – love song from crooner Vince Hill.

But this is the incongruous accompaniment to a terrifying title sequence which sees a young woman (the same Penny Spencer previously seen in the school-set TV comedy *Please Sir!* (ITV 1968-72)) parading unpurposefully about central London in a fur coat and a see-through blouse. We are of course supposed to be aroused by sight of her breasts through the gauze-like fabric, as she is photographed voyeuristically from a long way away. But as she stops off on various unlikely errands, like buying a bag of hot chestnuts (the seller, embarrassed, not aware that he's being filmed, looks like he wants to run away – how British), you will surely find yourself not titillated, but primarily worried about how cold and uncomfortable she must have been, as she marched unenthusiastically about amidst leering members of the public. She is, we eventually discover, portraying the unlikely patient of the titular 'doctor' himself, our old chum Barry, cashing in on his unfortunately-ended old TV role, playing an equally unlikely psychiatrist. A nymphomaniac with an unhealthy obsession with her step-father (verisimilitude is not, you'll have realised, paramount in this production), Penny's character is one of four women whose sexual confessions are inexplicably related through the film, portmanteau style, to Dr Barry, while he twitches, pulls faces and mugs so much that surely, if the wind should change, he would be at risk of staying like it.

Though it wasn't made by him, the film was originally distributed under Stanley Long's Alpha distribution banner. It would surely have played at the kind of sex cinemas where films of this kind played. But remember the Brit-smut paradox: as was so often the case, there's not much sex on offer here. At least the first tale contains some kind of fornication, albeit off-camera, with a bawdy butler (played by Peter Cleall, another ex-cast member from *Please Sir!*, intriguingly) but progressive increasingly-chaste segments seem to shift the focus, from scenes of getting it on, to scenes of *avoiding* getting it on.

The sex factor diminishes as the film goes on, like a drunkard's member, perhaps almost semi-erect at first, but slowly, inexorably drooping. Early on, the butler's at it and sex is signified symbolically – by a cork unexpectedly popping on a bottle of champagne. The woman is disappointed with his premature ending; but at least ejaculation has been achieved. By the time of the next segment, a strange period piece, which looks like an odd outtake from *Barry Lyndon* (1975), the sexiness has diminished still further. It features a duel between Evans (who plays multiple roles in this movie, but he's no Peter Sellers) and a bloke who was indeed in *Barry Lyndon*, Jonathan Cecil, as romantic rivals in regency era England. In fact, though, it becomes painfully clear, olde-England Evans has no phallus at all – as he reveals to the rampant nympho of this sequence, it was in fact shot off in the wars. So, instead of fucking, there's clucking – courtesy of a barn full of chickens. A nice set and some nice costumes in this bit as a matter of fact; perhaps explained by the fact that the Kubrick masterpiece had been shot just briefly beforehand, and the assistant accountant on *Barry Lyndon*, a chap called Ron Bareham, was in fact also the producer of *Under the Doctor*. Might he have bagged not only one of the cast, but also a location and some costumes? Certainly the expensive looking stately home set and these lavish costumes look incongruous all right in this bargain basement production. Barry would have loved a part in *Barry Lyndon*, don't you think? But he didn't get one. Instead, here he is, battling bad weather, his badly-written words frostily hanging in the air, cold cocks and cold cockles, in a bizarre *Under the Doctor* dream sequence. Sometimes life just isn't fair.

You'd think that you couldn't get much more sexless than knob-removal. Somehow, though, it does, towards the end. The film steps still closer to sterility with a long fantasy sequence in which unlucky Liz Fraser (a fine actress, also slumming it in the 1970s slump, and no more a natural-born porno player than Barry) attempts to seduce another Sellers-lite version of Evans, this time cast as a bored husband. She sings a song in Dietrich fashion, wearing the supposedly ever-popular red basque, serving up the sausage and mash to look like a cock and balls. The pair of them both look like they would rather be anywhere else, doing anything else, other than where they are. Neither are as young, or as beautiful as they ought to be, to even hope to get away with this kind of thing, if anybody could, which they probably couldn't; and the sequence seems, in fact, all rather creepy, if you allow yourself to ponder it for more than a few moments, which you probably shouldn't. Yet here we are discussing it.

Nobody at all, it would seem by the end, can get it up in *Under the Doctor*. It is a million miles away from being sexy, or erotic, or titillating.

They also perved: another splendid example of the Great British smut comedy, happily available in a 'new full length version' on this pre-cert VHS release. ›

Not only is it filled with fear of the vagina, it is also filled with fear of any kind of interaction, social or sexual, between the sexes. Barry's character does not want to deliver the 'money shot'. He spends all his time trying to avoid trying to deliver the 'money shot'. And ultimately, there are no money shots – or even, one surmises, money thoughts – here. In fact, by the end, as the doctor's nurse (another nympho, wouldn't you just know it?), appears and disappears in provocative poses around the office, we are left wondering (as with many other films in this perplexing but most absorbing genre) what exactly all the chaps in the macs could possibly have been getting out of it all; other than new complexes to complement their old complexes. It's all somewhat...complex.

Here, as in so much Brit smut, that old adage the foreign chaps have hooted about for donkey's years seems to be proven – that as a nation, we have always been somewhat uncomfortable with our sexuality. We'd rather hide the truth with a cheeky laugh and an innuendo than even begin to countenance the reality. We'd rather, it would seem, see Barry pull a funny face, go 'phwoarr!' and ride off quick on his bike, than acknowledge that we have sexual desires – or the chilling fact that they may forever be unfulfilled. Perhaps it was a particularly 1970s phenomenon, and things are all better, now we have ubiquitous porno all over the internet. Perhaps we have been somehow liberated. For a while, though, when you couldn't easily see anything stronger, films like this were about as explicit as you were legitimately going to get. Sexless, definitely; dreadful, assuredly so, when undergoing evaluation by any established critical criteria; but nonetheless endlessly fascinating and revealing in how they both conceal – and conversely, reveal – the issues at hand. Why are they still ignored by so many 'serious' historians?

And what of poor Barry, who was in them even though he didn't want to be? Is he forever doomed to shuffle around the eternity of our cultural memory with his trousers down around his ankles, or, worse, humiliated amidst the chickens in a borrowed barn? Not only limp dicked, but dick-less. No. Barry deserves better, far better. Let's remember instead the bright eyed boy, the talented actor of *Here We Go Round the Mulberry Bush*, the glorious career still unquestionably lying ahead.

'I saw the futility of it', says one of Barry's patients, half an hour into the 'action' of the limp comedy castration that is *Under the Doctor*, discussing her sordid sex troubles. And for perhaps the only occasion in the film, the words – unintentionally – ring true, all right. The futility is writ large all over it, under it, and runs straight through it – almost like the writing on a little stick of Blackpool Rock. Yet, at the same time, the film speaks so eloquently of the uptight sexuality of the masses in that supposedly 'permissive' 1970s Britain – and of the work that British actors did when they didn't have the luxury of saying no – and of that never-ending tension between commerce, cash, art and aesthetics. *VP*

So much for what the men in dirty-macs were miserably mulling over in the sex-cinemas. Meanwhile, in a rather more adult world, outside of the confines of 'commercial' cinema, women filmmakers and artists were looking for new ways to articulate the sexual aesthetics that had emerged out of the sixties counter-culture – with a new and distinctly female focus…

Phoelix

UK Film | 1979 | colour | 46mins
Director Anna Ambrose
Script Anna Ambrose
Cast Cosey Fanni Tutti, Philip Beaumont, Angela Coles
Production Company British Film Institute Production Board

Many considered at least elements of this new permissive society to benefit straight men – and straight men only. One last gasp of the old ways, before sex was subsumed into various forms of pornography, appeared to be the 1971 Wet Dream Film Festival in Amsterdam where the likes of Germaine Greer, underground organiser Jim Haynes and veteran exploitation filmmaker Stanley Long all rubbed along – these were strange times.

Thereafter women's and gay liberation emerged and British underground film for the most part dropped its sexual preoccupations. Abstraction and experimentation with perception instead became order of the day. With American finance being removed from more mainstream productions, it was a tough world for filmmakers to tentatively enter as on one-hand, exploitation and sex comedies went into the ascent, and on the other, independent and experimental film became fiercely debated and theorised.

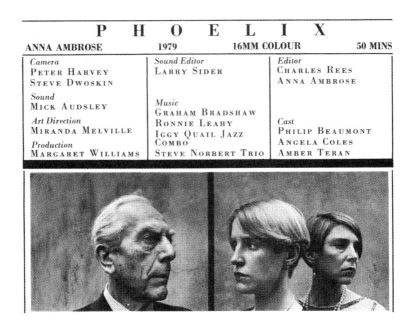

P	H	O	E	L	I	X	
ANNA AMBROSE		1979		16MM COLOUR			**50 MINS**

Camera	*Sound Editor*	*Editor*
PETER HARVEY	LARRY SIDER	CHARLES REES
STEVE DWOSKIN		ANNA AMBROSE
Sound		
MICK AUDSLEY	*Music*	
	GRAHAM BRADSHAW	
Art Direction	RONNIE LEAHY	*Cast*
MIRANDA MELVILLE	IGGY QUAIL JAZZ	PHILIP BEAUMONT
	COMBO	ANGELA COLES
Production		
MARGARET WILLIAMS	STEVE NORBERT TRIO	AMBER TERAN

All in order: Philip Beaumont, Angela Coles and Amber Teran, plus the credits for *Phoelix* (1979).

This had international repercussions as once lauded alternative filmmakers Walerian Borowczyk, Alain Robbe-Grillet and José Larraz became increasingly associated with pornography. Indeed, they struggled to find finance, and often porn became their only option.

But some resisted this equation of sex and the body with straightforward exploitation – even if this meant appearing distinctly out of step with their peers. Placed centre stage, the body was used to complicate or highlight assumptions about sexual dominance and control, as in the work of Austrian video artist Valie Export. Penny Slinger in the UK made cut-up photographs of her body, and, with Peter Whitehead, shot the unfinished film *Lilford Hall* (1969), exploring psychosexual geography on celluloid. Many of these works addressed, often in transgressive fashion, identity and identification.

Anna Ambrose, who died in 1985, was another UK independent filmmaker to venture into this controversial and not always well-received terrain. She had worked at the radical Everyman Theatre in Liverpool (where Julie Walters and Bill Nighy first started out) before training in film at the Royal College of Art in 1970. Thereafter she moved between commercial freelance editing at the BBC and associating with Film Work Group and the London Film-Makers' Co-op, an independent organisation supporting all stages in film production, distribution and exhibition by way of a co-operative model. ('She was always influenced by that experimental film world' – her partner, Michael Whyte.) Through the 1970s she explored formal ideas over a series of works and in 1974 won the Belgian Radio and Television Prize at the internationally renowned Knokke Experimental Film Festival with *Noodle Spinner* (1973). Footage of an Asian man spinning and drying noodles, filmed from different angles, is looped, inverted, duplicated and layered, all the processes undermining the visual integrity of his actions. Her 1979 film *Phoelix*, which she wrote and directed, would in all likelihood have been met with a mixed response amongst the experimental film community, at least at the radical LFMC, which resisted the presentation of bodies and sex.

Phoelix was, however, a carefully thought through work and drew on an interesting series of collaborators. Steve Dwoskin, who had been a founder member of the LFMC in 1966 and had taught Ambrose at the Royal College of Art, was cameraman for one section, whilst Cosey Fanni Tutti, of the abrasive experimental noise performance band Throbbing Gristle, also an artist in her own right, took a supporting acting role as a stripper. Fanni Tutti was unafraid to use her own body in radical and confrontational art performances and collages. Her work was particularly challenging as it didn't flag clear aesthetic connections to surrealism (though she has been interested in Georges Bataille), or for that matter any other forms of traditional high-art. Rather than distinguishing her work from pornography, she posed for pornographic magazines as a way of generating content for herself to then cut-up and incorporate in mail-art and other work, and latterly present unaltered in the highly controversial 1976 ICA exhibition *Prostitution*, whipping the tabloids into a frenzy. She was introduced to Anna Ambrose by Steve Dwoskin (having appeared in his *The Silent Cry* (1977) and later *Shadows From Light* (1983)). Her very presence brought a range of associated ideas and a frisson of controversy. At the very least, it meant that industrial music fans might be interested in a filmmaker who was actually little known – even in British experimental film circles. Even years later, the film would never be particularly promoted or written about, perhaps showing how out of step it was. It did screen on Channel 4 following her early death, and at the request of the channel's Chief Executive, Jeremy Isaacs, who held Ambrose in high regard and had commissioned her last film, *Handel – Honour, Profit and Pleasure* (1985).

Reflecting on cinema and performance, *Phoelix* was about a woman reclaiming the image of her body for herself. June (played by Angela Coles) is a middle-class out-of-work actor who moves between securing funds as a nude posing model, and indulging her elderly male neighbour in tea and conversation rituals in his upstairs flat – which is laid out like a museum. Statues and gold refinery overwhelm the space, and also its occupants. Bramwell, the man (Philip Beaumont), devotes his attention to June but never his actual interest, and his out-of-time pronouncements and oppressive flat depress her and drive her inward. So, she conjures a dream where Bramwell visits a burlesque club, one similar to the place where she poses, but in what appears to be the 1920s.

Each section of *Phoelix* was shot in a different way and the flat scenes were almost certainly shot by Dwoskin. He receives a camera operator credit. Having contracted polio as a child, the Jewish New Yorker, based in the UK since the early 1960s where and when he became a celebrated underground filmmaker, made a point of shooting in his crutches, highlighting the camera's presence and the viewer's act of looking by way of his fluid, hand-held, slightly lower-level eye view. In *Phoelix*, he focused more on objects in the room than people, and everything is brought oppressively close, and sometimes partially off-centre, creating a fragmented, claustrophobic picture of the man's strange, compressed, baroque palace. It is filled with shiny gold and kitsch opulent refinery. Heavy curtains hang by the windows, and small nude statuettes stare down, almost embarrassed, at the floor. The woman, June, remarks: 'he "has a guilt complex" he says. I think he means "gilt". I was in a manmade world.' Dwoskin's style complimented the aesthetic and ideas.

Each space in the film constitutes a kind of dream and a context for a different fantasy. The strip club, or rather the 'posing' club, is progressively revealed over the course of three scenes. First up, June and Cosey Fanni

Tutti sit in deck chairs, presenting themselves straight on, clothed. They obliquely compare notes:

'I didn't think I would get here actually. I couldn't get the bus'.
'I'm glad you did; I couldn't stand another day with Caroline. What do
  you do other than this? Anything?'
'Well, I'm supposed to be acting but I can't get any work at all at the
  moment. Could be worse. It pays the rent and it's tax free.'
'It's not very good though, is it?'
'I don't know, seems like easy money to me.'
'Nah, you can get more in pubs.'

The dialogue has a loose improvised feel and there's a sense that they might be playing themselves. It's not clear that they're on a stage yet, or indeed where they are. The lighting is bright and flat, suggesting something isn't quite right, and, as subsequent scenes reveal, the whole set-up is something of a comment on the theatrical dynamic of cinema. This is real, but not real. Melancholic electronic music pervades a later club scene and four rows of seats are glumly revealed, with various men sitting, expressing various levels of disinterest.

Posing clubs dated back to the early 1960s and were something of a strange and outdated concept by the time the film was shot in the late 1970s. But it suited *Phoelix*, with its brief inclusion of an eighteenth century Gainsborough nude. June even mirrors the Gainsborough pose later on, and the film draws a dotted line through these different art histories, highlighting the politics and history of voyeurism.

Cosey Fanni Tutti told us that the Blue City, on Peter Street in Soho, where it was shot, 'smelt damp with an undertone of cleaning chemicals to clear up "residue". The dressing rooms backstage were dusty, small, with minimal and very tired facilities. The stage was also small and in need of a makeover. The audience seating out front was small and in rows. It was very intimate and felt dirty and a bit suffocating, giving a distinct feeling that in its day to day use its main purpose was to provide a seat while the girls presented visual inspiration for masturbation.'

Despite being in central London, and in its pornographic quarter, Blue City operated under very specific restrictions. The age and inherent fire risks to the building prevented a music and dancing license, and thus it was illegal for women to strip or move to music on stage (consequently they take their clothes off in stages when the lights are out). At one level the strip club was the only legal and culturally designated space where women could be perceived as sexual – for the benefit of men, of course – and yet it was still policed and controlled in very specific ways. Cosey and June refuse these implicit rules and towards the end finally leave the stage, now topless, whilst telling their male audience: 'if you can do any better, come up here yourself'.

By way of contrast, the burlesque club that June imagines her neighbour attending is more fluid in event and character. A man, made-up and feminised, blurring gender boundaries, performs as Nefertiti, 'an old Egyptian queen' and the occasion takes place at night. Men and women, all dressed-up in 1920s refineries – the men in dinner jackets, the women in long, hanging flapper dresses – order drinks and politely flirt in the shadowy light. A stuffed owl surveys the proceedings. Later, police burst in and raid the joint. Though it assumes a sort of night logic, with a different but similar-looking actress functioning as a mirror side to June, curiously, of all the sequences, it is the most conventionally shot, incorporating different perspectives and illusions of continuity, and a sense of social inclusion. In conventional, long-established cinematic terms, the fantasy, the dream, becomes the most real and most natural seeming place of all. Weird. But it was all part of Ambrose's plan. (And this section was shot by the second credited cameraman, Peter Harvey, who, with his background, appeared to represent the independent narrative film scene in the same way that Dwoskin represented the underground. The film as a whole, then, conceptually, brought these two worlds together.)

Returning to Bramwell's curious, mausoleum like domain, June feels ever more repressed, frustrated and out of control. She couldn't find him or herself in the strange/normal imagined past, and neither can she here. 'His room was a setting for a drama that never took place. I would make him see the play, not just the stage.' She is an actress, she tells him and follows: 'I'm playing in a strip show. Would you like to see it?'

Reaching a kind of frustrated breaking point, she confronts the elderly man with the actual reality of her life. She takes off her clothes. On paper the event may sound like an attempt to seduce but the final scene is brief

Contemplating the fates: Anna Ambrose on the set of *Handel – Honour, Profit and Pleasure* (1985).

SPECTRE

a film-makers co-operative

has produced:

BEFORE AND AFTER THE MONSOON	*Keith Griffiths*	1982
GIVE US THIS DAY	*Phil Mulloy*	1982
JOURNEY THROUGH AN UNKNOWN LAND		
	Phil Mulloy	1984
THE WORLD OF CHILDREN	*Vera Neubauer*	1985
A PROFILE OF ARTHUR J. MASON ·	*Michael Whyte*	1984
HANDEL – HONOUR, PROFIT AND PLEASURE ·		
	Anna Ambrose	1985
MID-AIR	*Vera Neubauer*	1986
THE GOURMET ·	*Michael Whyte*	1986

* with Skreba Productions

and has in preparation:

FURTHER AND PARTICULAR	*Steve Dwoskin*
SONGS OF THE MACHINES	*Phil Mulloy*
END OF A JOURNEY	*Vera Neubauer*
IMMRAMA ERAINN	*Thaddeus O'Sullivan*
GIRL FROM THE SOUTH †	*Richard Woolley*

† with Tell Tale Films

Spectre's films have been financed by Channel 4, the Arts Council of Great Britain, the British Film Institute, and individual enterprise.

MEMBERS: STEPHEN DWOSKIN   JOHN ELLIS   KEITH GRIFFITHS   SIMON HARTOG   JANINE MARMOT
PHIL MULLOY   VERA NEUBAUER   THADDEUS O'SULLIVAN   MICHAEL WHYTE   RICHARD WOOLLEY

SPECTRE PRODUCTIONS LIMITED   41 & 45 BEAK STREET   LONDON, W1R 3LE
TELEPHONE: 01-439 1381   TELEX NUMBER: 946240 CWEASY G, "REF. 19016110"

Spectre: a list of their productions as advertised on the back of a brochure celebrating the twentieth anniversary of the London Filmmakers' Co-operative in 1986.

and functional, simply demonstrating that she has a body. The camera quickly passes up her torso in short broken shots in a way consistent with the fragmented images of Bramwell's flat seen earlier. It remains un-eroticised. Themes of display and voyeurism run through the film, but something different is happening here.

Still, it is too much for Bramwell who cannot accommodate the revelation. 'Do you think I'm a retired businessman from Birmingham or out-west somewhere? I don't like that sort of thing at all', he blusters. 'I think you'd better not come here again'. The woman realises events are not beyond her control and the man recedes back into his fantasy. (A parallel to what happens in the posing club.) June: 'there was nothing more difficult than to live up to men's dreams' and the film dares to venture into this world of sexual colonisation, addressing self-identity and control.

The end result was challenging and provocative, even for an experimental film. Cosey Fanni Tutti remembers the process of making it as a positive experience. 'It was good to work with other people, especially women, and Steve [Dwoskin] was so experimental and open-minded, easy to work with. Throbbing Gristle was really intense at that time so working with Anna and Steve was a release and refreshing.' Anna Ambrose 'was very focussed on the filming but I remember her as being a very warm person, easy to work with. I don't remember any real instructions other than to keep to what was permitted in the club environment which was very different to the pubs I worked in at the time. That was mainly in relation to the film rather than what was going on in the 1970s.'

Passivity threatens to dominate the film but June's internal monologues and interactions with her fellow stripper provide toughness and an edge. In fact, each space brings its own sense of expectation: the posing club, the models literally passive and stationary but then goading the audience out of frustration; the strange mausoleum that is the old man's flat; and then the risqué gentleman's club, back in time, somehow both acceptable and not.

Anna Ambrose's film signalled that it was possible to enter – or at least exit – these worlds on a woman's, or a person's, own terms. Context is everything and the appearance of the artist and noise musician Cosey Fanni Tutti brought associations that went beyond simply a person acting or appearing as a stripper; indeed her presence, like virtually every component to *Phoelix*, raised questions about what it meant to act and assume certain roles. A facet further reflected by a detail that few would be in a position to pick-up on: the actor playing Bramwell, Philip Beaumont, was in fact friends with Ambrose in real life. And their relationship, in part, paralleled the one explored in the film: Ambrose had visited Beaumont as a supportive neighbour and, being partially overwhelmed by him, imagined fantasy alternatives to both their lives – hence *Phoelix*. Beaumont was apparently happy to go along with it. To even have approached these subjects in the experimental, independent film world at this time, particularly with the film's sexual framing, would have been considered highly controversial, at least to some. It was also quite confusing – or highly mentally stimulating – if one chose to think about the connections going back and forth between the film's inspiration, its story and shape, and its internalised mode of self-reflection.

Anna Ambrose was forty when she died from breast cancer, just a week after completing the edit of her last film, *Handel – Honour, Profit and Pleasure*. According to her partner, Michael Whyte, Ambrose had had a premonition she would die at that loaded age. More fantasy, reality crossover. But what might have happened had she not passed on in 1985? Would she have made more dramas, as opposed to documentaries, her previous focus? Perhaps a feature?

In the 1970s, she had associated with the London Film-Makers' Co-operative and in the early 1980s she formed, with Steve Dwoskin, plus filmmakers Keith Griffiths, Phil Mulloy, Vera Neubauer, Thaddeus O'Sullivan, Richard Woolley, and Michael Whyte: Spectre Productions. This new group provided a pathway between alternative and commercial production, so as to ease and enable commissions from Channel 4. Many such groups were formed. In 1984, she made *The Cinema of Stephen Dwoskin*. Then she made the aforementioned *Handel – Honour, Profit and Pleasure*, a dramatic account of the life of composer George Frederic Handel starring Simon Callow and a young Hugh Grant. (The smooth, foppish actor and Cosey Fanni Tutti almost meet through Anna Ambrose's filmography.) What might have happened after that? Of course, we can't know. And it's difficult to speculate, given the rapidly changing media landscape of this period. One thing we do know – *Phoelix*: it was and is an unusual, dynamic piece that sidestepped the more familiar modes of 1970s experimental film production whilst still engaging with the issues of the day, and, importantly, on the filmmaker's own terms. In the wake of punk, on the precipice of the pop video explosion – and as experimental film was becoming increasingly engorged with theory – a different path had briefly emerged. *WF*

OUT OF TOWNERS

Cinema is only a century or so old. Down through the decades of its jolty journey towards becoming an ' artform' deserving of critical respect and academic analysis, there has always been a pronounced divide – for the critics, at least – between film that can be considered 'art', that is to say culturally valuable, and hence suitable for the discerning cineaste; and that which is considered 'entertainment', that which is popular fodder for the masses. The latter category is far bigger than the former, of course. Thus that path towards respectability has been a thoroughly thorny one; and, despite every 'great' film that has been made in the last hundred years, film is still sometimes viewed with suspicion – possibly perceived by some fancy folk as a worryingly populist medium – not nearly as respectable as fine art, opera or the theatre, and certainly disconcertingly popular with the grubby mass that were once known as the 'lower classes'.

Perhaps part of the problem is that like all mass-produced entertainment media, with ticket sales determining its direction, its development has proven dashed hard to control. Let's take a delightful mid-twentieth century example from long-ago 1962. In that far-off year, the more discriminating clientele could venture on a stylish, sand-swept cinematic journey across the desert, courtesy of the critically-lauded *Lawrence of Arabia*. For those of

‹ **I've got you under my skin:** a rare sight indeed; a man does the Padstow May Day Oss dance out of costume in *Oss Oss Wee Oss* (1953).

a more low-budget bent, there was an altogether more cheap and cheerful excursion available: *Carry on Cruising*. And still time for a couple of jars across the road after the latter film had finished, to boot. Who's to say which one is the best? Then, as always, audiences were prepared to pay for what they wanted to see – not necessarily what was deemed to be good for them.

Some years earlier, in the first half of the twentieth century especially, the divide between the guardians of good cinematic taste and the punters purchasing the tickets – many of whom were the new urban working classes, who a couple of generations earlier, might have worked the land, but might work now in a factory – was particularly pronounced. The film trade press, in those polite years gone by, did not think it at all unkind or odd to make somewhat patronizing statements like 'would play well in the provinces' in their reviews, when it came to alerting cinema managers about what to show on their screens around the country. Indeed, in the years after World War Two, independent producers made the most of this cultural and regional divide, generating specific content for localized working-class audiences. In Manchester, the Mancunian production company made films starring local lad Frank Randle, for instance, whose comedies played to packed houses in the North country, but often barely made it down south. Another famous Northern comic, the aforementioned George Formby, broke the mould to become popular nationwide – and overseas too – but his films were viewed with an aloof eye by critics – despite the fact that before too long George was grinning and gurgling his way to bringing in bundles of cash for Michael Balcon at erstwhile Ealing Studios.

Despite the fact that this 'lowbrow' fun could make big money, and pleased a heck of a lot of punters, such films weren't (and still aren't) accorded much of a look in when it comes to film criticism. British comedy always gets it in the neck. Some years further down the line, despite the fact that Norman Wisdom was bringing in the cash for the Rank Organisation in the early 1950s, he still faced snobbery from the upper echelons of the management there. And film critics – to this day – never miss a chance to moan about him. And while we're travelling down that road, don't forget to stop off at the 1970s, when much-sniffed at films like *On the Buses* (1971) were, despite a season ticket's worth of bad press, coining it in, bolstering the British Cinema industry when it was in the deepest doldrums.

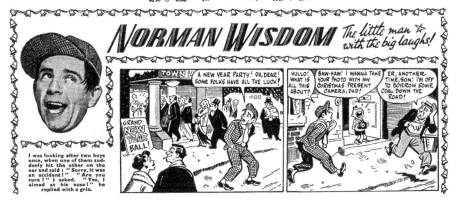

Little man, big laughs, big money for Rank: 'The Gump' as seen in his weekly *Radio Fun* comic strip, 1959.

Inextricably enmeshed with this highbrow-lowbrow dichotomy is the similar historic divide between 'town' and 'country'. Compare and contrast the elaborately artificial, pre-fab goings-on at the Festival of Britain in 1951 – swanky modern designs down at the Southbank, fancy sculptures, bri-nylon blouses, flouncy dance steps and what have you, supposedly reflecting the great new post-war nation – with the earthier rustic-realism of the strange old countryside ritual at the heart of *Oss Oss Wee Oss* (1953). The Festival of Britain posited that the capital was the cultural centre of the nation, neglecting to reflect the vital things going on far outside its urban orbit. While in Lomax's film, eerily Morrissey-like men danced their earthy dances in a remote village, or roguishly raided the lord of the manor's sycamore trees, the urban intelligentsia had other ideas about country living. They were busily dreaming up an artificial rural idyll, soundtracked not with authentically bawdy old folk songs, but with a politely polished Vaughan Williams orchestral score.

Townies are traditionally distrustful of those from the countryside, and vice versa. There is perhaps an undercurrent of fear, on both sides: fear of different kinds of people, from different backgrounds; fear that concrete will cover the cornfields, and town will encroach upon the countryside; or, conversely, fear that the old, mystical ways of the countryside will somehow engulf and obliterate the new ways of the town.

We reckon that the films and programmes discussed in this section somehow reflect these social antagonisms – dichotomies between town and country, upper class and lower class, rich and poor, valued and unvalued, or the urban and the regional.

Whatever anybody says, we all know we still do not live in a classless society; and the ideological and financial tensions between urban and rural expanses are more pronounced than ever, as the cataclysm of 'Brexit' continues to bewilder all and sundry. And whatever that brings, assuming we end up having isolated ourselves, our internal arguments will continue. One of which will always be this: with the creeping onset of concrete, is it better to adapt, alter and survive, or resist and risk being swept away? But, also, isn't it far easier to argue your case either way knowing that you've been to a good school and have a few quid in the bank?

…Back now to the 1950s. While cleaned-up country dances were being politely performed in the cities, in a distant Cornish village the old ways were earthily observed by the locals…and caught on Kodachrome in a most unorthodox manner…

Oss Oss Wee Oss

UK Film | 1953 | colour and black and white | 16mins
Director Alan Lomax
Producer Peter Kennedy
Script Alan Lomax
Production Company Folk Films
Cast The Hobby Horses of Padstow in Cornwall, The People of Padstow in Cornwall, Charlie Bate of Padstow, Charlie Chilton of London

'I must say, Sir, when I'm gone West, I hope the Oss will come down on my graveyard and dance over it,' said a person known as the Colonel after dancing through the streets of Padstow on May Day in 1951. He'd been wearing the heavy, black Hobby Horse or 'Oss (as it's known) costume/ construction for many hours and had followed 'the teaser' along the preordained route, mapping out the North Cornwall fishing town – like he did the year before. The Colonel danced this dance every May Day for decades, and so did many before him. And as several have since. The 'Oss is no-one, or no one specific person; it transcends life and the individual, and is continually reborn.

The tradition has enormous power, even for the increasing numbers of out-of-towners (or 'emmets', to use Cornish parlance) who fill up the place on May Day weekend. When the Colonel's words were recorded in 1951, however, it was very different. When Alan Lomax and two friends travelled down from London to make a film about the Cornish custom, visitors were very unusual.

Folk culture was perceived in a new way in the 1950s and Alan Lomax played a significant role in driving, radicalising and popularising that change. He arrived from the States at the very beginning of the decade and quickly established himself in the London folk scene. He played in a skiffle band (playing the English folk rock and roll – itself influenced by blues musicians Lomax had documented in the Southern States), travelled the British Isles recording folk singers and broadcast his distinctive, enthusiastic, loud American voice over the nation's airwaves courtesy of the BBC. In almost all these activities, he worked with Peter Kennedy, a folklorist with whom he would go onto make *Oss Oss Wee Oss*. The two young men had folklorists for fathers – John Lomax was the co-founder of the prestigious Texas Folklore Society while Douglas Kennedy was the director of the English Folk Dance and Song Society – and had bonded quickly. They were also technological pioneers.

The portable reel-to-reel tape recorder had been developed at the end of World War Two and was still considered something of a new machine in the 1950s: Kennedy and Lomax recognised its potential and used it. They recorded folk singers – usually rural people who'd learnt songs through their family or in the pub or at work – within their own environments and played these recordings back on the radio. Simple but daring. Folk songs had been featured on radio before but up until this point had always been transcribed and re-performed by a professional – i.e. 'proper' – singer. Hearing these new songs and singers on Light Programme slot *As I Roved Out* (1953-1958), and live TV show *Song Hunter* (1953), many viewers and listeners were shocked. Lomax and Kennedy (along with a handful of others at the BBC, including Séamus Ennis) privileged the original, raw

On parade: the Obby Oss on full display in Padstow.

voice and people weren't used to it. But then Lomax and Kennedy didn't just see folk culture as something from the past, something to be got at via corrupted words and tunes delivered by a modern singer: they saw it as something contemporary, alive and real now.

Social documentaries had up until this point typically included little or no spoken reflections from the people they purported to represent. There were both ideological and technological reasons for this: the class system was still very rigid and shooting mobile synchronised sound and picture remained virtually impossible until the early 1960s. Rather than grappling with this technical issue, most filmmakers used music and narration to tell their story and when including on-location spoken-word, employed a clapperboard to help with synchronising sound and image. The latter process was very formal and hardly likely to relax the person about to be questioned about some part of their life. The clapperboard would be whacked and a question barked. The procedure also perpetuated the power relationship between the interviewer and interviewee; the worker beholden to the boss asking the questions, waiting for permission to speak.

Lomax and Kennedy overcame these constraints by utilising their skills with the tape recorder. They were at ease with the machine and used to eliciting relaxed, personal responses from the people that they spoke to.

Working partly with a script and partly with informal interviews, they either post-synched their recordings with the film footage shot by cameraman George Pickow or happily left them loose. *Oss Oss* is a complex film and the interweave of these different elements with actuality and staged scenes plus the use of both colour and black and white film indicate that it went through a sophisticated and probably lengthy editing process. Alan Lomax was admittedly a busy man but this might account for the delay between shooting the film in 1951 and completing it in 1953, a long production process for a sixteen-minute documentary.

John Szwed briefly recounts the story of the production in his Alan Lomax biography, *The Man Who Recorded the World,* and suggests that the project began at least very casually. Driving down from London, the three men made their plans en route. Kennedy primed Lomax on the detail of the custom, Lomax worked-up a rough shooting script for Pickow, and Pickow played with his new spring-driven Bolex camera. On arrival, however, they realised that some key events happened on May Day eve and that they didn't have enough film – or even the right type. Had they been too relaxed about it? In a state of slight panic they searched for and eventually located more stock – black and white film that could be shot in low light – and a floodlight. The day – or rather the evening – was saved.

The people of Padstow helped Lomax, Kennedy and Pickow and truly entered into the spirit of the film, despite the fact the filmmakers were out-of-towner 'emmets'. Fisherman Charlie Bate welcomes the camera crew and invites them to meet the local characters: the beginning of the film. Cut to the pub and the footage shot in black and white. The Colonel slurs hello and then we're presented with an incredible sight: the 'Oss dancers drawing their hands over each other in animalistic fashion and moving to the beat of a thumping drum. They're doing the Oss dance out-of-costume. According to Peter Kennedy, anthropologist Margaret Mead later compared these moves to dances she'd seen in the Pacific.

Patrick, the Colonel's great nephew and current 'Oss, said at the 2011 Cornish Film Festival that this scene was shot in two locations, the Red Lion and the London Inn. Herein lies another story. There are actually two 'Osses; the Old 'Oss and the Blue 'Oss, or Peace 'Oss, and the Colonel and Charlie Bate and their friends belong to the Old 'Oss party – drinking in the Red Lion – while the dancers performing out-of-costume belong to the Blue – in the London Inn. Both parties are thanked in the credits but Lomax chose not to get into the story of the two groups, probably to keep it simple but also to avoid disagreement no doubt.

The use of black and white film helped glue the discrete pubs and teams together. This happened in the edit and so did the addition of an unseen Cockney, a visitor who asks the Cornishmen about their town and tradition. It works extraordinarily well and it's difficult to believe that this was an afterthought, but John Szwed says it was. We never see Charlie Chilton but he helps us make sense of Padstow and he's a welcome change from the more traditional forms of narration: the plummy, BBC-style voice. It's notionally Chilton that Charlie Bate welcomes at the beginning of the film and takes to the pub, not the filmmakers.

Charlie Chilton meets characters around the town. The greengrocer who's in charge of greenery and garlands on May Day says, 'about eighty years ago, some of the most influential people in Padstow did everything possible to prevent the Old 'Oss coming out but a few faithful ones,

Unite and unite for summer is a-come unto today: Charlie Bate plays the accordion in *Oss Oss Wee Oss* (1953).

including Old Mac, did it at the risk of losing their jobs.' While the Colonel, who we've already quoted says: 'you got to get permission from the Squire himself see [to cut the sycamore] but sometimes you take French leave. Well, I was caught once and the steward said...'you'll hear more about this.' Such confessions were not what you might expect in a British documentary.

These quotes clearly allude to class tension and a distinct indifference to authority, but the same could still be said about the tradition today. Many Padstonians feel considerable resentment towards the second-home owners who've pushed-up the housing prices in the area. And when they perform the custom now, there's a sense that they're re-marking their territory, letting people know who really owns the town. Lomax and company were an earlier generation of outsiders – but there must have been a feeling that these emmets 'got it' and that they could be trusted. According to Peter

Kennedy, a contract was made that stated the film would be premiered back in Padstow once editing had been completed.

It's perhaps also fitting that Lomax and friends shot *Oss Oss Wee Oss* at the same time that a very different type of culture was being celebrated back in London. King George VI opened the Festival of Britain at the new South Bank centre on May 3rd 1951, two days after May Day. The Festival was a wilful attempt on the part of the government to reinvigorate both culture and the spirit of the people after the War. It centred on commerce and a kind of State sponsored art, approved and contextualised by the government. The May Day custom in Cornwall was and is very different and the film absolutely reflects that.

The interactions between Charlie Bate and Charlie Chilton allow the route of the dance and the importance of the custom to be explored and explained in a relaxed, conversational way. Charlie Chilton's words, probably largely written by Alan Lomax, also contribute to the film's distinctive poetic quality. 'I first saw Padstow from the hill, framed by silver sycamore trees: a funny little fishing port where sailboats slept along the quays. Padstow: down on the Cornish coast, famous for wrecks and ships gone wrong,' he says. Poetry also lies in the way the song lyrics interweave with the lives of individual people. And it's in this particular interplay that a strange fusion of narrative and actuality somehow emerges from the happenstance. A young Padstonian woman sits amongst some grass and the May Day song seems to comment on her activity: 'where are the maidens who here now should sing, for summer is a-comin' today? They are in the meadows, flowers gathering in the merry morning of May.' And then she gets up and, with a look of pure joy on her face, runs to the 'Oss. It's quite magical.

These collages of song and people tell us that this 'tradition' isn't just something from the past. Instead it's a sort of once and future folk memory. The Padstonians remake and rejuvenate the custom each year and it remakes and rejuvenates them. *Oss Oss Wee Oss* doesn't overly explain or historicise the tradition but it does illustrate the custom's incredible local importance and enormous dynamic power. Yes, the film is very romantic but it's also very convincing.

So why isn't this visionary film better known? It's ground-breaking but for whatever reason it's never found a place in the documentary history books. It might be because it wasn't made through the government documentary movement or included in the Free Cinema screenings at the National Film Theatre, events that kick-started some long and prestigious careers. Instead, it was distributed by the English Folk Dance and Song Society (and presumably Lomax's people when he returned to the States) and was largely seen only within the folk community. Curiously though, another folk documentary from the period, *Wake Up and Dance* (1950), broke out of that enclave and won an award at Cannes despite being, arguably, a lesser film. It has a visionary quality – it's another film about how folk music casts a spell on people – but the dancers are middle class and the dancing, unfolding at an EFDSS sponsored festival in Stratford, is somehow both stiff and overly performative. Why didn't *Oss Oss* win an award? It feels too obvious to blame it on a class bias. Was it somehow too unruly, subversive even?

Charlie Chilton: 'Pagan or Neolithic, this Padstow 'Oss dance is pretty terrific'. The May Day custom in Cornwall doesn't descend from above or come with an official stamp. Alan Lomax's groundbreaking, little known film, celebrates precisely this. *WF*

…and if those townies had no idea what went on in the countryside, the opposite may also have been the case. Certainly the fee-paying public school education system was somewhat misunderstood by those who never attended…

Fun at St Fanny's

UK Film | 1955 | black and white | 80mins
Director Maurice Elvey
Script Anthony Verney
Producer David Dent
Production Company Adelphi Films (Advance Films)
Cast Cardew 'The Cad' Robinson, Fred Emney, Vera Day

Before we sit down to carve our names into the ink-blotted desks of St Fanny's, the silly public-school setting of this cheery, cheap, 1950s classroom comedy, let's stop fooling about and try to be serious for a moment. Let's think about a different kind of class. Yes, British society and class. Wake up at the back there! Was there ever a book about British film that did not mention it?

Play the game, you chaps: elderly schoolboy Douglas Cardew 'The Cad' Robinson, sporting a precariously balanced cap, on this 1950s music sheet.

If we flashback to the *St Fanny's* era, or thereabouts, but look towards better known examples of the comedy genre, you can spot a clear class distinction between 'posh' comedy and 'working class' comedy. Check out the two sides of the Rank Organisation's comic coin. Side one is *Doctor in the House* (1954) featuring well-scrubbed, sharp-suited, fearsomely Brylcreemed Dirk Bogarde. He's training to be a doctor, as all nice boys not training to be lawyers, not in officer training school, or working in the city should. He's getting into scrapes with blustery James Robertson Justice's senior doctor and deflecting the amorous advances of Shirley Eaton's not-well-bred-enough landlady's daughter – also as nice boys should. Side two is Norman Wisdom's first feature, *Trouble in Store* (1953). This features working-class Norman in his cloth cap and too-tight trademark 'gump' suit as a lowly stockroom assistant in a department store (the kind of person who would stack the jars of Brylcreem on the shelf for Dirk's doc to buy, perhaps) aspiring to romance with the shop girl in the record department (she's too good for him), dreaming of one day being a window dresser (forget it, Norman!). Quite a different kettle of fish, eh?

Note also, though, outside the diegesis, the cold hard commercial fact that scruffy Norman saved the Rank Organisation's bacon, in many ways, in troubled times, and they warmed to the scruffy little man once they saw how he could make them money. 'In the early days of shooting, everyone was as tense as a bowstring, from the director down to the clapper boy,' recalled Wisdom later in his excellent autobiography. After the successful premiere, however, previously icily-reserved execs couldn't wait to applaud their cloth-capped cash-cow. 'The Rank chiefs and their wives clustered round to pump my hand. Beaming smiles lit up the entrance like fairy lights…it's called the bullshit of show business.'

Away from Rank, and their nationwide screen ambitions, a plethora of small, independent filmmaking concerns made cheaper films, and fought fiercely for bookings, either on the major circuits, run by Rank and Gaumont, or at the numerous independent cinemas across the country. One such was the maker of *Fun at St Fanny's*: Adelphi Films, founded by Arthur Dent – indomitable, cigar-smoking, veteran film executive, who, having entered the business in its earliest days, had worked his way up through the ranks to become Sales Director for the prestigious Associated British Picture Corporation (ABPC). In 1940, he had finally struck out as an independent, forming Adelphi (and various other film-production related concerns, including Adelphi's sister company, Advance Films). Like the other small fish in the big pond of British film production, Arthur's outfit chased bookings in British cinemas with all the rest. Additionally, Adelphi constantly found itself in conflict with cinema circuit bosses who had no time for outspoken Arthur's virtuous vocalisation of the problems of the independent little men of British cinema.

Fun at St Fanny's was just one of Arthur's many modestly-budgeted comedy extravaganzas – ambitiously designed for circuit distribution, but, when it was turned down by big-boy exhibitors like Rank, one that ended up being played at independent cinemas. In common with most of Arthur's projects, it featured a mixture of new talent (he had a fine eye for stars on their way up: early on, he'd signed Goons Sellers, Milligan and Secombe for the Brighton based comedy romp *Penny Points to Paradise* (1951)). He also watched and waited for old troupers on the way down: he'd unexpectedly bagged wartime favourite Tommy Trinder for a nostalgic National Service comedy, *You Lucky People* (1955). On this particular occasion, Arthur signed up a star in his heyday: contemporary radio-comedy's most famous aged-schoolboy, Cardew 'The Cad' Robinson, for his feature debut. 'Who did that?' demanded the angry teacher in the weekly show on the wireless. 'Cardew the Cad!' screamed the schoolboys. Robinson had borrowed the name of his radio-persona from a schoolboy 'bounder' he'd read about, Ralph Reckness Cardew, created by Martin Clifford (aka Charles Hamilton), prolific author of the St Jim's stories of school life, as published in the weekly boys' paper, *The Gem*.

'My interest in and, in fact, obsessional love of public school life is possibly odd, considering I didn't actually attend one,' Cardew Robinson would recall in the *Daily Telegraph* in 1985. Definitely odd, you might conclude; as was the fact that he built a career around his unlikely stage persona as a gangly, gormless ever-more-aged public schoolboy: toothy Cardew 'The Cad' of *St. Fanny's*, sporting stripy scarf and precariously-balanced cap.

Perhaps odder still, though, was that he became a wireless comedy regular with the BBC, with his comic strip adventures seen every week in the pages of *Radio Fun* by a Commonwealth readership of more than seven million. Perhaps oddest of all, Cardew got the opportunity to immortalise his wacky world of creaky, corny 'schoolboy howler' jokes in a feature film: Adelphi's *Fun at St. Fanny's*, one of the very last in line – and perhaps the strangest – of British schoolroom comedies in the Will Hay mould. 'I had the thrill,' he also remembered via the *Telegraph*, 'in addition to playing Cardew, of seeing all the characters I had created come to life... the film was shown at the Warner's cinema in Leicester Square.' Not bad, considering 'The Cad' had been quickly knocked up for a monologue with music designed to fill a few minutes in a wartime RAF Gang Show.

The concept was undoubtedly Cardew's, but he was billed beneath the real star of the film: portly comedy veteran Fred Emney. Fred, popular on television at the time, having scored success with the BBC's *Emney*

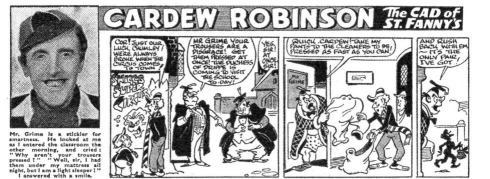

Your trousers are a disgrace: Cardew's special brand of high-brow humour gets an illustrated airing in this edition of his weekly *Radio Fun* comic strip, 1959.

Enterprises (1954-57), pocketed £75 per day on the three-week shoot, whereas Cardew made do on £20 per day; and for the rest of the cast, it was harder times still. We might spare a thought for poor Ronald Corbett, many years away from *The Two Ronnies* (1971-87), in aged schoolboy mode like Cardew, but well down the cast list, sufficing with a measly £5 per day for his time spent sweating over a hot classroom in his imitation Eton collar.

Relentlessly faithful to its radio and comic strip roots, and thus tailored to precisely that 'provincial' audience at which the 'intelligentsia' then and now might scoff, Anthony Verney's straight-down-the-line pun-stuffed screenplay was fashioned from raw material provided by industry veteran Denis Waldock and the 'Memory Man of the Movies', showbiz journalist Peter Noble. Shooting took place at Twickenham Studios in May 1955. Noble, more used to gossip columns than the scriptwriting game, threw himself enthusiastically into the project, but his fellow journalists were not impressed with the results. 'Some of the rottenest chestnuts I have had thrown at me in twenty years of film going,' moaned the *Evening Standard*. 'Farce of the crudest order,' griped *The Times*.

A small sample should suffice. Warning – hold your sides whilst reading. This is powerful stuff.

Dr Jankers (Fred Emney, sporting a mortar board, tapping a pointer on his desk, and doing his best Will Hay schoolmaster impression): Cardew, what is a circle?
Cardew: Why, sir...don't you know?
Dr Jankers: Well, er...I don't know...do you? What is it?
Cardew (beaming toothily): Why, a circle is a blob of nothing with a ring around it.

Of course, the critics were right. True enough, this was not a highbrow production. Here were, shamelessly delivered, enough achingly ancient jokes to fill a Christmas cracker factory, amidst the scraps of a jumbled plot that made little sense, bundled together with a selection of bizarre musical interludes; but, in retrospect, these attributes are precisely what lend this bewildering film a distinctive near-surreal charm all of its own. Perhaps the critic at the *Standard* understood its cheerfully unpretentious strangeness a little better, summing it up, with just the faintest glimmer of patriotic pride, as 'the British school joke stretched almost to infinity.'

None of which helped Adelphi boss Arthur Dent in his struggle to convince the big cinema chains to book his latest. He'd managed it with the previous Adelphi production, securing a full major circuit release for the aforementioned *You Lucky People!*, primarily because of the reputation of its star, Tommy Trinder (who, intriguingly enough, never mentioned the film after he'd shot it). However, despite Emney's estimable presence, the name of Cardew Robinson did not open the same doors. Besides, following previous battles with outspoken Arthur, the big chains remained sniffy when it came to booking films from upstart independents like Adelphi. In an attempt to avoid any stigma attached to the Adelphi name, *Fun at St. Fanny's* was even disguised as 'a Grand Alliance release', but to no avail. Released in January 1956, without a major circuit deal in place, though it played well in those 'provinces', ultimately Cardew's classroom comedy sadly failed its box office test.

Robinson decided afterwards that he might have outgrown his schoolboy persona, and put aside 'The Cad' to play roles of a more mature nature. Subsequent decades saw him penning comedy scripts for various performers,

‹ **Master of arts:** the greatest stage and screen school room comedian of all, Will Hay, as seen in a foldable stand-up postcard, circa 1940s.

including Dave Allen and Peter Sellers, writing for newspapers, making television appearances, providing light relief in awful Harrison Marks sex comedies, latterly appearing in a non-speaking role in an unloved Roman Polanski film, *Pirates* (1986), and authoring his own book, the splendidly titled *How to be a Failure*. Nonetheless, he was often asked to dig his cap and scarf out of the dressing up box, and, at a special screening shortly before his death in 1992, he proudly introduced his film to an appreciative audience of old-chestnut-collectors at the Museum of London. To them, as to everyone else, he would be forever Cardew, 'The Cad' of St. Fanny's.

All this being so, it is odd indeed, we might conclude, this enduring love of public school life, by those that never lived it. Intriguing, also, especially now, in our thoroughly modern and supposedly classless society, is that public school life has continued to flourish in so many fictional forms over the decades. These range from the Victorian days of Thomas Hughes' *Tom Brown's Schooldays*, via the Edwardian creation of St Jims and Tom Merry, and Greyfriars and Billy Bunter (all written by the wonderful Charles Hamilton, aka Frank Richards, aka Martin Clifford, for consumption by a largely hard-up working-class readership), on to the Narkover and St Michaels of Will Hay (notably playing a corrupt, sniffing incompetent in a battered mortar board and cheap paper shirt front – probably, one surmises, not properly public school educated). The mythology has continued, via the *St Trinian's* films and Ronald Searle cartoons (more mass consumption of a deeply embedded public school myth, with spivvy non-public school wide boy Flash Harry calling the shots), Jimmy Edwards in *Whack-O!* (BBC 1956-72), right on to the latest *St Trinian's* revamps and the mass-appeal magic of posh school Hogwarts and speccy wizard-type Harry Potter. Significantly, amongst the many both concocting and consuming this mythology, there were and are numerous that – like our chum Cardew – never went to a fee-paying school. Might we conjecture, then, that if they had, they may not have been so enduringly enamoured by the idea of it all? Yet still the cycle of fascination continues. Play up and play the game, you chaps. *VP*

...and, furthermore, and a little later on, what about all those expensively-educated townies invading the countryside: swanky urban types, full of liberal ideals, buying up properties in the late-sixties split from the city? Read on...

Robin Redbreast

UK TV | Transmitted 10/12/1970 | colour | 81mins
Director James MacTaggart
Script John Bowen
Producer Graeme MacDonald
Production Company BBC
Cast Anna Cropper, Bernard Hepton, Andy Bradford, Freda Bamford, Amanda Walker, Julian Holloway

This eerie and evocative *Play For Today* – emanating from key post-sixties punctum point 1970 – slowly but effectively polarises the tensions we've been speaking of, between town and country and old and new. In addition, this particular example builds towards an exceptionally eerie, effective ending – which will *almost* be referred to later on: spoiler alert!

It all begins innocently enough, though, with television script editor Norah Palmer heading for the sticks, where she intends to get her head together after a big relationship break-up in the city. A thoroughly modern woman, she takes up temporary residence in a quaint country cottage in a chocolate box village, where she will soon resolve upon a fiery rebound-fling with rough-and-ready local macho-man Rob. It all sounds idyllic: what could possibly go wrong? Yet it is in this supposed safe-space that she is first unnerved by an unsettling local resident, the thickly-bespectacled Fisher, who peers intrusively in through her kitchen window.

Fisher: I wonder if I might hunt for sherds in your garden.
Norah: What?
Fisher: One often finds them, you know, in freshly turned earth.
Norah: Sherds?
Fisher: I have an archaeological interest. I'm a student of that, in my own time. Old things generally.

> *Norah: I don't think there are any old things in the garden but what*
> *the builders left…broken bottles and old beer cans, mainly. But you're*
> *welcome to look.*
> *Fisher: You haven't noticed anything yourself as you walked about?*
> *Some small sherd or other?*
> *Norah: I don't think I should recognise a sherd if I were to see one.*
> *Fisher: It takes a trained eye.*

You'll discover – if you had to seek out the dictionary, as we did, after watching *Robin Redbreast*, superbly scripted by John Bowen, who also penned some other splendidly creepy scripts for the BBC's *Ghost Stories For Christmas* – that a sherd, or more properly a potsherd, is defined as a fragment of prehistoric pottery. These are ostensibly what Fisher seeks; but, enigmatic remnant of an indistinct age, he himself seems like a fragment of an elusive rural English past. And when you stop to think about it for a moment, *Robin Redbreast* seems narratively and thematically scattered with such sherds – fragments of ancient ritual tradition, pieces of cultural, folklorish pottery that Fisher and his mischievous associates gather together and strive to preserve, amidst the 'broken bottles and old beer cans' of a modern Britain on the verge of an austere new decade – a time of great change, pessimism and uncertainty.

As the pot-smoke cleared at the end of the 1960s, the dream was over, and the come-down was imminent. Despite what the Beatles had said, love was not all you needed, and the establishment was not about to yield to the new order. Business as usual in grey Britain; while the countryside was cheerfully churned up to build suburban fairylands of identical houses of the kind soon to be glimpsed in *Whatever Happened to the Likely Lads?* (1973-74).

Some of the battles of the 1960s seemed to have been won, though, as *Robin Redbreast* reminds us. Women were no longer expected to get married, have babies, and sit around being housewives. Script editor Norah Palmer, the thoroughly modern woman around whom the narrative centres, emerging from a failed long-term relationship, has the freedom to embark upon sexual flings galore, with no social stigma attached – unthinkable a decade earlier. Casual partners can be as carelessly picked out as rogue

Perfect body, empty mind: rugged Rob (Andy Bradford) throws some shapes for Nora (Anna Cropper) in this scene from *Robin Redbreast* (1970). ›

ROBIN REDBREAST

by

John Bowen

croutons floating atop the cheese in the dinner party fondue set, and as easily discarded. She can make flirtatious wisecracks with her boozy upmarket friends, before zipping off in her trendy sports car to a rustic retreat, where – like Paul McCartney, perhaps, escaping the break-up of the Beatles – she hopes to clear her head. But despite these liberations, symptomatic of the dawning supposedly 'permissive' society, there remains a void at the centre of her oh-so-modern existence.

The problem – for her, for the other trendy urban folk that she associates with, and perhaps everybody – is a crushing cynicism. There is a hollow void at the heart of contemporary existence. The old establishment may, perhaps, be withering away; but nothing much has replaced it. The unquestioned reassurance that religion and marriage was supposed to offer has dwindled in an increasingly secular society. Norah's relationship, she is forced to acknowledge, ultimately meant absolutely nothing. She and her partner simply 'cut their losses.' She feels she is supposed to be upset about it, so she cries to order for a few moments in front of her louche and somewhat disinterested friends. 'Let's talk about anything,' she suggests, flatly changing the subject, dabbing away the empty tears. But there's not a lot to say. And is there anything left to believe in?

We know what Norah and company don't believe in: the stuffy religion of the establishment (later on, Norah, tellingly, turns over the TV when a discussion gathering together the great and the good – including a Bishop – crops up. She'll talk about anything – except that). Tragic Rob, the chap she finds herself having a fling with in her country cottage, with ominous consequences, is blessed with a perfect body, but cursed with an empty mind, and seeks solace in martial arts and the regimented discipline of the Third Reich. Thanks to their hugely disparate backgrounds, Norah and Rob have nothing to talk about. As Norah becomes increasingly concerned that she is being prevented from leaving her rustic retreat, and that maybe there is some more sinister purpose that has somehow stage-managed their coupling, it becomes increasingly clear that what brought them together in the first place, aside from deep-seated sexual instinct, was their sense of doubt, and uncertainty. A spiritual lack, not known, but felt. For Fisher, meanwhile, meaning lies in the sherds of the past shored up around him; continuance of ancient pagan rituals, in which Norah is increasingly afraid that she has become unwillingly involved. But Fisher, at least, is somebody who knows exactly what they believe in – even if he has read it all in Frazer's *Golden Bough*.

And his beliefs are not quite as unusual as all that. *Robin Redbreast* reflects a cultural moment where witchcraft and the occult were no longer ludicrous. Since the repeal of the Witchcraft Act in the 1950s, there had been a steady growth in the practice of Wicca, as popularised by Gerald Gardner, author of *Witchcraft Today* (1954). Increasingly, it would seem, people were turning back to the old ways. In the face of a modernity devoid of authenticity and meaning, ancient superstitions seemed to some a viable alternative. Key cultural figures dabbled: hadn't Jagger hung out with Kenneth Anger, and recorded *Their Satanic Majesties Request*, after the Beatles snuck a picture of Aleister Crowley onto the cover of *Sgt Pepper*?

Meanwhile, urban development continued apace, the city encroaching worryingly upon the countryside, Fisher's precious sherds carelessly churned up and indiscriminately mixed into bland new-town pebble-dash. Perhaps something intangible but important was being lost; certainly the stark contrasts between town and countryside, new and old, were vividly apparent. The anxiety was reflected via various films of the period, which often showed no-nonsense modern folk challenged by dark superstitions of the past. *Night of the Demon* (1957) saw a distinctly Crowley-esque Niall MacGinnis challenge Dana Andrews' sceptical scientist, portraying a genial occultist who combines witchcraft with his sideline as a children's entertainer. *Night of the Eagle* (1962) had Peter Wyngarde's sceptical psychology professor falling prey to witchcraft both via folk charm and reel-to-reel tape recorder. Paganism is a matter-of-fact part of contemporary country village life in *The Witches* (1966). More closely aligned to *Robin Redbreast*, perhaps, though a period piece, was *Blood on Satan's Claw* (1971), where a sherd of sorts – a gruesome skull with an eye still attached, unearthed in a field – is the grisly emblem of ancient evil reawakened. All these were what is now being increasingly called 'folk horror' of one kind or another. Amongst others, still to come, were *Straw Dogs* (1971) – the logical mathematician confronts unpalatable countryside custom – and, perhaps most famously, *The Wicker Man* (1973): Christian copper versus heathen islanders.

Fuelled, like *Robin Redbreast*, by Frazer's *The Golden Bough*, *The Wicker Man* would shuffle into place astride the uncertain terrain of 1970s British cinema shortly afterwards; it's fascinating to compare the two. Both ask us to consider belief. Both wryly question how far we have progressed. Both suggest that the past and the present are inextricably bound up together, and to deny one is to jeopardise the other. Subversive ideas lurk within them, and as we half-glimpse Fisher in ancient garb in the brilliant closing seconds of *Robin Redbreast*, we're reminded once more that if ignored, if forgotten, if concreted over, the countryside, its traditions, and its ostracised peoples, may well return with a vengeance, one of these days, to wreak havoc on those too-clever city folk. *VP*

Conversely, though, some urban dwellers were attempting to do it all the other way round, and tried to change the ways of the big city by playing with alternative ritualistic modes of living, and by pulling the-out-of-town in...

Secret Rites

UK Film | 1971 | colour | 47mins
Director Derek Ford
Script Derek Ford
Producer Morton Lewis
Production Company Meadway Productions Ltd.
Cast 'King of the Witches' Alexander Sanders, Penny Beeching

In the latter decades of the twentieth century, witchcraft came out of the countryside and into the city. The vibes were strong in Notting Hill – a counter-cultural London enclave in the 1960s and early 70s, contained and to a degree closed-off, a sort of Haight Ashbury for the UK. In *Getting It Straight in Notting Hill Gate* (1970) men and women bustle in kaftans and bright, tight clothing whilst the camera tracks down the busy Portobello Road, moving through the crowds and pushing into the hippies and members of the local black community, almost all of whom eye up the device suspiciously, as if to freeze it out. Elsewhere Caroline Coon offers advice about what to do if found with drugs on your person and local band Quintessence, hanging out in a local church, explore raga rhythms and toot on a flute.

It's all happening. Or is it? Witchcraft mondo film *Secret Rites*, by way of contrast, painted an, if not more sedate picture of the area, then certainly a more complex one. Witch couple Alex and Maxine Sanders set-up their home in Notting Hill as a sort of drop-in centre and support station for potential Wicca initiates and people in trouble. Their sorcery had an urban base. Their reputation extended beyond West London and they often appeared in the press, and even on TV. The second scene in *Secret Rites* sees hairdresser receptionist Penny travel across London to visit them in a local pub, and as she emerges from the subterranean depths of the underground, the Notting Hill tube sign is presented clearly for the viewer.

Penny says she is nervous and her friends and family think she is crazy. But not too crazy presumably as she has clocked-off from her job as normal – waving goodbye – and travelled alone. This is the strange thing about *Secret Rites*, it criss-crosses between the everyday and the exotic. We don't see much of Notting Hill but the pub is quiet and modest and everyone gathered is calm – is this just the power of witchcraft? Certainly, the urgency in *Getting It Straight* is far from view. And yet director-on-the-make Derek Ford had reputedly heard about Alex through a television report and approached him about making a film thereafter. He may also have seen *The Sun* newspaper headline 'Satanic Witch Cult in Notting Hill.'

Ford was an exploitation filmmaker and had a reputation for sleaze. He regularly worked with Stanley Long in the late 60s and early 1970s and had assumed directorial duties on Long's early mega-hit *The Wife Swappers* (1970). He directed but also wrote scripts and with his brother worked on TV shows *Z Cars* (1962-78) and *The Saint* (1962-9) early on. His output could be padded if not outright tedious but at times he brought a concentrated focus to proceedings, utilizing his fascination with extra-marital sex, manipulation and secrecy to ramp things up. *Sex Express* from 1976 was certainly strong and existed in a virtually everything-goes export cut – *Diversions* – which encompassed both Nazi nastiness and the removal of a penis with a knife. Although uncredited, Long said Ford wrote the narration for *Primitive London* and that bounces along, the snide irony coming thick and fast. Ford provides the narration in *Secret Rites*, and that's, by way of contrast, remarkably measured (relatively speaking), even if by the end it talks about a rite that is so

SECRET RITES
featuring

ALEXANDER SANDERS
KING of the WITCHES
A Film Paperback

GSP

SECOND PRINTING
75ₚ

The true story of witchcraft: published to enable closer study at home, this film paperback tie-in of *Secret Rites* was sufficiently popular to go to a second printing.

SECRET RITES

Here, for the first time ever filmed, is the true story of witchcraft, performed by actual witches.

Unexpurgated eyewitness pictures of initiation ceremonies, witches wedding, and some of the highest degrees in witchcraft — never before witnessed by outsiders.

secret that everyone not actually actively participating has to leave the room. Except of course the camera, which keeps hungrily rolling, sucking in the images, suggesting that this 'never photographed, rarely witnessed' evocation of the Egyptian Rite of Ra is not really actually that secret, or for that matter, important.

Ford, at least on the surface, sought to dispel the myth that witchcraft was a depraved act of satanic abuse, but he initially revels in the association. 'It is the Devil's Night' says narrator Lee Peters at the very beginning, before we get to meet Penny, before anything. A sinister castle flashes into view with a lightning strike, while inside robed figures scream and lunge at each with decadent abandon, the camera twisting and turning, trying to immerse the viewer in the camp satanic revelry. The frenzy centres on 'an innocent victim', a woman dressed in white who is 'dragged towards unmentionable obscenities'. Two practicing witches audibly groaned at this point when we screened it at BFI Southbank. But it's okay: John Goodfellow, the would be victim's true love, interrupts the scene and the assembled wretches recoil at the sign of the cross, and his Hammer hero good looks that beam out across the cheap film set.

The narration and Alex Sanders' cool delivery provide a deliberately very different tone to the film thereafter. It immediately cuts to Sanders who says 'that is a lot of rubbish', commenting inadvertently not just on the aforementioned Dennis Wheatley-esque theatrics but in a sense the whole post-war British horror tradition of the last fifteen years. 'Reality' and the horrors of the 1970s were all creeping onto cinema screens as part of the permissive post-sixties malaise and the long-running Hammer studio did what it could with, amongst others, *Dracula A.D. 1972* (1972), but otherwise struggled. *Secret Rites*, by way of contrast, was a weird amalgam: part-mondo movie, part news exposé, part counter-cultural artefact, part sex film, part horror film (sort of); the blurred lines all being part of Ford's strange new aesthetic.

So, let the 'real' witchcraft begin: three individual rituals performed for the benefit of the camera, and framed in part through the eyes and ears of Penny, who like the general viewer, knows something of the strange practice but not the intricacies of ritual and coven membership.

Alex sets the scene, establishing the magical circle and invoking the Goddess Kahani. As the initiation proper begins, 'candidates' Penny and 'a man called Brian' enter the space, surrounded by men and women in black gowns. The Spindle, a band about which nothing appears to be known, produce fluttering stabs of Hammond organ, the thick tones bending through the use of a wah-wah pedal before settling into an insistent rhythm. The light is kept low and mysterious – though bright enough to fully reveal everyone's naked bodies once the black robes are discarded!

Ford cleverly structures the action and dialogue, moving between Penny's subjective impressions – 'when I first saw the temple I got quite frightened. Every terrible thing I'd heard about witches suddenly seemed only too possible' – to Alex Sanders' ritual incantations, and then to the narrator describing what's 'really' going on: 'the circle is cast and created as a meeting place for man and the gods'. Penny stands rigid, and then, once the initiation is complete, the coven begins their circuit dance, gradually moving faster and chanting the witch's rune, eventually getting quite frenzied and wrapping their hands and arms around the new initiates.

Penny, with her quavered blonde hair, must attend two other ceremonies and she looks increasingly uncomfortable as each event takes place. Standing naked and biting her lip, she watches a man and woman join as if in marriage through a ritual hand-fasting ceremony, however, she does wisely ignore the man sitting on a throne, dressed as the horned god, essentially doing nothing. (Does he normally do that or is just for the benefit of the film?!)

She looks more alarmed though when it comes to the Great Rite of Ra, our third ritual, an act also known as the 'Union of Souls'. This, if you remember, is 'rarely witnessed, never photographed'. The camera films at least part of the proceedings through a warped mirror, twisting and abstracting the strange deeds as they unfold. Curiously, Alex suddenly appears with a giant dog's head on his shoulders – he wears the visage of the great Egyptian jackal God Anubis! The intensity increases, tabla and piano joining the stabbing Hammond sounds, everything getting ever more groovy – and the cutting speeding-up. And yet the coven members look bored, perhaps distracted by Alex's new costume. Or maybe the mood on the ground was different to that conjured by the film? Ford uses other effects to ramp-up the tension: notably even the narrator's voice is treated with echo and reverb, and then, as more footage is warped and twisted through the strange mirror, and Alex stands there in his unusual costume, the main couple adopts the 'pyramid position', somehow both kneeling and engaging in ritual sex at the same time.

Penny says 'as the guardians closed the doors, I felt they were shutting out the twentieth century' and yet the scene is very much a melting pot of times and late counter-cultural codes and symbols. Egyptology; hallucinogenic imagery; phased, psychedelic sounds; plus heavy beards and gothy, hippy long hair; all these things place the nude, thus 'neutral', participants in the time in which the film was made.

It's 'happening' and weirdly psychedelic but Notting Hill is not overly prefaced, probably because the essentially straight and close-to-middle aged Derek Ford was not plugged in to or overly concerned with the broader counter-culture of the time. He would have been thinking about national distribution and the world beyond London, plus the immediate subject matter was no doubt already considered racy enough. Whatever the reason, Ford chose not to shoot the ritual acts on location and in fact decamped to Film House Studios, London. Authenticity was further eroded by the use of non-coven members in the ritual sequences, with writer and sex-film historian Simon Sheridan stating that many of the gyrating pagans also featured in 8mm works by underground hardcore pornographer John Lindsay. Penny, meanwhile, appeared in *Up Pompeii* (1969-1970), with Frankie Howerd. Titter ye not. She was also on the books for Askew Models International.

None of these revelations ultimately affect the film. Certainly, the idea that the film presented an un-mediated, rarefied glimpse of a private ceremony and that the reality of modern witchcraft had somehow been revealed is cast into doubt, but then it was hardly the first time that a 'documentary' had been set-up or that extras were employed to fill out a scene. Admittedly the personal involvement of Alex Sanders might have suggested a more authentic approach, however.

But then Alex had a tendency to court the media or at least go along with their whims and requests for photos and action. Maxine Sanders, his wife and collaborator, had long blonde hair and was notably taller than Alex. Press photographers gladly took pictures of her in her 'sky-clad' state, i.e. naked, and Alex was happy to set it up. Maxine appears in the pub and in the private scenes in *Secret Rites* but curiously not in the ritual moments where ordinarily she would have participated as High Priestess. Perhaps she smelt a rat.

The man, his myth and his magic: Alex Sanders graces the cover of the iconic supernatural and unexplained phenomena magazine.

Alex Sanders had a tendency to play with the media, both enjoying a kind of rock star mystique while also seeing how far he could take it. He told one journalist that he wore dark glasses to conceal his eyes because they 'were too powerful for the public to bear' whilst elsewhere he recommended using a pint of Guinness to scry or peer into the future.

The common view is that Alex liked the attention but a desire to promote the craft and dispel popular misconceptions played at least a part. The visibility of the Sanders brought many conversions to the craft and interestingly they also provided a kind of alternative family role model. Marriage didn't have to mean a traditional English lifestyle, and both husband and wife were active in the press (even if the traditional gender dynamic often went on behind the scenes). Their house in Notting Hill also became something of a safe haven for many people; journalist Stewart Farrer was so struck by their set-up and way of life that he wrote the book *What Witches Do* and subsequently converted.

Their place in Notting Hill also put them in touch with the counter-cultural and broader freakscene. Alex released the album *A Witch is Born* through Occult Halloween Records and A&M (who very quickly deleted it) and the couple performed with heavy psych band Black Widow at, amongst other places, the Lyceum. Sanders later performed the show solo in an Ilford discotheque.

He and Maxine also appeared in another exposé documentary made the year before *Secret Rites. Legend of the Witches* (1970) took a different approach and presented Wicca as a timeless ancient craft, both emerging from and belonging to the rural sphere. Beautiful black and white images show the sun rising at dawn and witches dancing by a burning fire, leaping over the flickering flames and chanting. A new initiate must follow one of his colleagues through streams and woodland floor, and then down into a cave, all the while naked and blindfolded. It's all part of his initiation. His female friend leads him on: 'Michael……Michael'. He stumbles on a loose stone, the moonlight catching his face. 'Michael,' and then again, 'Michael.'

It's a beautiful, stunning piece, if overloaded and arguably too wide-ranging. It seeks to tie-up the historical case, complete with accounts of persecution, whilst also illustrating different rituals, and exploring the philosophy of Wicca. It even asks – and attempts to explain – how it works.

The film is conceptually rigorous and a compelling advert for the cause, but it's not without its exploitation elements. Sanders is happy to perform what is called a 'black mass' and, wearing Christian vestments and kneeling in front of a very large crucifix, he calls out to Lucifer, asking for help and companionship. Thereafter follows a more traditional nude Pagan ritual. It all gets rather confusing – aren't Paganism and Satanism supposed to be distinct and different, any confusion the result of Christian propaganda?

Director Malcolm Leigh shot sex comedies but also documentaries, including *The Sword and the Geisha* (1971), *Pillars of Islam* (1973) and *Manifestations of Shiva* (1980), suggesting he held an ongoing interest in religion. He was friends with Derek Jarman, too, and helped him shoot his first film: the 16mm Warhol-esque *Electric Fairy* (1971), and they were still in touch in the early 1990s when Leigh lived in the Chelsea Hotel, New York.

Despite its rural locations, *Legend of the Witches* had more overt links to the counter-culture than *Secret Rites*. The film discusses scrying as a means of looking into the future – Alex, if you remember, said he could do it using a pint of Guinness – and the narrator here refers to water and mirrors, but also a Stroboscope, an electronic lighting device that flashes fields of light at predetermined intervals, changing the rhythm of the brain. 'Modern witches combine old and new techniques to get the scryer into the right frame of mind' says the film, and the presence of both this strange new machine plus lights and mirrors evokes both Derek Jarman's early films – was he inspired by *Legend*? – and, with its hallucinogenic drugs and light shows, evoking and bringing forth new forms of consciousness, or rather old forms newly transposed, the broader hallmarks of the sixties counter-culture. The man seen operating the Stroboscope is in all likelihood William Grey Walter, an experimental neurophysiologist and one-time contact of Brion Gysin and William Burroughs.

Leigh's film is more reflective and enquiring in tone than Ford's but, moments such as these aside, is also – curiously – often drier for it. *The Monthly Film Bulletin* noted that its 'relentless atmospherics' were 'so artily contrived that one sometimes wishes the director would cut the pseudo-poetics and simply get down to tabloid tack.'

Derek Ford's pithy forty-seven minute picture, by way of contrast, proved ultimately more satisfying: 'An unusually sympathetic and selective addition to the recent spate of witchcraft documentaries. Though some of the rituals contain an erotic element, there is no black magic, no wax images and pins,' said *MFB*. All things considered, *Secret Rites* was actually pretty modest, particularly given Ford's background and penchant for salaciousness. It was as though the subject matter was raw and tantalizing enough; the public was still new to Wicca as an everyday activity at this point, and yet sufficiently primed through the racy headlines and saucy pictures that appeared in the press. Wiccan ritual was like old anthropological photos and practices, sort of de-sexualised as pure reportage and yet also clearly not. Indeed, witchcraft was confusing in this respect. It was by its very nature all about sex and gender polarity and yet the rituals were for the most part solemn and stoic, purely representational and yet again confusingly performed naked. What was the sex obsessed voyeur to do?

Ford did ramp things up, of course. The very concept of 'secret rites', plus the conceit that the film will reveal the truth behind the rumours of satanic abuse, did increase expectations and create a dramatic arc. Ford also peppered the proceedings with nude close-ups and strange eccentric details, like the 'free-expression dance' after the handfasting (marriage) ritual. Figures shimmy in stoned abandon, shuffling unenthusiastically in a circle whilst Alex Sanders finishes-off the paperwork. And then of course there's the finale to the 'Great Rite of Ra' – actual sex, sort of. The spaced-out couple embraces awkwardly, somehow – in theory – linking coitally whilst kneeling on the floor. The man wearing Arab headdress shrieks at orgasm and yet appears bewildered and confused, crying out more from fear than anything else, also clutching at his companion.

Secret Rites was far out and unusual in staging an urban portrait of modern Wicca, rather than relocating to the countryside, as in *Legend of the Witches*, and several TV reports from around the same time. That Penny is a hairdresser receptionist seeking a bit of paganism in her spare time does, however, cut quite a contrast with, say, *Getting It Straight in Notting Hill Gate*, where counter-cultural activity is seen as spilling out into all parts of life, and even effecting interactions with the law. It was as though alternative lifestyles could just be a hobby in *Secret Rites*, life otherwise going on as normal; taking in quiet drinks at the pub, hanging out at home, chatting, painting. Perhaps that wasn't unusual by 1971. The counter-culture was beginning to be subsumed.

But it also tapped into Derek Ford's particular kinks. Friend and collaborator Stanley Long said Ford 'trod a thin line between the mainstream and the illegal'. That the 'Penny' character would go from upstanding hairdresser to group nudist and flagellator would have no doubt excited him. He'd recently directed *The Wife Swappers* and was into backroom salaciousness. His desire to get into mischief behind the closed doors of respectability also fed into his practice of shooting hardcore scenes after hours, once the main cast had gone home. The strong sex itself might have been exciting but it was probably the secret, illicit nature of the filming itself that was as much, if not more the kick. Ford and Alex Sanders had different drives and different lifestyles but equally both were far from straightforward and both relished a mixture of privacy and public exposure. How did they get on? Did Sanders know about Ford's other films?

There's also the question; did Ford make a hardcore version of *Secret Rites*? Stanley Long recalled that 'often the film laboratories wouldn't develop anything vaguely pornographic for fear of getting caught by the police. Directors like Derek got around this by paying backhanders to certain staff members late at night.' Also, as already noted, sex film historian Simon Sheridan has identified several 'actors' here as having also appeared in hardcore Super 8 films shot by John Lindsay, plus an 'adults-only' photo-book tie-in of the film has emerged, presenting – alongside more familiar scenes – witch couples apparently having missionary-position-style sex in the faked-up ritual circle. Rendered in tightly-cropped, grainy black and white, the photographs frequently appear considerably sleazier than the actual motion picture. This doesn't necessarily mean that such acts were actually filmed, however, or indeed that the couples obliged with anything other than static poses.

Whilst certain evidence grows, we might ask – or those that care might – if this was one of Ford's first films after working with Stanley Long; would he so soon jump to shooting hardcore? The answer may of course be, yes! Curiously there is another, longer film called *Secret Rites* from 1972 but this is American and it concerns itself with rituals from all around the world. Any alternative versions would have to exist abroad, given censorship restrictions, and probably under a different name so as to avoid upset and legal confrontation with the backers, Meadway Productions, who were British based.

It all sounds like hard work but then the film is itself something of a mystery and only came to light very recently when we discovered a copy in the BFI National Archive, a lone 35mm print. The production history and the nature of the actors/coven members, plus the use of a set, also leads to confusion and murkiness as to what this film really is, and what it's about. For all these reasons, it's been easy for commentators to essentially write it off as a sensational Derek Ford fake job, with the equally sensational Alex Sanders playing his part in the ruse. Of course, it was a money-making exercise, but does that make it all unreal or entirely untrustworthy? Rituals are followed through and Penny's initial Wicca contact, Wendy, is serious yet reflective enough on camera to seem like an actual witch, i.e. not an actor or a model. We also know that Alex was a witch – he was the *King of the Witches* according to the 1969 book by June Johns. Maybe it depends on your beliefs but in theory Penny, whether an occult enthusiast ('I was interested in the occult') or not, was inducted into a coven, receiving 'the purely symbolic act of scourging' for her efforts and also witnessing other deeds and rituals. In theory then, yes, she is a witch, may be even still now. Which is a strange thought. Unless of course the presence of non-coven members nullifies the power and results of what happened?

For all its trappings and sexploitation lineage, *Secret Rites* does not lie down easily. Other mysteries – did it actually show nationally? Why was Maxine Sanders only in parts of the film? And who are the Spindle, the strange group that provided the manipulated keyboard sounds and tabla? All films have their mysteries but in this case the director would probably not only be happy for it to stay that way but probably get a kick out of it. Poor Derek Ford, he loved transgression, voyeurism and most of all, secrecy; yet when he died he did it in a very British public place; in a WH Smiths on Bromley High Street, in 1995. He had a heart attack. *WF*

It's all to play for in this next entry when once again the country and the city collide with leather against willow in a great British game of cricket. But, it transpires, there are spinners and googlies aplenty in this match – and neither side is revealed to be exactly united...

Playing Away

UK Film and TV | 1987 | colour | sound | 98mins
Director Horace Ové
Producer Brian Skilton, Vijay Amarnani
Screenplay Caryl Phillips
Production Companies Insight Productions, Film Four International
Cast Norman Beaton, Robert Urquhart, Ross Kemp, Neil Morrissey, Ram John Holder

British film was struggling in the 1970s as American finance was withdrawn and the British public were getting more excited about what was on TV than at the local picture house. Cinema-going was in decline. But several initiatives eventually attempted to revive and maintain the dream of a British cinema of which we could be proud. One was *Film on Four* (later *Film Four*) initiated by the new Channel 4 which arrived at the start of the 1980s. Their early films were the multi-platform hybrids of their day, broadcast rights being already written into the production deals whilst the potential for an international roll-out in cinemas was also firmly inscribed into the script and production process. Sometimes titles remained TV films, sometimes they received wider distribution. Not be left out, the BBC initiated *Screen Two* and adopted a similar model.

Early *Film on Four* productions included Neil Jordan's *Angel* (1982) and Stephen Frears' *Walter* (1982) and *My Beautiful Laundrette* (1985). These films told British stories that expanded the basic creative, theatrical stylings of *Play For Today* and – hopefully – opened them up to potential Transatlantic audiences. Indeed, producer David Rose had moved over from one strand, by way of his base in BBC Pebble Mill in Birmingham, to the other; and in 1990 he programmed, on Channel 4, a repeat run of his favourite *Play For Today* films, calling it: *Film 4 Today*. Geddit?

Playing Away was one of these. Funded by *Film Four International*, it was directed by another *Play For Today* graduate, the Trinidadian filmmaker Horace Ové who'd overseen *A Hole in Babylon* (29/11/1979), and directed the first Black British feature film *Pressure* (1975). *Playing Away* appeared to straddle both the worlds of TV comedy and more ambitious, serious film. For one, featured actors were, or would become, very familiar to TV

Conquistadors: Norman Beaton and his cricket team in *Playing Away* (1987).

audiences. They included Norman Beaton, Neil Morrissey and Ross Kemp, plus Joseph Marcell who would, perhaps most intriguingly of all, later play the part of posh English butler, Geoffrey, in *The Fresh Prince of Bel-Air* (1990-96).

Playing Away sees The Conquistadors, a black British cricket team from Brixton, invited to play a match against the local team in the Suffolk village of Sneddington. The film initially cuts between country and city, displaying the tensions and differences within each side, exploring and expanding the frame beyond the simple black/white, country/city divisions.

London life, it would appear, is all fast cars, berating punks and crowded, smoke filled rooms; but rural Sneddington is also not without its tensions – primarily arising around class. The local oiks resentfully guard their spot by the benches outside the local pub, while their leader, Ian (Morrissey), keeps everyone at bay with his frozen, comic-book sneer. Meanwhile, Derek (Nicholas Farrell), of the more well to do in the village, keeps his distance in the exclusive, club-like atmosphere of the saloon bar. Never the twain shall meet, unless it's on the cricket green – when they must unite to play the Conquistadors. But the tensions within ultimately break the team, leading to Sneddington's defeat.

Playing Away was an unusual and at times provocative comedy of manners that, rather than attempting to unite its characters, continually emphasised difference and conflict – an unusual reflection of television's potential to juxtapose and then, paradoxically perhaps, hopefully unite different perspectives – on screen and in the hearts and minds of the viewers. It was released at cinemas in 1987, and broadcast on Channel 4 in 1989.

When Cambridge University sports film *Chariots of Fire* won best film at the 1981 Oscars, the scriptwriter Colin Welland famously declared: 'the British are coming'. The phrase would float around for some time and evoke frothy confidence based around idealistic views of England and a newly revived cultural Empire, after years being beholden to American finance and American movie tropes. It implied the need for an export industry and a turning of the back on small scale interest films, movies that only made sense to British audiences – maybe like strange television adaptations and eccentric independent films about cricket teams. It was perhaps ironic then that *Playing Away* featured *Chariots* actor Nicholas Farrell as the Sneddington team captain. The film's score, during the climatic cricket match, mixed moody electronic music in the style of Vangelis' iconic *Chariots* theme with steel drums, colliding Imperialist style heritage cinema with traditional Trinidadian music.

Although made only a few years after *Chariots of Fire*, *Playing Away* picked-up on very different issues. The world had changed in the years between: 1987 saw several 'State of the Nation'-type films being released: Jarman's *The Last of England*, Mike Grigsby's *Living On the Edge* and Jack Bond's lighter *It Couldn't Happen Here*, starring the Pet Shop Boys; on television, there were the documentary series *The Lie of the Land* and *Viewpoint '87*. Margaret Thatcher began her third term as Prime Minister; and each of these filmic missives, in their own way, took the temperature of the country, whilst providing an implicit critique of institutional power and those who wielded it in the wake of the suppression of the miners' strike, the dismantling of British industry and the privatisation of public services.

Grigsby had been making documentaries for television for two decades at least by the time he came to make *Living on the Edge*. The film was simultaneously released in cinemas (on a limited run) and broadcast on television through producers Central Independent Television. Again, television tried to play into the film world as the media industries continued to reform.

A powerful collage film, *Living on the Edge* utilised archival film, adverts and actuality; it was in fact reminiscent of Humphrey Jennings' benchmark documentary *Listen to Britain* (1942), if rendered in much darker, more contemporary tones. In Grigsby's film television is itself presented as a social problem, building expectations for a lifestyle that for most people, and for the most part, does not exist. It traced different working communities around the country struggling with social changes, economic difficulties and encroaching unemployment, having been left behind by the so-called dream of nationhood, as money became centralised around the new financial centres of Canary Wharf and the City.

Playing Away is similarly filled with disenchanted social groups increasingly alienated in a shifting world they are unable or unwilling to fully understand. There are numerous divisions here, and not always the ones you might expect: between the immigrant generation of the Conquistadors and their children; between the Jamaicans and the Trinidadians; between the blacks and whites; between countryside and city; and, finally, between the local white working-class and the village well-to-do. The Brixton contingent are made up of first-generation immigrants plus their British born children: the tough rude boy Errol (Gary Beadle), who attracts the attention of Sneddington local girl Sandra (Elizabeth Anson); his nerdy friend Stuart (Brian Bovell), who sleeps with his teddy bear; Willie Boy's uptight daughter Yvette (Suzette Llewellyn) who misses her mother back in Jamaica; and Masie (Femi Taylor) who makes the winning catch.

The film effectively held a mirror up to a country still trying to get a measure of itself after tumultuous years of internal conflict. Quips about a waiter at the vicar's tea party being oppressed, and the waiter not understanding, or the Conquistadors setting the village on fire – referencing the 1981 Brixton riots – are drily despatched and then swiftly moved on from as the story progresses. The more upwardly-mobile Jeff (Trevor Thomas) of the Conquistadors, for example, reaches an understanding with

A dream betrayed: stark promotional postcard for *Living on the Edge* (1987).

the disappointed wife of the opposing side's captain. Both are married – but do they in fact 'play away', as the saying goes?

Director Horace Ové had first come to Europe from Trinidad to appear as an extra in *Cleopatra* (1963), and eagerly absorbed the new European cinema of the era. As a devoted cinephile with a particular interest in realism and the internal workings of the mind, he was fascinated with the links between identity and behaviour. He brought these preoccupations to bear in the dynamic sensibility with which *Playing Away* is so richly imbued; exploring these areas, and encouraging the actors to play themselves as much as possible. Many of these, along with the crew, had worked with him before.

Despite points of contact, *Playing Away* had a distinctly different style and shape to *Living on the Edge*. It was of course a narrative piece rather than a documentary, and far more light-hearted. When Willie Boy, the Conquistador captain portrayed by the magnetic Norman Beaton, is hassled and asked to leave the saloon bar, he ricochets from melancholic drunkenness to out-of-control rage. 'Ejected? What do you think I am – a fucking rocket?' he shouts. The film fizzes forward with speed and momentum, moving through scenes with great economy and packing pithy character sketches concisely and effectively together. The light-touch tone and style entertainingly takes the antagonistic edge off many of the confrontations and sometimes even helps to alleviate the bitter taste of the racism on display.

At one level it could be seen as a radical update of the Ealing Comedies of old, films that gently probed social differences and collisions in class and society through the niceties of daily interaction. Yet *Playing Away* also looked more fiercely forward to 2016's *Pride,* in which politicised gay men and lesbians from London head to the Welsh valleys to show their solidarity with the striking miners under siege by the Conservatives. Here too the question would be asked: how would these seemingly different cultures get on and negotiate their connections and divergences? The way in which the two films conclude neatly confirm the main differences between the then and the now, however.

Whilst *Pride* ultimately ends in extremely upbeat, socially-unifying fashion and is unquestionably a feel-good film – with the young gay Welsh man reuniting with his mother from whom he had so long been estranged – *Playing Away*, by way of stark contrast, sees its symbolic cricket match centrepiece descend into relative chaos, with compromised umpire judgments and departing players highlighting the class divisions within the Suffolk side. The Conquistadors ultimately win; but if it is a victory, it is an ambivalent, bittersweet one. Willie Boy reflects upon the day's proceedings as he and his teammates head off back to the big city: 'At least they could have offered us a drink in the pavilion.' 'These people have difficulties of their own,' his friend decides. Willy Boy's response to this is sad, but telling. 'You don't think we have ours?'

It's true. Each character expresses varying levels of sympathy and antagonism to their friends and rivals, and alliances come and go. But, as viewers, if we step back and return, or try to return, to that fiercely protected space, the saloon bar, with its special permissions and pervading sense of exclusivity – where some are welcomed and some are 'ejected' – perhaps in *Playing Away*, at least, it is ultimately class, and not colour, that presents the most persistent barrier to integration. *WF*

KIDS' STUFF?

Children's film and television remains a wide ranging, bold and sometimes distinctly overwhelming universe. Raw in its horrors, its effects, affects and logic can be difficult to fully comprehend. The initial imperative behind children's film and TV was predominantly a moral one, however. With a paternalistic form of government being played out through the television screenings, it was meant to encourage good behaviour, a sense of nation and community. In its earliest days, many were mindful of the commercial, provocative – potentially corrupting – material being served up to the young; and by the 1950s, J. Arthur Rank and Mary Field set-up the Children's Film Foundation as a way of, in part, countering the perceived threat of morally unsuitable films and horror comics emanating from America.

Strange though it might seem today, Disney's groundbreaking feature-length cartoon *Snow White and Seven Dwarfs* (1937) was granted an 'A' certificate on first release, meaning children wishing to see it required an adult chaperone. Perhaps the idea was that the accompanying parent was almost reading the book to the child, potentially comforting them at the first mention of the wicked witch. It serves as a reminder, nonetheless, of the darkness at the heart of our most beloved fairy tales.

‹ **The great bear:** Sooty waves his magic wand and appears on the back of a kids' game playing card, circa 1955.

Black-eyed boys: 1950s children at the cinema, their excited, unwavering attention documented by way of infrared photography.

Years later, with the advent of television in the early 1950s, the child would be deposited in front of whatever screen with little care, trust in the establishment presiding. Early kids' slot *Watch With Mother* (1953-75) and its equivalent later manifestations were, one conjectures, not, for the most part, a communal viewing experience, but actually just an occasion for the adults to deposit children in front of the screen – and then go about their business. With the true horrors of the world – post-war crime, and atomic-era anxiety – being so readily brought to the screen elsewhere, it was perhaps as though fairy tales and children's stories had somehow lost their edge.

Adult sensitivity can be misplaced. Folk tales and nightmare visions have frequently been reinterpreted for the modern age, the results both firing the imagination and drawing out psychological undercurrents, updating and reinvigorating classic fears. Weird kids' drama show *Escape Into Night* (19/04 – 24/05/1972) (later remade as feature *Paperhouse* (1988)), presented a young girl troubled by dreams of a sick boy in a dreamlike house, disturbed by large, monstrous stones with big blinking eyes that move ever closer to the building. The horrors become increasingly real and the story progresses into ever more unexpected, strange shapes; the boy is trapped in a feverish protracted sickness, unable to leave his bed. To challenge the basic spaces where a child hopefully feels safe – the home, the bedroom, sleep – was, perhaps, peculiar; but especially memorable and effective.

A tangible, affecting darkness has pervaded many children's programmes. The delicate yet dangerous *Tottie* (1984-86), made by Oliver Postgate and Peter Firmin, who'd made the brilliant *Ivor the Engine* (1959-64 & 1975-77) and *Bagpuss* (12/02 – 07/05/1974), even saw animated characters praying that bad things would be kept at bay. At one point a malicious, too-beautiful doll takes her revenge on simple, domestic Tottie and her friends, setting their doll's house ablaze and melting the celluloid-made Birdie in the process. Bad things happen to good people, or even good dolls, it seemed to say. A powerful lesson to us all.

The eyes have it: spooky, strange 1970s stones come to life in *Escape into Night* (1972).

Everybody thinks I'm asleep, but I'm not: naughty Hartley Hare, up to no good in
Pipkins (1973-81).

Many archive children's films and television programmes were, and
remain, just plain odd. The buying in of overseas productions for UK
broadcast introduced British kids to whole new worlds of imaginary
landscape. The dubbed, weird, uncanny French adaptation of Tintin that
screened on the BBC in the 1970s, *Tintin and the Golden Fleece* (1961),
discussed in this section, impressed kids with a strange continental Europe
that appeared both familiar and recognisable, and yet was somehow alien
around the edges.

Kids' programmes from abroad were sometimes shot on film, as
opposed to on video in a studio, and this also made things seem more exotic
and strange, giving programmes a location-based photographic sheen

that significantly disrupted aesthetic expectations. For example, smash hit series *The A-Team* (1983-87) (which quickly became a kids' show, despite its original design as a more adult entertainment) made guns and violence seem distinctly exciting by ways of its bigger budget and film veneer finish, whilst Euro-drama *Silas* (1981), about a parentless boy who escapes from the circus with his horse, made by a German production company, shot in France and based on a Danish book, came across like an extended medieval epic. The latter screened in multiple cut-up episodes in the UK through the summer holidays of 1984 (16/05 – 01/08/1984).

On the flipside, the crudity of low-budget productions also created strange, unexpected and sometimes chilling aesthetics that in retrospect can be hard to appreciate. Glove puppets, perhaps ridiculous and painfully cheap to adults and modern viewers, could be distinctly eerie, as life was conjured from strangely-shaped pieces of knitwear and cardboard. The names of these programmes almost don't matter as individual moments often linger long after a show, its name, cast and other details have been rejected by the mind. Did it even ever exist? (Just for the record, *Pipkins* (1973-81) would be one such show. And it existed. Like the similarly unintentionally sinister *Hickory House* (1973-77), featuring delightful pretend chums Humphrey Cushion and Dusty Mop.)

Adults may never have truly realised what was going on in children's minds as their little ones tried to process this oft-weird fare; but broadcasters did occasionally try to blur audience interests in the goal of making 'family' television, in a sense drawing the generations together. Offering 'something for the dads' could be confusing for junior, when the likes of a scantily clad *Doctor Who* companion appeared on screen shortly after the Saturday evening football results, as in the classic case of Leela played by Louise Jameson in 1977 and into '78. And what did junior make of it when well-known page 3 girl Samantha Fox appeared, admittedly fully-clothed rather than topless, on *Roland Rat: The Series* in 1986? The mind boggles.

In the world of children's television, different, unclear rules of suitability sometimes seemed to apply. Certainly wayward suggestions that would be rejected or considered unacceptable elsewhere crept in, perhaps planted by naughty aged hippy-types. For instance, when the Television South West (TSW) mascot Gus Honeybun jumped on a red and white fly agaric mushroom as birthday cards were read out, the punching of the psychedelic

Don't trip on that mushroom: Television South West mascot, Gus Honeybun, jumps up and down for the viewers' amusement.

toadstool triggering a change in background. He could be seen inhabiting a strange chocolate factory, where gloopy brown sweetness dribbled onto passing biscuits.

The big hitters in children's film and television, like *Blue Peter* (1958-) or *The Railway Children* (1970), are often spoken of, and revisited. But the worlds of less well-known children's film and TV are vast, labyrinthine and fascinatingly obscure. Everyone has something buried in the back of their mind – something old and forgotten they remember with either fondness or bewilderment. In the less regulated entertainment world of the latter part of the twentieth century, it would be easy to think that in some ways adults pushed their fears and dream images away from themselves and instead into children's films and TV; and of course, it's a world of instant nostalgia, for that very reason. But analysis of this odd world on the fringes of remembrance can be dangerous indeed. It may turn out to be stranger, more daring and darker than even your own memories will allow you to recall.

Ah, the good old days of childhood nostalgia. And to get started, what could be more innocent than a cute little glove puppet bear…running his own cute little chemist's shop?

The Sooty Show: Sooty's Chemist Shop aka *We Dispense With Accuracy*

UK TV | Transmitted 19/02/1957 | black and white | 12mins
Script Harry Corbett (uncredited)
Production Company BBC
Cast Sooty, Sweep, Harry Corbett

The odd and unusual is not always pushed to the sidelines of popular culture. Occasionally, something eccentric and strange – that you'd never dream could possibly work – is the unexpected recipient of mainstream acceptance; once in a blue moon, it becomes a national institution. Such was the case with Harry Corbett's odd little glove puppet bear, Sooty.

It's hard to imagine if you take a look at the cute animated Sooty of recent cartoons that there was ever a time when the quiet yellow bear sold drugs, clowned around with live wires in the back of television sets, or hit his owner on the head with a hammer. But he did, and it was funny. Back in the early days of *The Sooty Show*, perhaps unwittingly, it was all just a little bit subversive. It was a kids' show, sure enough. But early episodes were shown twice, once in the afternoon and once in the evening, so that older viewers could enjoy them too. We should also note that as early as 1950, Corbett was doing live shows for adults (and reputedly going down a storm at Pudsey Conservative Club). Sooty was refreshingly lacking in the well-scrubbed goody-two shoes niceness of his puppet competition: *Muffin the Mule* (1946-55), politely presented by vaguely haughty Annette Mills. Sooty, like Muffin before him, came along at just the right time, the early

Bad-ass bear: thousand-yard-stare Sooty packs a mean-looking hammer as he becomes a delightfully disturbing egg cup for 1950s kiddies.

1950s – ITV did not begin until 1955, and so competition was limited – and with a good spot on the BBC at tea time of a weekend, anybody who had a set saw the naughty little bear.

Harry Corbett, the Bradford-born engineer who came up with the idea, infused the Sooty programmes with his own peculiar brand of dry North Country wit. According to Geoff Tibballs' indispensable *The Secret Life of Sooty*, the puppet – originally known simply as 'Teddy' – had been bought on a rain-spattered Blackpool pier in July 1948, to entertain his kiddies, primarily because it had 'a cheeky face'. But before long Harry – who'd always been bitten by the showbiz bug – was including the bear in the magic act he did at children's parties around Leeds. Shortly afterwards, as the act developed, he was being asked to skip the magic, and just do the bit with the bear. Corbett and his little yellow friend made it on to BBC TV's *Talent Night* in May 1952, and caused a sensation. Harry wisely blacked in the ears of his bear, to distinguish him from all other yellow bears bought from seaside toy shops, and registered him for copyright under the name of SOOTY.

Harry got the opportunity to do six Saturday night slots with Sooty on television. He seized it with gusto, even though his boss had refused to give him time off, telling him 'you can't mix television and engineering'. Possibly true, but Corbett was aware that the *Muffin the Mule* syndicate was turning over £30,000 a year in merchandising royalties. So Corbett, a canny character unafraid to take a risk, decided that his career in engineering was over. The gamble paid off as Sooty caught on and became a regular fixture on the BBC. His early programmes were bizarre little ten-minute flights-of-fancy, all flavoured by the idiosyncratic imagination of Mr Corbett, that were like strange music hall sketches in miniature. Corbett played the straight man, endlessly suffering by his own hand, at the paws of his naughty little glove puppet. Sweep, the squeaking, sad eye-browed dog, came along in 1957, providing another foil for Sooty's mischief, and the foundations for some fine situation comedy. He was operated by Harry's brother, Leslie, squeezing his Sweep duties into annual leave from his job at the Electricity Board, while family friend Bill Garrett provided some astonishing sets for the little bear's antics.

Much of Sooty's early popularity grew out of his violence towards Mr Corbett. Steve Race, a pianist who worked with him in 1953, spoke on *This is Your Life* of the fateful night that he heard Harry, alone with Sooty in an adjoining hotel room, in 'gales of laughter' as he came up with his masterstroke: 'he'd just had the first thought of hitting himself – via Sooty – on the head with this hammer…and of course it was the beginning of everything – in fact, very soon it caught on.' Even the Queen enjoyed seeing Corbett smacked on the head with a hammer. Introduced to Harry and Sooty at a British Industries Fair, her first words were 'Has he bonked you on the head with his hammer this morning?'

Working with Sooty had dangerous consequences, as Gerry Marsden, later a regular on the show after his flush of pop fame as lead singer of Gerry and the Pacemakers had faded, found out, and recounted on *This is Your Life* years later. One fateful episode set in *The Laugh Shop* saw Marsden, already covered in custard pie foam, attacked by the puppet with a prop-mallet.

He had the accidental misfortune of being hit not by the soft spongy prop head, as planned, but by the hard solid wooden handle within. The pie foam took on a vivid red tinge, as the blood gushed out. 'Sooty! You've killed Uncle Gerry!' cried one concerned child. Marsden, rushed to hospital, had to tell the doctor stitching him up, 'I was hit over the head by Sooty with a pick-axe handle.'

But supposing a child should copy such behaviour? With great power comes great responsibility; and as the yellow bear grew ever more popular with the nation's schoolchildren, there came demands to clean up Sooty's act. Soon, taking the advice of Harry's agent, the hammer was quietly dropped from the act, and content considered unsuitable to children was, over the years, phased out of the programme. But still, even in latter years, the vague air of cottage-industry mischief lingered on.

We Dispense With Accuracy is a ten minute episode from 1957 that has a joyously irresponsible air of fun about it that viewers young and old must have loved. Jolly organ music ushers us into Sooty's chemists' shop: an incongruous setting for a children's programme. What's more, this is a pharmacy where the puppets mix the powders, and encourage the customers to buy sleeping tablets. 'How do you like Sooty's new chemist's shop?' Harry grins. 'Smashing, isn't it?'

Harry, apparently celebrating his wedding anniversary for the purposes of the drama, wants to buy a nice present for 'the wife'. Sooty, whispering in Harry's ear as always, suggests lipstick. Sweep – emerging from the dispensary, where he's been mixing 'conditioning powders' following an explosion off screen – is the unwilling model for the lipstick, as Harry and Sooty decide whether it's a nice shade. It isn't.

Further suggestions grow ever more absurd, and each proposed gift is tested on Sweep, who is successively powder-puffed, tooth-brushed (with sawing noises), tied up in a hairnet, doused in perfume ('Pong' and 'Niff'), and covered in shaving foam. Sooty suggests a comb would make a nice gift. 'Does it have strong teeth?' says Harry. Sooty forces Sweep down on to the counter and scrapes a hefty comb across the hapless dog, while teeth snap off like pine needles. Sooty, laughing at Harry's baldness, also attempts to sell his master hair restorer. 'None of them make the slightest difference – I've tried every kind there is,' Harry grimaces. Sooty demonstrates his new concoction on Sweep – hair sprouts out all over him. So Sooty uses hair

Nutcracker sweet: the beloved bear whacks Harry Corbett on the head on this postage stamp.

remover – and Sweep reemerges patchily bald. 'He's down to bare skin now!' complains Harry.

Eventually enraged, Harry smacks the counter with his hand, and ends up with a splinter. 'I've got a spell in me finger!' he complains. Treatment for this ailment sees Harry end up bandaged to Sooty and Sweep. Keen to take Harry's pulse, Sooty takes Harry's watch and ends up smashing it into pieces with a pestle and mortar; by which time Harry has a headache. Help is at hand: Sooty has made some headache pills – in order to demonstrate their effectiveness, he smacks Sweep on the head, and makes the dog swallow one. Sweep freezes bolt upright for a moment then races off the set – the pill is a laxative. 'I could do with a good sleep at night,' Harry confesses. So Sooty tries to sell him sleeping tablets, which he uses Sweep to demonstrate. Forced to swallow the tablet, Sweep promptly falls over. 'He's falling!' warns Harry. 'He's all right now, all right,' Harry says soothingly as

Bear necessities: Sooty's hammer has been swapped for a jolly trumpet – but he remains under police surveillance – on the cover of this 1960s kids' annual.

Sweep passes out cold on the counter. Sooty must use 'pep' pills to bring him round- at which point Sweep squeaks with joy and starts running about. 'Don't get too excited,' Harry intones crossly, as Sooty chases the hound with a net, before Sweep chases Sooty. But it is now time to go; time for Harry's soothing sign-off catchphrase. 'I'd better say bye bye…bye bye, everyone, bye bye.' The programme ends, with more jolly organ music, as Sooty pins a squealing Sweep to the counter.

What makes it all so entertaining – aside from the devil – may-care inclusion of subject matter that would nowadays be frowned upon – is the way the humour escalates to ever more absurd, dreamlike and childish extremes, with, seemingly no limitations imposed by ideas of what is a 'good influence' on the kiddies. Sooty's suggestions are the kinds of things a child might suggest, and his mischief would surely appeal to any small child. But the action – paced and structured like the kind of 'tit-for-tat' sequences of slowly escalating destruction seen in some of the best Laurel and Hardy comedies – also has the air of music hall about it, lending it an adult appeal. Corbett is the ideal straight man, and makes the most of his slightly stodgy, respectable air. Thin strands of hair neatly flattened down, smartly dressed in a suit, wearily searching for a gift for 'the wife', he brings just the right air of lower-middle class dignity and tired disgruntlement to the proceedings; making his frustration at the hands of his infantile charges – which he truly seems to believe are real – all the more amusing.

Intriguingly, the prospect of Sooty selling drugs was less controversial at the time than another taboo: the idea that Sooty might get a girlfriend. The BBC were appalled at Harry's latest idea, claiming that it was 'sex creeping in,' and refused to countenance such filth. Harry, undeterred, and always a shrewd operator, 'accidentally' mentioned the subject to a *Daily Mail* reporter. 'Fleet Street went mad,' Harry revealed in a television nostalgia-fest entitled *Sooty: The First Thirty Years* (1983). Such was the media hoo-hah, he remembered, the BBC eventually caved in. One newspaper headline proudly proclaimed 'Sooty will get his sex life – so there.' Marjorie, Harry's wife, operated Sooty's new friend, Soo, who joined the cast in 1964, and provided her breathy voice, and made her dresses – which soon numbered over three hundred – from leftover scraps of cloth.

Storm clouds were on the horizon, however. Cruelly and unjustly bundled into the same category as the less-inspired helium-voiced twitchy-headed singing pigs Pinky and Perky, Sooty was, in 1968, unceremoniously dismissed from BBC1 in a revamp instigated by a new controller who did not like puppetry, or Harry either, who was considered too old. Demands that he should wear a wig on screen had not gone down at all well with the presenter. Harry left the BBC forever and signed for a new series with Thames Television.

Brother Leslie – who had gone back to the Electricity Board – was replaced as Sweep operator by Harry's son, Matthew; and Matthew put aside his dreams of becoming a serious actor and eventually took over the family business; even providing his own songs for the show (recorded in his custom-built recording studio). ITV offered bigger budgets and lots of location shooting and Sooty went from strength to strength. The air of oddness lingered through the years but it wasn't quite the same. Matthew approached Sooty very much as a business concern; the shows were still highly entertaining, but they weren't quite the labour of love that his father had made them. Matthew was well aware that Sooty was a puppet; it was different for Dad. 'If you look back at the old black and white programmes, you can see the affection between the puppets and myself on screen,' Harry revealed to biographer Geoff Tibballs later. 'You can see that I think they're real.' When he replaced an old Sooty with a new one, Harry would break out in a cold sweat, he confessed, and always make a quiet apology to the deposed puppet.

Harry's obsession was not good for his health, and he'd always worked too hard. A heart attack on Christmas Day 1975 meant that Matthew – busy on his own behalf in another fondly remembered children's programme, *Rainbow* – had to take over the family business. Once he'd recovered, Harry couldn't take it easy, however, and before too long, though he had sold the rights in Sooty to his son, there were two Sooty stage shows playing the provinces.

Matthew had taken over the television show, too; and unlikely as it may seem, in 1980, Sooty was in trouble again. In an unexpected echo of *We Dispense With Accuracy*, an episode featuring an overactive Sweep saw the dog forcibly calmed down in the unfortunately-named 'tranquilizing booth', a cubicle which pumped out soothing smoke. Sooty and Sweep were on tranquilizers, screamed the tabloids, and it wasn't long before the IBA were watching and self-censorship in the form of 'The Sooty Rule Book' – a list of television dos and don'ts – was imposed upon the programme.

Through all of this the air of cheeky subversion remained, as became evident in a 1989 edition of *This is Your Life* honouring Matthew's illustrious father. Though surprised on stage during a Sooty extravaganza with his son on the occasion of his birthday, Harry seemed only mildly perturbed when a hot and bothered Michael Aspel lumbered on stage in a bear suit to thrust the big red book at him. As the programme progressed, Harry behaved himself as he was paid tribute to; but by the end of the show, he could not resist taking control for a grand finale. It was no doubt supposed to have been a cute, cuddly coda for the cameras: the show was to end with Aspel presenting Sooty was his own little red book to match Harry's. But it wasn't: Harry had other plans. Operating Sooty through a little black box, just as he'd done when he met the Queen all those years ago, he was less concerned with such cuteness than with slipping a well-filled water pistol into Sooty's paw. Grinning naughtily, Harry proceeded to give Aspel a good unexpected squirt in the face, as well as dousing anybody else unwise enough to get in his way, before he proudly strode forward to take centre stage. Matthew grinned tolerantly behind his esteemed but naughty parent. Bye bye, everyone, bye bye. Here was a glorious reminder of those early days of mischief, and of all that anarchic magic somehow wreaked by a simple seaside glove puppet. Then – and now – it was a long, long way from the taut-stringed antics of Muffin the Mule. *VP*

And if this wholesome, homegrown fun seemed somewhat strange, the bought-in stuff from abroad brought still more bizarre bafflement to mould childish minds…

Tintin and the Golden Fleece

France Film (Dubbed Soundtrack: UK) | 1961 | colour | sound | 94mins
Director Jean-Jacques Vierne
Script André Barret
Producer André Barrett, Chantal Riviere
Production Company A P C Paris
Starring Jean-Pierre Talbot, Georges Wilson, Georges Loriot

Recall, if you can, a time before the smartphone – before the internet – when your only source of information about the world was books, newspapers, radios and television. Great chunks of historical data – hugely important or hugely irrelevant – were entirely obscured from view. Of course, our Wikipedia world brings its own perils – unsubstantiated opinions masquerading as truths – but at least there's somewhere to look for basic bits of trivia. Not so on Bank Holiday Monday, May 1st 1978 – the morning, many years ago, that *Tintin et le Mystère de les Toison D'Or* had its one and only scheduled screening on British television as *Tintin and the Golden Treasure*.

Pop culture history you thought you knew can suddenly seem supremely strange if you pause to reconsider. Revisit for a moment the other delights on BBC television that day designed to appeal to young viewers, as listed in the *Radio Times*. The morning's programmes included *The Postman*, a story from Czechoslovakia: 'out looking for mushrooms, four boys discover a postbag, and this provides temptation for one of them.' Intriguing. So very foreign. If you didn't fancy that, you needed only wait until teatime for Billy Smart's *Children's Circus*, which boasted a performance by Silvano and his eight-year-old daughter Maraika with their comedy contortion act. Later the same evening you could enjoy the *Little and Large* holiday special (with guest stars Petula Clark, the Stylistics and Boney M). Whither this stuff in the celebrity-fronted nostalgia programmes?

Before the coming of the internet, you may have been familiar with *Tintin* solely through the series of cartoon books that were available at the local library. Accurate information was in short supply. It was apparent from close scrutiny that they originated somewhere 'on the continent', as it was called in those far-off days, when even France seemed a million miles away, and that they all, according to their striking covers, emanated from 'Hergé'. But who knew what a 'Hergé' was? Was it a man, woman, machine, a company? Why didn't he have a first name? Was it, then, the acronym for a strange, faceless conglomerate of cartoonists? Did anybody know for sure? Was there really an accent on the end?

As far as the film was concerned, all there was to consult was the latest issue of the *Radio Times*. You may have had a smart leather folder to put your copy in (available by mail order from the BBC) but the magazine housed therein did not help solve the mystery of Hergé. It didn't even confirm how you might spell 'Tintin'. According to the somewhat sketchy schedule listing,

Tin Tin and the Golden Treasure was 'a feature film', yet it was not reviewed on the films page with the rest of the week's movies. Why? Furthermore, the film seemed to have been unceremoniously dumped at 11.00 between early learning programme *You and Me* at 10.45 and *The Life of a Lake*, a documentary about Lake Windermere in spring, at 12.35. In retrospect, you might surmise that the BBC were just filling a gap in the schedules and that the *Radio Times* film editor thought this kiddie stuff unworthy of review. And so there was no review. So there is nothing for us to look back on years later, except this rather lacklustre listing – but it gives an idea of the plot:

> *11.0 Tin Tin and the Golden Treasure*
> *A feature film*
> *Captain Haddock is left an old, rusty sailing boat. But when he, Tin Tin and Snowy go to Istanbul to claim it, they are offered a fortune. The boat obviously hides a secret. In solving the mystery, the three have many adventures across the Mediterranean.*

Like the boat, this listing hides a secret – what was that film really like? Luckily, the English language dub of *Tin Tin and the Golden Treasure* ended up in the vault at the BFI National Archive. Rewatched years later – now that a quick google can provide valuable contextual detail, like the fact that Hergé was in fact Belgian cartoonist Georges Remi, and that his character was called Tintin, not Tin Tin – and the film is easily available on DVD – you can get a fuller sense of it. Filled with charmingly silly intrigue, absurd action and catchy 1960s twangy guitar euro pop, it remains both a hypnotically nostalgic viewing experience, and a potent counterpoint to the better remembered kids stuff of the same era.

Compared to the books, it's no substitute for the real thing, of course, but it manages to capture a lot of the flavour of the stories. And while it's all still darned odd, the action scenes – crucially – are played straight, and there is a decent smattering of the kind of slapstick and character comedy that is so typical of the books. A big bonus, now as then, for the shamefully mono-lingual Tintin fans that populated bits of Britain in the 1970s, is that splendidly entertaining if strangely foreign English-language audio track. Luckily, this screen Tintin and Haddock do seem to act something like the comic strip originals we know and love – even if the Captain uses insults we never heard him shout in the books, and the stiff, wig-like hairstyles and painted on facial hair stretch verisimilitude to the utmost. But these were things that the *Radio Times* never told us.

In that pre-video recorder age, you had to catch films when you could. There was no guarantee that they would ever be on again. Up until the last couple of multimedia decades, that was the case – things were on at the pictures, or on the telly, and then they were gone. Time went by, memories slowly faded. Had that mysterious film ever been on at all? Perhaps you'd dreamed it. How would you know?

Take another flick back through the browning pages of the 1970s era *Radio Times* and you'll find similarly Spartan listings for all manner of bought in overseas programming, some of which may trigger your own half-remembered memories of long ago sunny school-holiday mornings, or miserable wet and rainy afternoons. Many of the programmes you see listed there may no longer exist. Luckily, some of them do. Examples are the brilliant French *Robinson Crusoe* series that seemed to be on every summer, with the hauntingly beautiful music, suggestive of the restful monochromatic lapping of the waves on the beach; the almost Pythonesque fake-moustachioed swashbuckling madness of the narratively-incomprehensible French period adventure drama *The Flashing Blade*, with its great theme song; those bewilderingly strange 1970s *Sesame Street* (1969–) episodes which interspersed crazy pinball animations with a weirdly eerie white-face clown painting numbers in the street; programmes from a time when European and American culture seemed equally remote. But not everything survives. As we mentioned in the introduction to this section, less easy to track down are things like those dubbed European fairy-tales, *Tales of Europe*, where you would swear you could hear the incompletely erased foreign voices buzzing mysteriously somewhere deep beneath the overdubbing; the strange unending oddly scary serial about the on-the-run circus boy, *Silas* (16/05 – 01/08/1984), racing anxiously about on a horse, hiding in barns, evading a sinister strong man; and a bizarre, incomprehensible undateable cartoon about a giant sad-faced dog on a bicycle, *Maxi Dog Fig*. It may have been Czech. Was it even called that? Were the English language versions of programmes of this kind thrown away long ago? How would they seem if we saw them now?

Don't bogart that bong, Captain: *Tintin and the Golden Fleece* (1965).

Historically there has been a hierarchical, subjective structure to archiving old films and TV, just as there has been with writing about them. These foreign programmes are surely the responsibility of other nations, you might argue. But even with our own visual heritage there are worrying gaps which speak volumes about those who, historically, once called the shots when it came to doing the archiving, or documenting the past. Note, for example, the existence of a bumper bundle of Lord Mayor's Show broadcasts, while many *Doctor Who* episodes were wiped.

There was a sequel to that Tintin film: in English it would have been called *Tintin and the Blue Oranges* (1964). And, again, in the absence of any decent or authoritative contemporary documentation from the time, there are some contemporary Tintinologists that say that this subsequent Tintin film screened once on television in Scotland in the late 1970s, with a dubbed English soundtrack, too. Others have attested that it screened down south, regionally; others assure us that it was once screened in cut-down instalments on Saturday mornings on ITV. But, as yet, the authors have been unable to turn up any definite documentary evidence of any of these possible broadcasts. At time of writing, no English language track is known to exist. Perhaps it never did. But we'll keep looking and hoping.

Somewhat startlingly, when you think about it, thanks to the wonders of modern technology, both *Golden Fleece* and *Blue Oranges* are now endlessly available for all to see, ripped out of the past and pasted into an ever-bulging present. Whilst this serves as a reminder that we must always guard against the blinkers of nostalgia and inadvertently becoming suspicious of the new technology, it is also a reminder of how important it is to remember that old stuff – though eminently available – is still old stuff, and contextualization of it all is more important than ever. We can appreciate new and old simultaneously now, and the lines of history are becoming increasingly blurred as a result. But while we can't rationally impose the sensibility of the new on the old, or the old on the new, and shouldn't attempt to clumsily reconfigure the past, we are in a better position than ever to re-examine it all. We have more research tools at our disposal now than ever before, should we wish to use them, to try and understand the past, and how it relates to the present.

Television in those days was surely just as immersive an experience as the internet is now. In many ways it was perhaps more isolating than the worldwide web. You were truly alone in your world. There was none of the sense of community – albeit illusory – that something like Facebook or Twitter now creates, and there was no possible contact with others who had the same interests – there were no forums, no networks, no discussion groups, nothing.

There was no additional reference context then for what you saw on TV. Not even the barest background details. This was back before the days when pop culture was being thoroughly analysed and investigated. You couldn't whack anything you liked into Wikipedia to get some basic facts (or even half-facts) about it. Sure enough, none of us can rely on what we read on the internet, and research rightly continues to be an evaluative process across multiple sources; but back then it was surely more difficult still: you'd frequently only have access to often exceedingly ill-informed hearsay, rumour, legend or urban myth.

Short of going down to the local library to do some research, you were on your own. And often that library visit wasn't much use, either. For while a five-year-old edition of *Encyclopaedia Britannica* was still reasonably okay on the life cycle of the frog, it was hardly hot on critically-dismissed pop culture. Of course, you can't take anything you read online or off it for granted. But it sure helps that you can google the life cycle of the frog and get some consensus of opinion; or alternatively find the dates of those Tintin films, which we now can be sure aren't Tin Tin films, just as easily, and without one of those areas of research being hierarchically positioned as being more important than the other. With that in mind, at least now we might be able to begin to document, discuss, reevaluate, and debate our film and television history in a more open environment. Perhaps, one day, we can think about chucking away all those out-of-date encyclopaedias. *VP*

Sometimes not everybody can decide what's for kids and what isn't – and this was certainly the case by the latter days of the original Doctor Who…

Doctor Who: The Trial of a Time Lord

UK TV | Transmitted 6/9/1986 – 6/12/1986 | colour | 14 x 25mins
Directors Nicholas Mallett, Ron Jones, Chris Clough
Producer John Nathan-Turner
Script Editor Eric Saward
Script Robert Holmes, Philip Martin, Pip and Jane Baker
Production Company BBC
Cast Colin Baker, Nicola Bryant, Bonnie Langford, Michael Jayston, Lynda Bellingham, Joan Sims, Brian Blessed

Though adults and kids enjoy it today, back then, not everyone appreciated the history and legacy of this sci-fi perennial. Far from it. Indeed, by the time of Colin Baker (the sixth incarnation of the Doctor, originally played by William Hartnell when the show began in 1963) he and the show were often derided or gently mocked when they featured on anything but *Blue Peter* (1958–) or *Saturday Superstore* (1982–87). Presenter Selina Scott was curt, dismissive and aloof when Baker turned up on *BBC Breakfast Time* (1983–89) in 1984. A clash of personalities? Or something more? Consider also when, in 1986, on *Open Air* (a sort of chat show, BBC audience feedback programme) a group of adult fans are told repeatedly that *Doctor Who* (1963–89, 1996 & 2005–) is for children, not people of their age. But to many people, a man wearing a funny costume, traveling through time and space in a beat-up Police Box probably seemed somewhat old-hat and childish in the post-*Star Wars* (1977), post-*Blade Runner* (1982) age. Baker's costume hardly helped. His collars were stamped with ridiculous question marks and his coat was brash and colourful in the extreme. Cut from at least fifteen different types of cloth, it was a strange garment for a character to wear every day. This overtly garish costume turned the eccentric traveller into too much of a stereotype. 'I'm a bit crazy, me' it seemed to say.

But we would argue that Colin Baker was one of the most imaginative, riskiest, perhaps even best Doctors of the whole original run of *Doctor Who*. It's not a widely held view and not one that anyone else would have likely voiced – at least confidently – when the programme was cancelled back in 1989. It didn't matter that he'd been out of the role for some three years; then and thereafter many fans used him as a whipping boy for the sins they felt had been committed by the series in its final years. The Doctor as played by Colin Baker – not to be confused with Tom Baker, perhaps the most loved and admired of all Doctor Whos – was bright, brash, mean and self-absorbed. A bit like the 1980s generally.

You'd be forgiven for not remembering Colin Baker. His tenure was short and the release of his eleven stories on VHS, then later DVD, was a long time coming. You might remember seeing *Trial of a Time Lord* back in the depressing, wintry early months of 1986 and thinking that its fourteen episodes of relentless courtroom scenes went on forever – and that nothing ever happened. The sixth Doctor wasn't very good, right? Weren't the stories quite poor?

Through those long-delayed DVDs and the internet, we can now very easily watch, re-access and make up our own minds about whichever Doctor or *Doctor Who* story we're told is contentious. Revisionism is possible. But it wasn't like that in the 1980s or early 90s. The show's history weighed heavily upon its shoulders and yet it was exceedingly rare to see, say, a whole black and white story featuring William Hartnell or Patrick Troughton (Doctors One and Two). You'd have to reach for that local library staple, the *Doctor Who* novelization, to get anywhere close.

The weight of an inaccessible history plagued the series through the 1980s; and Colin Baker suffered for it the most. For those that don't know, he was effectively fired by the BBC after only two-and-a-bit seasons in the role. The Doctor survived *The Trial of a Time Lord*, an overarching narrative season broadcast in 1986, but Colin Baker didn't. The regeneration – a process whereby the eccentric Time Lord rejuvenates himself as a means of staying alive – kicked off the next series but without Baker being present, and the series limped on for a further three years. Briefly revived in 1996 with Paul McGann in the lead, it wasn't until 2005 that *Doctor Who* truly found its feet again. In 1986, Colin Baker had been a sacrificial lamb for a series slowly losing more and more support internally at the BBC. And the fans hated him for it.

Eighties *Doctor Who* proper began when Tom Baker left the series at the end of story *Logopolis* in March 1981. For many, it meant the end of the Doctor himself – such was the degree to which Tom Baker had captured people's imagination with his mixture of childish naivety and confrontational mania. It didn't bode well for the series and *Doctor Who: The Unfolding Text*, a rather dry sounding tome produced to examine the series, predicted its demise as early as 1983.

John Nathan-Turner, the *Doctor Who* producer from 1980 onward, began to make changes to the show, even before his star had left. He was understandably keen to propel the series out from Baker's shadow and amassed a whole arsenal of tools and techniques to grab and hold the viewer's attention: 'exotic' foreign locations, 'famous' guest stars and attractive, occasionally scantily-clad female companions all regularly featured. He also dug deep into the series' past and revived old villains, old friends and even

Arresting threads: Colin Baker is resplendent on the cover of this 1985 comic that came free with crisps.

old storylines. Peter Davison and Colin Baker (Tom Baker's successors) faced not just Daleks but also more esoteric villains such as the Time Lord Omega. Whole seasons could even be historically themed; season 20 saw an element from the series' past revived for each and every story while season 22, Colin Baker's mainstay, featured a whole array of classic villains and characters: the Daleks, the Cybermen, the Sontarans, the Master and the return of Doctor number two, Patrick Troughton.

It sounds like the pudding may have been over-egged but many loved seeing elements from the show's past revived and pouring out into their living rooms. The use of old *Who* clips during Tom Baker's regeneration scene had been incredibly popular, for example, and montage sequences of archival *Who* footage were regularly squeezed into the show from there on in. The Cybermen got the treatment in *Earthshock* (08 – 16 /03/1982): the first story to feature the robotic villains in seven years. They were, of course, revived at John Nathan-Turner's behest.

Eric Saward, the show's script editor (1982–86), would say in an infamous interview for *Starburst* magazine that John Nathan-Turner was actively courting the fans, particularly in America, and often gave interviews for fanzines rather than working on the show. The referencing of the old is approaching excessive but surely we can understand why people would have liked it so much, particularly the old clips. *Doctor Who* fans were in heaven when BBC2 repeated a story from each Doctor's reign in 1992 and '93. There's a story in the new *Doctor Who* where Christopher Eccleston's Doctor tells Charles Dickens that he's a fan but also something to the effect that it's the job of fans to be critical and to appreciate that some books – or stories in the case of *Doctor Who* – aren't as good as others. Some may even be quite bad. We agree, but when you've been starved of your love object, critical judgments of this sort become something of a privilege. You can't afford to 'not like' something when the material is so rarefied: it'd be a threat to your identity as a fan – something perhaps easy to forget in the age of the internet. Sometimes we need glimpses of the past, whatever form it takes, and *Doctor Who* fans appreciated the glimpses they got in the early video, pre-DVD days of 1980s Britain.

Who was enlivened by its past but laden down by it too. Self-parody lay in the wings and ageism came at it from all quarters, even traditionalists: Mary Whitehouse's complaints about the programme reached a zenith in the mid-1980s. It was as though her self-appointed, unregulated group the Festival of Light thought *Who* should be behaving as it had been two decades earlier, or at least how they remembered it: wholesome, educational, and devoid of violence. More significant though was the attitude of BBC commissioners. For a brief moment in 1984, they cancelled *Doctor Who.*

It was surprising if not shocking news. Viewing figures had been very high for season 22, Colin Baker's first following his introductory story *The Twin Dilemma* (22 – 30/03/1984) broadcast the previous year. In fact, the figures showed an improvement on the average for the whole of the Peter Davison era. Fans went into overdrive and inundated the BBC with complaints. There was even a novelty single: *Doctor In Distress*, written and produced by *Doctor Who* uberfan Ian Levine. The broadcasting corporation, now in its own state of shock, adjusted their statement and said the series only needed a rethink and would be back in eighteen months. What was going on? It was popular; why did it need a rethink?

For all its obsessions with the past and reuse of elements sucked out of old stories, the Colin Baker era of *Doctor Who* is arguably one of the most distinct within the whole of the 'classic' era. The character of the Doctor had always had an irascible quality – he could be difficult, manipulative and unreasonable, 'un-human', to paraphrase a powerful moment between Tom Baker's Doctor and companion Sarah Jane Smith in *The Pyramids of Mars* (25/10 – 15/11/1975) – but not until Colin Baker came along, had he been such a bastard. He's arrogant, self-obsessed, unpredictable and rude to almost everyone he meets. When he storms off to rescue what he assumes is a creature in distress at the beginning of *Attack of the Cybermen* (05 – 12/01/1985), he does it for the glory, not for the sake of doing good. He's as jarring and difficult as the more aged first Doctor but with more energy – in fact it's almost as though he has too much energy. He bounds around the TARDIS dispatching orders and judging his increasingly long-suffering assistant, Peri (played by Nicola Bryant), appearing not to care about her feelings or even her well-being sometimes.

Doesn't this make for an interesting character? More intriguing than the Doctors with which we might be more familiar? Sure, it can be exhausting and Colin Baker's energies don't always hit the mark or work with the environment around him; but when it does work, it's totally compelling. The Doctor has an edge and subsequently all his relationships have it too; there's always a negotiation going on, something unpredictable. Dialogue doesn't just advance the plot or raise a laugh; it has tension.

The tension in *The Twin Dilemma* (22 – 30/03/1984), Colin Baker's first story, is extreme. The Doctor taunts Peri and eventually tries to strangle her: a type of violence and situation never before seen in *Doctor Who*; an act in theory explained away by post-regeneration instability. The Time Lord's literally not himself. Regardless, it's shocking particularly when you consider that 'nice boy' Peter Davison (the fifth Doctor) had only just left the show. But then Baker and Bryant (Peri) were still wary of each other when they made this four-parter, still testing each other like the old girl and new boy that they were – and you can see it in their body language. Genuine mistrust and antagonism dominates the story, so much so that subsequent tiffs between Doctor and assistant – and there are many – seem light, fluffy and pretty unconvincing in comparison. (Baker and Bryant liked each other by season 22, even if their characters didn't.) *The Twin Dilemma* may not be a fan favourite but it has a real edge to it and the trajectory and the performances are brilliant. (When the story proper kicks in in the last episode, it gets very, very boring, very, very quickly, however.) Baker's whole way of being gave *Doctor Who* a shake-up and complicated the way that good might be victorious, and frankly what 'good' might even mean sometimes.

Baker's sensibility was right on cue with that of script editor Eric Saward – and vice versa. In both *Attack the Cybermen* and *The Mysterious Planet* (06–27/09/1986) (the first part of *The Trial of a Time Lord*), there's no real 'goodie' to root for (aside from the Doctor), just a sort of general need to save the Earth and to stop people squabbling. Saward set characters against each other like birds in a cock-fight. They battle it out with wisecracks and brutal violence. If anything, perhaps that's where the problem lay. Colin Baker's difficult character might have been better off in a universe where good was celebrated and his reactionary ways had something more to react against. It worked well in stories *Vengeance on Varos* (09 – 26/01/1985) and *Mark of the Rani* (02 – 09/02/1985), even if Kate O'Mara arguably stole the show in the case of the latter.

Fans did struggle with Baker's Doctor. Some disliked the complicated morals; others hated the costume and feelings of excess. The show returned after its controversial eighteen-month break with *The Trial of a Time*

Lord, a fourteen-episode story that subdivided into four further separate narratives: *The Mysterious Planet*, *Mindwarp* (04 – 25/10/1986), *Terror of the Vervoids* (01 – 22/11/1986) and *The Ultimate Foe* (29/11 – 06/12/1986). The first episode begins with a stunning model sequence of the TARDIS being dragged into a space station; it was shot on 35mm and features powerful, moody music. It then cuts to a decidedly cheap set and the Doctor clambering out of his time/space travel machine the TARDIS and walking into a courtroom. He's been summoned by his fellow Time Lords for interfering in the lives of others; something that goes against their very code.

Like a sort of sci-fi Scrooge, the Doctor watches adventures from his past, present and future on a giant video screen. (All the stories are new to the viewer, however. The self-reflective act of watching TV screens had featured in both *Vengeance of Varos* and *Revelation of the Daleks*. Postmodernism had invaded *Doctor Who*.) The show and Colin Baker were both on trial – but in such a scenario, a scenario where there is no room for moral ambiguity; all judgments and answers look predetermined. It can only be guilty or innocent, good or bad: the basic moral binaries that Colin Baker and the show had been trying to avoid or at least complicate over the last two years.

We know the ending before we even get there. Or do we? Things actually get quite odd by the time we get to *The Ultimate Foe*, the final sub-story to this *Who* portmanteau yarn. Plot spoiler alert. The Valeyard, the strange shadowy man who'd been trying to prove the Doctor guilty – with considerable delight and earnestness – is in fact... the Doctor. Or rather a sort of possible, future evil version of him. (It's never quite explained.) He's got into the Time Lord Matrix and having manipulated the Time Lords' understanding of both the past and future, hopes to take over the Doctor's life. It's true mythic narrative; like the end of TV show *The Prisoner* (1967–68) where Number 6 discovers that Number 1, the authoritarian figure he's been trying to unmask for the whole series, is actually himself. (Note the conclusion to that series also takes place in a courtroom.) Or like *Apocalypse Now* (1979) where Captain Willard travels up the river to meet, confront and kill Colonel Kurtz and then unwittingly sort of becomes him too. Good and evil confront then collapse in on each other in all three cases.

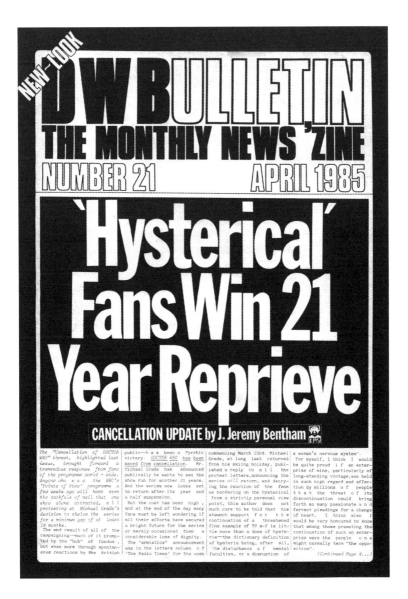

Headlines scream: front cover for forthright news and opinions 'zine *Doctor Who Bulletin.*

Looking back, it was as though that battle between good and evil, light and dark, was going on within Colin Baker himself. If he'd had his way, his costume would have been black from head-to-toe – a look associated with the Master, another Moriarty type character in *Doctor Who*. It was like he wanted to be both the goodie and the baddie at the same time. Villainous roles had been his stock-in-trade. He played the mean Commander Maxil in Doctor Who story *Arc of Infinity* (03 – 12/01/1983) just a year before he got the leading part.

Eric Saward had intended the whole *Trial* affair to end as the veteran *Who* writer Robert Holmes had drafted it: the Doctor and the Valeyard tumbling into space, fighting each other forever, like Sherlock Holmes and Moriarty. It's the final logical end to a mythic metaphysical story about the battle between good and evil. Or rather, there is no end, no final judgment: the battle just goes on forever – inside the Doctor's head and outside of him too. Perfect. John Nathan-Turner wasn't so keen. He wanted the show – and the Doctor – to win and fight another day and the final episode was frantically re-written. In the version that went out on 6th December 1986, the Doctor defeats the Valeyard, Bonnie Langford joins the TARDIS (having appeared in *Terror of the Vervoids*) and everything is left neat and tidy. The stakes had been raised but essentially it was business as usual. The later sacking of Colin Baker aside, that is.

Whatever his motivations were and whatever dynamic fresh qualities he brought to *Doctor Who*, it didn't really matter: Colin Baker was out. Executives at the BBC thought *Doctor Who* was old, tired, boring and dull and ignored the fact that the general public still watched it in their relative droves – until after the hiatus, that is. In a way, the fallout of punk was still rolling out and *Doctor Who* was a prog-rock dinosaur. With Channel 4 beginning in 1982 and Youth TV and pop videos taking over, an old show like *Doctor Who* was practically an embarrassment. Better to rip it out like an old fireplace, as was the trend in Thatcherite Britain. Baker was sacked and three years later, the show cancelled. It didn't matter what he had or hadn't done.

It's totally different world now, though. The BBC is rightly proud of its flagship programme and considers it legacy, heritage viewing, something that actually distinguishes the broadcaster from other channels. In a way, we live in *Doctor Who*'s world now too. We embrace old and new TV alike – and music and fashion and everything else – and we've finally gotten over the jokes about wobbly sets and *Doctor Who*'s general rubbishness. New *Who* had quite a task on its hands but it swept that all away, and now a woman, Jodie Whittaker, has taken on the leading role. But did team Baker, Saward and Nathan-Turner take the programme to its natural end point back in 1986? *The Trial of a Time Lord* could have been a rich and shocking end to the entire show. But then maybe that's what it would have been: an ending, no reprise, no revival many years later, just an end. Colin Baker: the last *Doctor Who*. It could be worse. Couldn't it? *WF*

TRUE STORIES

The French are supposed to be poetic and philosophical and the British concerned with empiricism and facts. Maybe that's why British cinema has been associated with realism and documentary, and, in its early days, actuality. Early cinema could certainly be fantastical and experimental; but more frequently it exploited the spectacle of work places emptying out at the end of the day. Thus it documented the economic and social fabric of the time. Concerned explicitly with the recording of people and place, in those early days, it also captured more exotic sights: beautiful foreign locations, 'savages', even death and other transgressions. Images of sex undoubtedly formed a part of the early cinema palette too; but were not so easily accessible, and were not promoted in the bills and posters, catalogues and by hawkers on the streets, all trying to sell tickets to the latest show, perhaps in a circus tent, or at a fun fair.

The concept of the film camera as an instrument of truth and witness remains compelling; it has always been a commodity both to pull punters, and to sell ideology. John Grierson headed-up filmmaking at the Empire Marketing Board and the General Post Office in the 1930s and 1940s, in both cases selling the idea of proud citizenship and Empire, to be celebrated at home and abroad. Film magazines made for the colonies promoted

‹ **Britons never shall be slaves:** a marching kazoo band in *Spare Time* (1939), made for the 1939 New York World's Fair.

both British values and British industry. Grierson spoke of the 'creative treatment of actuality'; and he and his colleagues and acolytes, Basil Wright, Humphrey Jennings and others, created a series of powerful, creative works that resonated with audiences, particularly during the War. Accompanying music was carefully placed: it sold national industries as if they were well-oiled machines in *Night Mail* (1936), and it connected diverse places in *Listen to Britain* (1942). Editing, that old trick that changes what was seen through the camera lens, was carefully employed; influenced, somewhat ironically, by the montage cinema of the Communist Soviet Union. The films attempted to rouse, and often did; but by way of their official, voice-of-the-state tone. They were frequently sober and wedded to ideas of detached objectivity and higher authority.

Documentary as a revelatory process, a means of lifting the lid on the obscured and misunderstood, has been a guiding principle of non-fiction filmmaking. Grierson and those that followed him opened up the car bonnet of the nation and peered within at its cultural, industrial and military engines (or, rather, fabricated a layman's image of them for the viewer). The previously-mentioned mondo movies of the 1960s and 70s became a notable yet critical maligned pseudo-documentary form that thrashed about wildly, exploitatively harvesting whatever mixture of actuality and tall tales they could to fill-up each title's circa seventy-minutes plus. The genre's commercialism and frequent lack of ethics remain distasteful to some but its broad cultural mix and strong stomach has made for odd, unlikely connections that, you might argue, get closer to the 'true' schizophrenic reality of modern life than almost all other films. Desperate homeless drunks, a hair-transplant operation and the phenomenon of the peacock-Mod all contributed to the 'creative treatment of actuality' in British mondo title *London in the Raw* (1964), by way of example.

We've mentioned before that the form's first major international flourish came with Italy's *Mondo Cane* (1962); and the UK capital itself eventually went under the Italian microscope in *Naked England* aka *Inghilterra Nuda* (1969). Like other mondo films, it lifted the lid on all manner of minutiae and, on this occasion, it sifted through the shit that made-up the backside of Swinging London. Far stronger than Arnold Miller and Stanley Long's string of mondos (which began with *West End Jungle* (1962) and included *London in the Raw* (1964) and *Primitive London* (1965)), it unflinchingly

Shock and awe: press material for Italian mondo film *Naked England* (1969).

sought out all manner of transgressive deeds and vices, taking in heroin injection in the toilets at Piccadilly, trepanning (re-enacting the moment when Amanda Feilding, seeking mental, neuro-physiological emancipation, drilled a hole in her skull), a crucifixion on Hampstead Heath (see also Andy Milligan's *Body Beneath* (1969)) and a vicar who frequented Soho strip bars – offering advice and counsel only, of course. These eye-opening exploits were further peppered with a round-up of novelty restaurants (also a favourite of Miller and Long's), on this occasion extended to the inclusion of a (clearly made-up) Nazi-themed eating establishment where the waiters dressed as SS officers and a 'joke' gassing took place half-way through the meal. Apparently, the place could be found in Mayfair.

Naked England reversed the older tradition of selling the virtues of the British Empire abroad. Instead, it used an Italian eye to make dear old Blighty look like a cesspit of decadence and depravity, the permissive society having already ruined the jewel. Or, maybe, the film just peered under the stone. Britain's place in the world was changing and it could no longer control the narrative; or rather those at the top could no longer control the narrative, in the way that once they had. Contentious content had increasingly become the order of the day; and new mobile 16mm technologies helped cameras go places they'd never been to before.

More independent voices were heard as hard-hitting documentary proliferated. Independent cinema shone a light on marginalized lifestyles as in the separatist rural existence documented in *The Moon and the Sledgehammer* (1971), and a mental health commune in *Asylum* (1972). The group Cinema Action made films as a way of spreading alternative information, and screened their films in factories and at union meetings. Television took-up the slack by combining these modes with the point-of-view of an intrepid journalist, positioning said centre as the voice of authority managing to combine both subjective and objective points of view and thus upholding the medium's power. Complex social issues could be simplified and the presenter became like an adventurer; an explorer striking out on new soil. Louis Theroux can be seen to be a current manifestation of this phenomenon. Television documentary partially renewed the revelatory impetus of early cinema whilst unpicking and trying to make sense of an ever-more rapidly changing world.

Of the first-flush of intrepid journalist TV presenters, Daniel Farson stands prominent and fascinating. As a gay man, and a regular boozer around Soho, he was himself already immersed in what were then seen by many as 'alternative' lifestyles, and had worked for various papers before joining the new London-based, independent TV company Associated Rediffusion in the early 1950s. Though occasionally subtly condemnatory, in his programmes he maintained an air of balance. He was also highly charismatic and capable of weaving multiple perspectives together as he spoke both to his interviewees and to the viewers at home. Though he appeared fully clothed in the *Nudism* episode of his show *Out of Step* (transmitted 02/10/1957), his wish to understand, and not to condemn, seemed genuine. The show revealed naked female flesh to British television viewers for the first time, or so the story goes, and provided the impetus for a steady flow of nudist films that began to appear in cinemas shortly thereafter. Thus reportage of this kind both reflected social change, and drove it forward, whatever the views were of those involved. More than half a century later, the internet and especially the ubiquity of YouTube are current manifestations of this phenomenon.

As prejudicial, partial and personal as documentary film itself, this section does not venture even to attempt to tell the historical story of the form. Rather it focuses on films and programmes we find interesting and, in some cases, oddly inspiring. Like the plane that sets-out at the beginning of *Primitive London*, leaving the capital, only to re-arrive at it – having cast fresh eyes on a revitalised familiar – we invite you to accompany us as we revisit and re-evaluate a further small and curious collection of strange cinematic artefacts.

The line between fact and fiction could be easily blurred in the early days of cinema as raw actuality footage and trick films were intermixed and 'performed' by way of a hand-operated projector; projector speeds might deliberately be changed and separate music and sound were added for effect...

Cricket Match on a Fishing Smack During a Heavy Sea

UK Film | 1899 | black and white | c.2mins
Production Company Warwick Trading Company

The alternative canon, or an alternative canon – if we can call it a canon? – can be an difficult terrain to navigate, particularly when, tragically, some films no longer even exist. What is to be done then, if we are to construct a fuller, richer film history? The exceedingly strange and compelling sounding *Cricket Match on a Fishing Smack During a Heavy Sea* is one such lost film.

Back in the late nineteenth century, the cinematograph was received as an astounding new machine, capable of capturing and presenting photographical images in movement, but it was also part raw spectacle, part sideshow entertainment and performances took place in music halls, circuses and revues, and even as part of magic shows. Stage magician regular at London's Egyptian Hall, David Devant, for example, whipped up hysteria with *An Over-Incubated Baby* (1901), where a newborn baby turns into an old man in less than a minute, and he later became a sales agent for the cinematograph developed by R. W. Paul.

No change in the weather: rough sea postcards were popular in late Victorian England.

It was curious, then, that simple and rather sober sounding footage of waves crashing on rocks or piers became a major cinematic phenomenon as the nineteenth century met the twentieth. *Rough Sea at Dover* (1896), *Waves and Spray* (1897), *Rough Sea on Stone Ground* (1897) and *Rocks and Rough Sea* (1899) were all shot and screened in the early years of cinema. And even as late as 1905, some ten years after the first public film presentations had taken place, *Waves Breaking Against Cornish Cliffs* was turned-out in the assumption it would bring in bookings, screenings and, most importantly, cash. Narrative development, multi-part films and even films of some length were in vogue at this point as the standardization of cinema loomed, but, whatever, *Rough Sea* films still kept being made, and eventually lost.

Charles Urban was a real champion of the form and made thirteen rough sea films through first the Warwick Trading Company and then his own company, The Charles Urban Trading Company. His enterprise and mode of filmmaking was centred on actuality and documentation and he used the adage 'putting the world before you' to advertise his catalogue and appeal to the Victorian desire to know and experience the wider world around. Curiously, the witnessing of rough seas via film would have been distinctly novel for some, even in a small island like the UK. Holidays and picture postcards required money and were associated with the upper classes. Urban was one of a few who tried to bring unusual sights to the general public.

But the power of the sea's image went beyond simple rarity and democratic function, in fact it seemed to resonate in a multitude of ways. The *Rough Sea* film is usually held up as an illustrative example of early cinema's power and ability to capture dynamic movement. It was as though cinema had tamed the wild beast that was the sea, man and technology together finally slamming down God's virile arm. A not inappropriate analogy as the sea had been a powerful symbol in the Bible, variously pre-existing the earth, laying sinners to waste in the time of the flood, and later washing away sins, via baptism. Indeed, Victorians had picked-up on the latter association particularly, advising visceral contact with the waves as a way of curing melancholia and renewing the spirit. Filming the stuff finally meant capturing it as if it were a trophy or treasure for a museum, sort of like mounting a stuffed animal on a wall. Manpower and Imperial power were primal and primary.

It was certainly seen in this both conquering and threatening light when the very first *Rough Sea* film, *Rough Sea at Dover*, was used to promote the Edison associated Vitascope camera and projector at the Koster and Bial's Music Hall, New York on 23rd April 1896. British duo Birt Acres and R. W. Paul, its makers, were present and, lasting roughly a minute, it showed a violent, fierce sea breaking on Admiralty Pier in Dover Harbour. The East Coast glitterati lapped it up:

> *'This was by the far best view shown, and had to be repeated many times. One could look far out to sea and pick out a particular wave swelling and undulating and growing bigger until it struck the end of the pier. Its edge then would be fringed with foam, and finally, in a cloud of spray, the wave would dash upon the beach. One could imagine the people running away,'*

reported the *New York Evening Mail and Daily Express.*

It was a powerful advert for Edison's new gizmo and exceedingly influential. That same year, Edison's company made *Surf At Long Branch* (1896), 'a remake of *Rough Sea at Dover'* according to historian Charles Musser, and then when visiting the UK for Edward VII's coronation they gleaned *Waves at Dover, England* (1902).

The aforementioned Charles Urban had travelled to New York from Michigan especially for the Koster and Bial's Music Hall screening and shortly after joined the Continental Commerce Company, one of three main licensees of Edison's film equipment in the USA. In August 1897, he moved to the UK to become the manager of their London branch and changed the organisation's name to The Warwick Trading Company to make it sound more British. He was dynamic and had shrewd business sense, persisting with *Rough Sea* film production and later making the frenetic sounding *Cricket Match on a Fishing Smack During a Heavy Sea* (1899), a work that used the raw drama and power of the sea to heighten spectacle and feelings of play and the bizarre. It was very different to *Barque Sortant du Port* aka *Boat Leaving Port* (1895), an early French film more about longing and romance than force and shock.

It's quite possible that either consciously or unconsciously the sea evoked patriotic or nationalistic associations in the UK, an island nation and imperial naval power. The latter part of the nineteenth century was a

EDISON'S NEW WONDER, THE VITASCOPE.

Hold on to your hats: America's gents were blown-away by *Rough Sea at Dover* (1896) when it screened at a special Vitascope presentation at the Koster and Bial's Music Hall on 23rd April 1896, according to the *New York Evening Mail and Daily Express*.

strange time for the UK. The Crimean War and the unifications of both Germany and Italy as nation states, plus the defeat of Napoleon III in France had drastically re-drawn the political map of Europe and Britain sat in the uncomfortable sidelines. It remained a respected world power but the sea that separated it from the rest of Europe represented contrary feelings. 'Splendid isolation' and the former glories of Nelson and a well-respected Royal Navy sat uncomfortably close to fears of invasion and the memories of loss of life during the Napoleonic wars. Films tapped into these mixed feelings and served to emphasise nationhood and a sense of the 'collective interest'. Cecil Hepworth made a film simply of a Union Jack flag, fluttering in the breeze, hoping to stir patriotic feeling. Meanwhile, Lord Kitchener arriving first at Calais after victory in the Sudan in October 1898, and then Dover, encountered an overwhelming audience reaction when screened on film at the Palace Theatre, London. *The Morning Leader*:

'They saw six feet odd of hard, wiry humanity, framed in an ordinary lounging suit of grey, alert and smiling. They saw him exchange a hearty shake of the hand with the steamer's skipper – and they rose to a man, aye, and to a woman, cheering loud and long. And when the cheers had died away they were succeeded by volley after volley of British 'hurrahs', which spread from floor to ceiling, from pit to gallery, from the back of stage even into the fashionable atmosphere of the tiers of boxes. The demonstration was renewed when the second scene was presented – representing the reception of the Sirdar, hat in hand, walking down the Admiralty Pier to meet the Mayor of Dover.'

He'd traversed the English Channel by way of a jump cut and arrived at the very pier smashed by waves in *Rough Sea at Dover*, the film that had driven everyone crazy in New York just four years earlier. The watery passageway between Dover and Calais, being rougher than in other areas and loaded with symbolism, became something of a psychogeographic hotspot in the nineteenth century. Naval writers referred to it as a divine 'deep moat' and in 1870 four times Prime Minister, W. E. Gladstone, called it the 'wide dispensation of the Province' and 'that streak of silver sea', in the *Edinburgh Review*.

The UK's waters were loaded with symbolism, and trick and novelty films riffed on the sea's collective mythological, and physical powers. Some may have found *Jig Aboard Ship* (1900) and *Dance Troupe in A Storm* (1900), both shot on boats during rough waters, distasteful, disrespectful even. Simple actualities developed as entrepreneurial filmmakers honed their craft and stretched their imaginations, content and mode changing before say the introduction of editing and other formal developments. Filmmakers went abroad to capture exotic sights, not unlike adventurers or explorers, and again these fed in to the patriotic narrative of the day, while others toyed with more outré subjects – animal deaths, for example. *Jig Aboard Ship* was similarly proto-mondo, or even proto-*Jackass*, its maker using the unpredictable forces of nature to affect their heavily staged scenario for audience guffawing. There was something rather novel and decidedly immediate about documenting the sea in a state of continuous motion. *Cricket Match on a Fishing Smack During a Heavy Sea* (1899) went even further in mining its predictable yet unpredictable nature. You can easily imagine the players flailing about as balls are lost over the side and the boat rocks to and fro, lashed by explosive waves. This *Jackass*-like effort was made, as were all the others mentioned here, by Charles Urban.

But, as noted, given *Cricket Match on a Fishing Smack During a Heavy Sea's* absence from the archive, imagine is all that you can do. Early cinema was dynamic and highly experimental but it was also commercial – very much so. Films were made by small businesses that did all they could to keep up with the competition, probably also scared that the novelty might just wear off one day. Times moved fast and as the sound era gathered pace and the studios began to exert their power, governments and passionate individuals began to realise that this early work was disappearing and many of the major international film archives were founded. Whilst it is hard to know exactly how many films were actually made between 1895 and the mid-1920s, given that films were often remade and titles changed, it is estimated that as little as 20% of films from this early period survive in the UK's collections.

Early cinema is really the stuff of legend now. The films discussed here are over a hundred years old, and yet the stories and contexts that surround them still hover in our imagination. If you play charades and act out a film, that first strange action you make, turning your hand, dates back to when cameras were manually operated. The early days of cinema are virtually the stuff of myth and folklore now; its symbols and rituals hide in plain view, out of sight.

The very first widely shown film *L'Arrivée d'un Train en Gare de la Ciotat* aka *Arrival of a Train* (1896), made by the Lumière brothers, has become one of those modern, symbolic legendary films and events. Reputedly the audience was terrified when they saw the train approach and enter the platform and the occasion was parodied in *The Countryman's First Sight of the Animated Pictures* (1901) – a country-hick grabs his floppy hat and runs-off in a state of fight-or-flight terror. Framing a film within film was a way of offsetting the feeling that the novelty of cinema might be wearing-off whilst also reminding city folk of their natural urban sophistication. It was to early film what Wes Craven's *Scream* (1996) was to mainstream horror in the 1990s.

The Lumière brothers' original has come to represent or stand in for all of early cinema, the train representing modernity; it runs down a track and takes us to other places; all things that film did and does too. And it has helped to preface France as the true nation of cineastes – the home of cinema – plus there's the story of people running away from the image of the train at the film's first screening, fearing for their lives; which given the predominance of other pictorial and photographic projection devices prior to the cinematograph actually sounds like a myth.

Taking a cursory look at the records it appears that *Rough Sea at Dover* actually had as much if not more of an influence than *Arrival of a Train*, in terms of subsequent production and ongoing audience interest – in the UK at least. R. W. Paul and Birt Acres re-made their *Rough Sea at Dover* many times over and Charles Urban made *Waves Breaking Against Cornish Cliffs* in 1905 when others filmmakers had moved on to narrative and editing. Demand was still there. But the sea is just too timeless and romantic, too devoid of modernity and technology, to represent early cinema for us today.

How do our stories and histories get written? Survival and visibility certainly helps. The legend of *Arrival of a Train* persists; Martin Scorsese made a remake for the centenary of cinema in 1996. Patriotism aside, wouldn't you rather see *Cricket Match on a Fishing Smack During a Heavy Sea* and other lost efforts by Charles Urban? As it is, we can only imagine the cricketers tumbling about and the audience back in 1899 laughing along as part of the show and spectacle. Or if not that then some other vulgar piece of cinema: a magician's trick, something played at a funny speed, maybe even a fake beheading. These films, particularly the dancing and sports films shot out at sea, are unique, unrepeatable in their exactitude, made solely for the camera whilst exploiting the unstable yet inherent truths of the natural environment. By way of contrast, looking back, *Arrival of a Train* feels planned and rigid, set to a timetable; the moneymen arrived at the station with it, about to take over, poised to turn film into big-business cinema. *WF*

Half a century later, the early days of television also negotiated with commercial concerns whilst trying to bring new sights and visions to people slouched in armchairs around the country...

Out of Step Nudism & Out of Step: Witchcraft

UK TV | Transmitted 2/10/1957 & 4/12/1957 | black and white | 2 x 14mins
Director Geoffrey Hughes
Written by Dan Farson, Elkan Allan, Stanley Craig
Cast Dan Farson, Charles Macaskie, Gerald Gardner
Production Company Associated Rediffusion

The investigative documentary series *Out of Step* arrived at an unusual time in British social and televisual history. Less international, more modest than the likes of *Whicker's World* (1958–94), but keen on weirdness and sensation, the series dug into its subjects with relish, and explored anarchism, vegetarianism, spiritualism, Scientology, nudism and witchcraft, to name just a few. Also, it became about opinions, not facts, and even the person on the street was given an opportunity to pitch in, something very unusual at that time. Questioned about nudism for the show, a rather stiff-looking young man responded: 'I don't think a girl looks so beautiful when they are in the nude, quite frankly I'd rather see them walking along with a nice suit on,' furthering the view that the general public could often be the most eccentric group of all.

The Suez crisis of 1956 had emphasized a decline in British influence abroad and people were looking for new forms of identity, and new ways of expressing themselves. Things were changing and Associated Rediffusion – the ITV franchise who made *Out of Step* – actively courted viewers in new and different ways. 'Let's face it once and for all. The public like girls, wrestling, bright musicals, quiz-shows and real-life drama. We gave them Hallé Orchestra, Foreign Press Club and visits to the local fire station. From now on, what the public wants, it's going to get', they said following a slow start. It was very different to the BBC and by 1959 the newly streamlined 'Rediffusion' had earned as much as five million pounds. Which wasn't bad as they only broadcast on week days, and only in the London area – the new ITV was divided into geographical constituents. Brittle post-war consensus had started to fracture and these independent television networks peered into the cracks, enlarging the fissures. Nearly fourteen million pounds were spent on TV advertising alone in 1957 – the very year *Out of Step* was broadcast.

Television changed with the introduction of the 'third channel' in 1955, but *Out of Step* was especially alive and unusual. It was shot on 35mm, looked good and had a clarity of purpose. But more than that it had Daniel Farson. A print journalist by trade, this well-travelled, likeable, yet mercurial and very English individual was actively interested in eccentrics, and appeared not only comfortable in their presence, but almost in semi-bemused awe. This fascination went back to his charismatic, alcoholic father who had loomed large in his early life, and had also been a journalist.

Farson deliberately incorporated wayward, widely-varying views in the show, and often managed to make traditional commentators appear as, if not more, out of step than the actual fringe-interest practitioners under scrutiny. He was skilled at drawing out soundbites and for the Nudism episode gently gave space to a Reverend Dr Davis to enter what can only be described as a fluster. The practice is 'abnormal' and practitioners are 'odd in their ideas'. Plus 'it may lead to other irregularities, such as peeping toms' said the psychologist and mental health hospital chaplain, breaking into a sweat. Everyone on Farson's show seemed strange and of interest as he naughtily created sparks and highlighted variations in points of view. The landowner and high Tory, Mr Wentworth Day, a regular contributor, was a man made of considerably tougher stuff than the Reverend Dr Davis. He barked, [nudism], 'it is a "cult", a dreary parade of rather revolting bodies, bulging stomachs and sagging bosoms'. Farson enjoyed these no-nonsense views, though he was also capable of quietly dismissing them with a subtle sideways grin.

For the most part, he did appear relatively open, however, just a man attempting to find out what people did in their spare time – anyone might be a nudist, a spiritualist, an anarchist, etc. His presentation style, speaking to the camera at the beginning and then again at the end of the programme, also suggested that the investigation was personal, just his opinion, and his opinion was almost always inclusive. (Though a gentle suspicion regarding the merits of whatever it was or wasn't could often be inferred.)

The programme incorporated a curious mixture of tones and registers and Farson was popular and a major draw. Slowly turning into something of a celebrity, he was even mimicked by Benny Hill, the comedian donning a special wig – despite the fact he and the TV presenter had the same fair, neat, straight hair! But this actually quite eccentric journalist, Daniel Farson, was not interested in hobnobbing with other TV types and, whilst almost certainly appreciating the attention, he would have given Hill a wide berth. Rather, he regularly headed for Soho and boozed it up with the likes of painter Francis Bacon; celebrated Vogue photographer John Deakin; and, much later, artist Damien Hirst. Farson was himself something of an active participant in this new, post-War, free-for-all, changing, commercial world. Or was he just trying to escape it?

He was surprisingly suspicious of the aforementioned nudists. Having interviewed the founders of the Spielplatz nudist camp, Charles and Dorothy Macaskie, and having advised their daughter that nudism was a waste of time, he concluded – with a pensive turn of his head – that most people were tolerant of nudism, but he would be opposed if it became a cult where people condemned those that did not take part. Looking at the smiling people playing tennis, it's hard to imagine anyone getting particularly aggressive. In fact, sitting in his would-be utopian domain, the bearded, hirsute Charles Macaskie is quite possibly the most relaxed person in the entire programme. He says quite calmly that he can't understand why people would expect bodies to look pretty, and if anything looks slightly bored. By way of contrast, Farson appears fully – and awkwardly – clothed at every point, which although perhaps something to be thankful for, becomes increasingly bizarre as the episode goes on.

The programme was not without its consequences. A newspaper the next day announced: 'The first appearance on TV of naked women. Some historian of the future might care to have the date – Wed. Oct 2nd, 10-30 P.M. 1957'. *Nudist Paradise*, the first commercial UK nudist film, was made and released in 1958 (so just after the *Out of Step* episode) and others duly followed: *Nudist Memories* (1959), *The Nudist Story* (1960), *Naked as Nature Intended* (1961) and *World Without Shame* (1962), amongst others, leading to further racy 'documentaries' as the years went by. In each case the narration voiced concern or even condemned those on screen while the camera got as close to the action as possible, which wasn't always very close. Still, it was the one relatively sure way of making money and those in charge both exploited and in some respects brought forward what was considered permissible on screen, and in daily life.

Farson was also very much ahead of the curve when he interviewed founder of modern witchcraft Gerald Gardner. The old ways, and the

Where to look?: reportage documentarian Dan Farson tries to cover everything when visiting the Spielplatz naturist resort for new television series *Out of Step* (1957).

new ways, were in a slippery state when *Out of Step* devoted its attentions to them, on 4th December 1957. Witchcraft, or Wicca, was, according to its followers, as old as time itself, and yet it had re-appeared as a phenomenon following the 1951 repeal of the Witchcraft Act – a law that made it punishable by death to practice the forbidden art. Slowly it attracted followers and by the end of the 1960s it was rarely out of the news, becoming something of a hip counter-cultural pastime. It was daring, virtually taboo, to publically discuss such things when the UK was still, at least on the surface, very much a Christian country.

Gardner's text *Witchcraft Today*, published in 1954, outlined the basic tenets of Wiccan ritual as if in the manner of an anthropological, historical account, but it is now largely accepted that the descriptions of blindfolding, tying of cord and light flagellation reflected his personal enthusiasms rather than any long-standing historical tradition; all things that would have further wound-up and confused the moral majority, should they have heard about it.

But Gardner was not quite the sensational figure the public might have expected, or indeed hoped for. Far from proselytizing aggressively, like a counter-cultural Wentworth Day, the man of the 'bulging stomachs and sagging bottoms', Gardner spoke softly, and with attention. Traced to his home in Castleton, on the Isle of Man, the grandfather of modern witchcraft chuckled gently. 'They've got their own god, a very nice god; they're the old gods of Britain'. Gardner reported that he was properly initiated and that at that time there were as many as four hundred witches in the UK. Nudity is a part of witchcraft, and it is because of this that it had remained partly secretive, he continued. His witchcraft sounded quaint; we 'mainly have a nice dinner and a dance.' And yet somehow, in part because of his stiff white hair and beard, and his electric light bulb eyes, he did still manage to appear intense and unusual.

Others in the *Witchcraft* episode were more straightforward. Young people join witchcraft circles because they think it 'daring and adventurous' insisted the petite, sharply dressed 92-year-old anthropologist Margaret Murray. These people 'prefer to be called the member of a witches' coven than a nudist colony' because it sounds 'more romantic'. Far from impressed, she even considered one specific witch, an old woman, 'one of the most disagreeable people I had ever seen'. Louis Wilkinson, a friend of Aleister Crowley's, was more sanguine: the 'Great Beast' used mystery and shock to his advantage, winding-up anyone who asked about Satanic rites and child sacrifice, an observation that inadvertently highlighted Farson and *Out of Step*'s own prurient quest for transgression – and the public's desire to be appalled.

Nudists, witches and latterly beatniks all seemed to get lumped together and received similar accusations of unlawfulness and licentiousness in the 1950s and 60s. It wasn't so much the nakedness that seemed to upset people, it was the assumption that it meant: SEX OUTSIDE OF MARRIAGE. Or maybe just sex. There was fear, and also jealousy, and it symbolized the first crack in the social contract that bound the country together, highlighting how radical the notion of 'free love' could really be. And yet ironically it was exactly this tension, and the promise of sensation, that drew audiences to commercial television in the first place.

Farson's concluding thoughts in the Witchcraft episode demonstrated that he and *Out of Step* could be thoughtful and reflective, however. An unspecified African tribe dancing intensely to drums, and then a sequence of a Nazi rally with a ranting Hitler, 'perhaps the greatest witch of all', demonstrated examples of mass hypnosis and hysteria. The inferences were sinister and overlooked the participatory nature of ritual and self-inducement into alternative states, but for mainstream television in the late 1950s it would have been extremely unusual. (Imagine if he had considered the suggestive influence of television itself.) The show finally closed with images of gyrating rock 'n' roll drumming and dancing; hysteria (or just sex?) very much in action. Farson: 'these cats certainly seem to be bewitched', and the charismatic host reverted to his usual practice of lightening the tone and reassuring the viewer.

Daniel Farson had been curious about covert, outsider groups perhaps because of his personal homosexuality, a practice which prior to 1967 had yet to be decriminalised. The viewers of course had no idea but when the bombastic Wentworth Day (nudists: 'bulging stomachs and sagging bosoms') was interviewed for an un-transmitted episode of Farson's *People in Trouble* (1958), saying all homosexuals should be hung, something changed. As noted by Robin Carmody on the transdifussion.com website, Wentworth Day was brought in to speak about a range of subjects for Farsons' programmes, always representing the extreme position. In the case of *People in Trouble: Mixed Marriages* (21/05/1958) he referred to 'coffee-coloured little imps' and claimed that black people must be 'inferior' because 'a couple of generations ago they were eating each other'. The Tory was a hunting and agrarian farming enthusiast, and he wrote supernatural stories about his beloved Norfolk. It was perhaps on the latter point that he and Farson, the great-nephew of Bram Stoker, author of *Dracula*, initially found common ground. No matter: after the homosexuality remark, they never worked together again, and to be fair to Farson, he stated, and then restated, his divergence from Wentworth Day's opinions at the end of the *Mixed Marriages* episode.

Farson was a gifted host and undoubtedly a major part of *Out of Step*'s success. He gave space to different views but also managed to counter those views in a non-aggressive way, as and when he felt it appropriate. But he couldn't stop his drinking. It had led to a black eye in a brawl the weekend before the *Witchcraft* show, preventing any two-person camera shots (and breaking with the programme's established style), whilst later he gently edged away from Soho and took to living in Devon, his original family home, again still drinking. Nonetheless, even to the end (when at one point he appeared on radio apparently drunk) he was still able to turn on that spark that had illuminated *Out of Step* and made its issues and questions feel pertinent and prescient, and entertaining.

Through *Out of Step*, he teased and tantalized but also gently schooled the public in the ways of a changing world. And notably *Out of Step* was part of that changing world. It prefaced a new kind of voyeurism, cameras peering into people's lives and vacillating between either emphasizing difference and/or reaffirming convention, the politics of the process depending on the nuances of the film or TV programme in question. Television and film journalism became itself 'permissive.' This was the stuff that enabled the 1960s, as we understand it, to happen: internationalism, communication, enquiry, reportage – like reports from the frontline in Vietnam; fostering a form of criticality in the viewer's mind whilst simultaneously often reaffirming their values. *Out of Step* is not particularly well known now but it was and is historically significant in the UK, approaching new, often-controversial subjects through the platform of commercial television, its very status affecting consensus. More often than not, Farson gently sidelined truly controversial viewpoints by foregrounding his own opinions, ensuring that nothing was too threatening for the viewer. He also approached his interviewees with a sense of humour and somehow – and this is not easily done – with a simultaneous sense of polite respect, meaning that their views, no matter how outlandish, no matter how much they might cut against the grain, (for the most part) they could somehow still have value, and a space – of sorts. Who knows what events he inadvertently brought about in peoples' lives? Only one person complained about the episode on nudism, in Farson's words: 'a mother whose teenage son came into the room unexpectedly and came face-to-face with life in the raw'. *WF*

Meanwhile, other filmmakers were also interested in exploring 'life in the raw'…but they were not investigative journalists…

Primitive London

UK Film | 1965 | colour | 85mins
Director Arnold Louis Miller
Script Arnold Louis Miller
Production Company Searchlight Films

Under the Table You Must Go

UK Film | 1970 | colour | 52mins
Director Arnold Louis Miller
Script Arnold Louis Miller
Production Company Global Films

Strongly influenced, like its more restrained predecessor *London in the Raw* (1964), by the worldwide success of the Italian shock-documentary *Mondo Cane* (1962), which gathered together strange or nausea-inducing actuality footage from around the globe, all presented with dry voice-over commentary, *Primitive London* is arguably one of the most important and definitely one of the most entertaining examples of the mondo genre. Made for British exploitation production maestros Tony Tenser and Michael Klinger, its value as a social document is more clearly apparent with the comfortable benefit of hindsight: the mirror-image of the capital it offers can now be more clearly enjoyed as a fractured, often lopsided, but nonetheless distinctly revealing reflection of a Britain still struggling to emerge from the austerity of the post-war decade.

A bizarre and tenuously linked hotchpotch of documentary sequences and staged footage, *Primitive London* (1965) cheerfully mixes the salacious and the shocking with the shamelessly banal, the weird and the downright ridiculous. In keeping with the ideological paradox at the heart of all good mondo, the film simultaneously permits and forbids: sternly delivered commentary (by Canadian disc jockey David Gell) infers strait-laced disapproval of all the thoroughly depraved activities taking place in modern London. Meanwhile, the visuals – contradictorily – offer an intermittently lurid sideshow spectacle in which the voyeuristic viewer is invited to revel. So, don't be shy – step right up, folks!

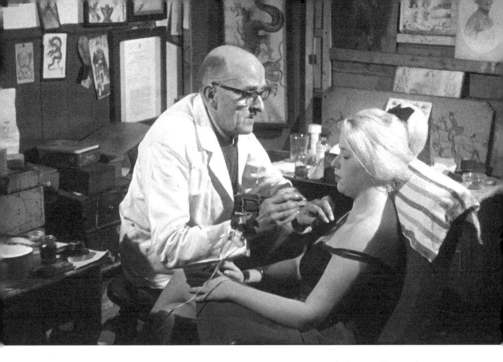

Beautiful people: note the thoroughly hygienic tea towel carefully spread over the tattoo parlour chair-back in *Primitive London* (1965).

Amongst the diverse delights on offer are mods, rockers and beatniks chatting with an unseen but rather uptight sounding interviewer (he almost sounds jealous); bloody footage of a birth; a grisly re-enactment of a Jack The Ripper murder (inserted at the last minute to ensure that the film was given an 'X' certificate, and which has the distinctly grimy flavour of the horror films that were to be a mainstay of Tony Tenser's Tigon productions); flabby men in a sauna bath (for our money, the most horrific footage the film contains); women modelling topless swimsuits; the difficulties inherent in accurate hat sizing; the daily life of a Soho stripper; and a chiropodist enjoying his work. The viewer also bears witness to a disgraceful, debauched party game involving dancing around an umbrella (if a walking stick is not available), which soon escalates into a full-scale family-wrecking 'key party' – the inspiration behind the notorious pseudo-documentary that was later to make Stanley Long his first million, also narrated by David Gell, *The Wife Swappers* (1970).

Time cannot diminish the sheer weirdness and variety of the material juxtaposed here; and footage of battery chickens being killed – made creepier

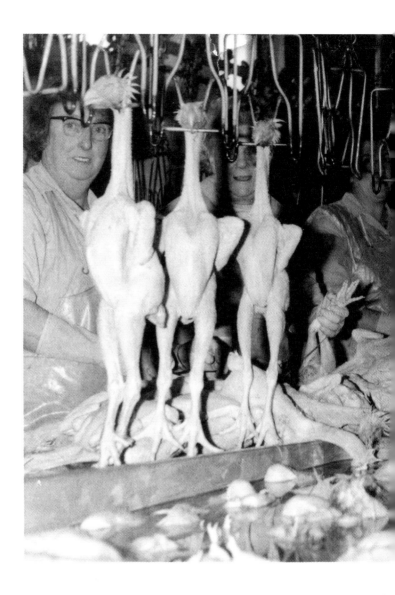

PRIMITIVE

Directed by **ARNOLD LOUIS MILLER** Photography by **STANLEY A.L**

Playing chicken: delighted factory workers pause from their fowl antics to grin for Messrs Long and Miller, on this delightful 1965 lobby card.

ONDON X EASTMAN COLOUR

Executive Producers **MICHAEL KLINGER** and **TONY TENSER**

thanks to an eerie, monotonous, other-worldly electronic accompaniment by soundtrack notable Basil Kirchin – retains its power to shock. Vegetarians (and guilty meat eaters, for that matter) still might wish to look away. Stanley Long, who handled the camerawork for most of the main sequences in the film, never forgot it. 'I never ate chicken for a year after shooting…I came home and burnt all the clothes I had worn that day.'

Amidst the sensational imagery, *Primitive London* is imbued with a dry, self-awareness of the conventions of mondo. It is constructed to play upon cinema audiences' growing familiarity with the already firmly established and rapidly dating stylistic grammar of a sub-genre in which viewers are teased by the promise of the sensational and the taboo, but – with everybody fully aware of the power still held by the by-then somewhat socially out-of-step censor – in which spectators also expect to be conned, and to receive less titillation than they had hoped for. At one point, the commentary unexpectedly takes a more obviously self-conscious turn, as the voices of the 'director' and the 'editor' suddenly obliterate the sanctimonious voiceover and, in heavy American accents, discuss what the audience want to see (girls in topless swimsuits) and what they actually get to see (a splendidly arbitrary cow and swan). This strange sequence speaks volumes about exploitation filmmaking and film censorship in Britain in the pre-permissive 1960s. When *Primitive London* was released in 1965, the sequence featuring topless swimsuits was entirely removed by censorial snipping, and has only in recent years been restored to its rightful place.

First screened at London's famous Windmill Theatre, 'exotic dancers' were hired to celebrate the premiere. Capitalising on the unforgettable 'Taming the Wild One' dance performed by 'Trainer' Willy Martin and 'Leopard' Anne Delyse in the film, and which inspired a strikingly effective image used on posters and publicity for the production, Soho dancer Vicki Grey, resplendent in a borrowed fur-coat and leopard skin bikini, 'toured' the West End before relaxing in the foyer with a cheetah on a leash, loaned by Colchester Zoo (a leopard wasn't available). Apparently this was an effective promotional gimmick – 'the box office has never been so busy', enthused *Daily Cinema* – but (sadly?) it is perhaps one that might not be so easy to replicate today.

Supermarket sweep: an average housewife strikes a pose in the well-stocked tissue department of a self-service store, in this *Primitive London* promo photo. ›

Snootily damned and dismissed at the time by *The Monthly Film Bulletin* as 'hideous', and a 'modishly cynical and negative expose of the obvious' (incidentally, one wonders how it was that 'Taming the Wild One' seemed 'obvious' to the reviewer – unless, of course, he was a regular at the Soho night spots included in the film) in retrospect the film is more interesting precisely because of its unusual and vaguely seedy counterpoint to the still-prevailing myth of 'swinging sixties' London. Indeed, as an artefact of its era, Primitive London provides a fascinating antithesis to the frothy fixed-grin joviality of its more respectable documentary contemporary the *Pathé Colour Pictorial*. Besides, what's wrong with exposing the obvious? It might seem constant, omnipresent, but we all know it isn't. The everyday relentlessly trickles away, largely unnoticed, like sand through the hourglass; and before long the familiar, along with the world in which it was so, has vanished into oblivion. So, however modishly cynical, hideous, negative and obvious it all seemed at the time, we're lucky that Arnold Miller and Stanley Long were on hand to put together *Primitive London*. It was never built to last, but unexpectedly still standing, it remains a strange and potent reminder of a time and place in the British consciousness when, as ties were loosened and hair began to creep towards the collar, lascivious cinematic thrills were desperately wanted, but could not be directly supplied.

1969 saw Miller and Long return once more to mondo. But by then, the permissive society had arrived. The grey comedown of the 1970s loomed in fact, but drink, drugs and free-love were – if the tabloid propaganda was to be believed – de rigeur. Taboos were in tatters; and the hip new generation of cinemagoers demanded more from their movies than chicken-horror. Both Miller and Long, dissolving their partnership after *Under the Table*, embraced this slightly more liberal era in filmmaking: Long shot the aforementioned lucrative erotic pseudo-documentary *The Wife Swappers*, while Miller ventured uneasily into sex comedy with *A Touch of the Other* (1970). You might have thought, then, you could expect similarly seedy delights *Under the Table*. But you'd be wrong.

It begins like the early 60s mondo film time forgot, opening with a conversation between two parked cars, followed by a creaky can-can dance that might almost be an outtake from *London in the Raw*. It transpires that we are on a splendidly random excursion to the outermost bargain-basement fringes of late 1960s pop culture, stopping off for swift halves along the way with sportsmen past their prime, half-forgotten celebrities and light entertainers who may never have made the grade, at a plethora of London pubs, many since demolished or altered out of all recognition. It's quite a ride.

Watching this, you may perhaps be struck most not by how much has changed in the capital since *Primitive London* but how much has stayed resolutely the same, and also how much was quietly going on in '69 that the media never reminds us of today. Take music, for example. You will find no groovy psychedelic freakouts here. Instead, there is middle-of-the-road Country and Western (of which DJ narrator Murray Kash, seen here, was a champion), dusty early-Bonzos-style novelty jazz from The Seven Syncopators of Justies (an offshoot of the better known Temperance Seven) and a bri-nylon clad cabaret duo politely frugging their way through The 1910 Fruitgum Co.'s bubblegum hit *Simon Says*.

As for the coming sexual revolution hinted at in Miller and Long's earlier works, well, somehow it never happened. Everyone here in 1969 is still repressed, and doing – or not doing – what they always did, or didn't. Bunny Girls at the Playboy Club are still having their nails checked by the 'Bunny Mother' and being scolded for forgetting which glasses to serve the drinks in. Bored belly dancers in a smoky tavern are still grinding their hips to squeaky Hammond organ music while sweaty, embarrassed men are still clutching their jugs of bitter and not knowing where to look. 'Choose which one you want,' leers the club compere suggestively as the girls gyrate; 'it could happen to you.' Not likely. Suits are grey and ties are narrow. Sex remains distant; mentioned in awkward innuendo, or a saucy song.

Flat hi-hat and rinky-tink piano accompany a Max Miller-style comedian singing of some unlikely woman named Josie Josephine in a music-hall style pub where aged patrons proudly wear their medals. The War still looms, barrage-balloon-like, over everything. Forces favourite Tommy Trinder is here to remind us of the good old days. Venerable old stager Fred Emney, as seen eternities ago in *Fun at St Fanny's*, still peering suspiciously over his monocle, is dismayed at being unable to order roast beef and Yorkshire Pud in a swanky Italian eatery (cutting edge then; now demolished). A pre-*Doctor Who* Jon Pertwee can't wait to don a spiked WWI era German helmet for a bizarre bierkeller sing-along: patriotic British standards are belted out with the obligatory affected

Ich bin ein Berliner: Jon Pertwee gives a sensitive, low-key performance, carefully crafted for overseas audiences, in *Under the Table You Must Go* (1970).

German accents. Oliver Philpot – one of the very brave chaps whose escape from Stalag Luft III formed the basis of *The Wooden Horse* (1950) – chats with 'Big Hearted' Arthur Askey's wartime comedy-hoppo, Richard 'Stinker' Murdoch.

All is as it was, and there's probably honey still for tea, until the time warp is rudely ruptured by hollow-cheeked Scots disc jockey Stuart Henry. An upcoming 'personality jock', he is relentless in his icky attempts to chat up the girls in The Bird's Nest, at the Green Man, Muswell Hill. This was one of a chain of trendy Watneys discotheques boasting 'telephone tables' that could be used to order food and drink; and – if the libidinous Mr Henry is to be believed – to arrange a date, too.

Disorientating modernity is glimpsed again later in the film's final minutes as the then-hep hit-making record producer Jonathan King, reporting from the Plough and Harrow, Leytonstone, mischievously quizzes a sleepy-eyed young lady about the future of pubs. 'When the older generation dies out, it won't be public houses any more,' she proclaims, before concluding naughtily, 'it'll be pot houses.' Forgotten Brit beat group John Hale's Time cover a Geno Washington number; confident mini-skirted girls dance provocatively and flash their knickers at the camera. Perhaps time has not stood still after all. Visually intoxicated by this seeming youthful abandon, you might almost be ready to believe that Britain did loosen up a little until you find yourself sobered up somewhat by the glimpse of a stiff-backed old chap standing rigidly amidst the teens, looking on. What's he doing there? Is he the father of the girl who mentioned pot houses, waiting to give her a good talking to? Is he with the film crew? Did he sneak in the back door? Then, in a flash, it's those daft talking cars once more, some more cobwebby *London in the Raw* style cabaret club dancing, and it's all over.

The past, as *Under the Table You Must Go* fragmentarily demonstrates, is a weird, confusing, mixed-up place, riddled with contradictions and inconsistencies. A fascinatingly awkward filmic artefact, it reminds us how tricky it is to get your head around history. Old and new, important and trivial, and truth and fiction, it screams incoherently, don't neatly stand apart, but are inextricably linked. Watch it as a triple-bill with *London in the Raw* and *Primitive London* for full effect, if you dare: and be reminded that the more things change, the more they stay the same. *VP*

There were others who sought to shock not for cash but in the name of serious scientific research. Reportage has often been used to push back barriers and drive change, and in the case of our next startling entry, it was in ways largely invisible to the general public...

The Savage Voyage

UK | 1971 | colour | 26mins
Director Eric Marquis
Script Eric Marquis with Peter Goodman
Production Company Unit 7 Film Productions
Cast Jerome Willis (narrator)

Huge budgets and costly marketing campaigns ensure that even the dullest mainstream movies invariably penetrate the consciousness at some level. Underground films, short films and other independent ventures, by way of contrast, have considerably less resource to pull on and have historically instead relied on notoriety, press stories and other breadcrumb trails for the dedicated cineaste to follow-up on. But what about the films that, no matter how unusual or extreme they might be, never reach a cult audience, let alone go out on general release – the movies that leave virtually no trail or imprint at all?

Cinema is extremely diverse and there are countless examples of 'industrial films' or 'corporate sponsored films' that have no direct connection to profit, commerce or the general public. And this in no way reflects their merits, cultural context, or even their strange or abrasive qualities – or otherwise. The overwhelming, transgressive, richly imaginative films of Eric Marquis are a powerful case in point. Titles *Survival* (1961), *Time Out of Mind* (1968) and *Time of Terror* (1975) were made for educational purposes only and sent to very specific organisations to be screened behind closed doors. Several have won prestigious awards but they have been rarely screened to the general public.

What is very notable about Marquis's efforts is how sensual, violent and informed by exploitation and commercial cinema they are, despite their institutional, documentary contexts. Alarming film *Time of Terror* was

A bloodied-up loo-roll in a shoe: eye-popping special effects as evidenced in the police training film *Time of Terror* (1975).

made to warn the police about the realities of terrorism, and to highlight the need for vigilance. Featuring a mixture of direct reportage and agitated, visceral reconstruction, the film appears aimed at the general public, but until BFI DVD release *Shadows of Progress*, viewing was confined mainly to the police or police-affiliated individuals.

'We don't want to find your dead body' instructs the narrator as a rigid figure is hurriedly carried off into an ambulance after a bomb goes off. Probing cameras then rush around at ground-level, like hungry foxes at night, desperately looking for further explosives. The film brings on panic and agitation, mirroring the horror as a way of neutralizing sensations in advance of a similar real-life event. The goal appears to have been to prepare the individual policeman, despite the 'your dead body', creating both identification and distance. (It raised challenging questions about genre films and their potential to desensitize. The more you see, the less you react?)

The isolated image of a charred child's foot, blown-off, is hard to forget, and it tells the film's story in microcosm. (It was in reality a bloodied-up, made-up toilet roll, shoved into a sock and shoe.) Many viewers will reel from the onslaught of shocking details and rushing camera work but it's hard not to also appreciate the creative imagination and compacted story telling that went into this and other heavy signifiers. Hitchcock might approve. It's possible to admire its aesthetic in the same way you might an effect-laden Lucio Fulci film, with its spectacular, theatrical viscera.

Adept at effects and visceral pressure points, Marquis also thought about shape and conceptual narrative; scenes and their development were imaginatively addressed. This could be powerful in a form associated with 'truth' and 'reality'. *Time of Terror* begins in an English Civil War museum, in black and white, thus connecting back to another period of social, sectarian division, before then ricocheting, with the bomb blast, into the bright, colourful present. It was a curious, highly alarming play on the dream/real-life, colour/monochrome dichotomy brought out in *The Wizard of Oz* (1939) and portends danger and death.

Commissioned films should deliver specific messages, and Marquis pushed hard. He regularly got work. *Seven Green Bottles* (1975) saw a gang of delinquents, made up of non-actors and a young Danny John-Jules, latterly of *Red Dwarf* (1988–), progress through a series of escalating street crimes with plucky, bored determination – stealing from parking meters, breaking and entering. Scenes include point-of-view shots as the lads are confronted by difficult stepfathers and insistent police officers, and they fall, one-by-one, like seven green bottles. Intricate, sweeping crane shots lend the film a thrilling urgency.

It is not clear if it was intended to train police officers or if it was to warn young people off a potential life in crime, but risk is clearly signalled. Screening it at the BFI we met one of the boys, now grown-up. The film, it turns out, had been something of a criminal 'how-to' guide and several of the gang (John-Jules aside) had subsequently acted-out for real many of the deeds that had been legitimized in a fictional context for Marquis's camera. The man we met had been to prison whilst the fierce gang leader had become a notorious football hooligan and was still serving time. Weird, sad, unexpected news. And whilst Marquis can't be held responsible, and without meaning to aestheticize and make poetic the situation, it indicated that some kind of power existed in his work, and in Marquis's relationship to his actors – or non-actors. And this sometimes complicated the works' outlined function. Rebecca Vick, author of the only Marquis career overview ('Savage Voyages: Eric Marquis' in *Shadows of Progress: Documentary Film in Post-War Britain*) notes how the director wouldn't shout action during shooting but instead used what are known as 'board on end performances', pretending each sequence was a practice.

Effective, affecting performances were key as Marquis drew the viewer into an unusual cinematic world. *Time Out of Mind* tried to foreground the symptoms of depression, a state of mind then rarely acknowledged or recognized by sufferers, or sometimes even health professionals. Doctors – who it was intended for – should thereafter ideally be more sympathetic and perceptive to patients and also, controversially, the anti-anxiety drugs developed by the film's sponsor, pharmaceutical company, Roche Products/ Hoffman-La Roche. Opening with an elderly woman slashing her wrists inside a grubby, claustrophobic public toilet, the film set the stakes high, as was Marquis's signature, and a middle-aged man experiencing a panic attack in a supermarket later in the film showed how good he was at combining intense performances with careful, confident camera work.

But it would be wrong to portray his films as incessant blocks of high-octane drama. Marquis found space for emotional reflection and even sadness too, with the said panicky middle-aged man later nodding calmly and quietly as he begins to understand what has happened to him. And in an earlier scene-setting tableau, a working-father stares at his modest breakfast – and prospects – with monosyllabic glumness, before then getting into a taxi and, in a state of confusion, forgetting where he's going, or even what he's doing. Whole life stories are compacted into glances and the shrugging of shoulders. Marquis could also include moments of absurd humour; a grinning skeleton peers bizarrely at the camera as a woman approaches a potential bomb in *Time of Terror*. And a caller to the local newspaper can be heard saying 'I want to advertise a crocodile for sale' in *Tomorrow's Merseyside* (1974). (There is at least one moment of sort-of playful humour in the about to be discussed *The Savage Voyage*. However, due to the extremity of the piece, it is very hard to register on early viewings. Sexual references abound in the film and at one point a man leans over a woman's shoulder as she is looking at some test samples. Is he flirting?)

Time out of Mind

This is a film that adds depth and insight to the general practitioner's view of psychiatric disorders. Relevant and significant in content, it is both original and compelling in style and represents an entirely new approach to the filmed presentation of case studies in a field which contains many intricate problems for the general practitioner.

A film to promote the pharmaceutical industry: *Time Out of Mind* (1968).

Here lies the uneasy side to industrial filmmaking and documentary more broadly. Whilst no viewer is completely bowled-over, or blinded to their larger agendas, films can be very effective at leading opinion, and in all sorts of directions. Marquis was a master of the form, forcefully and convincingly drilling into each concept and commission whilst making works that, once removed from their original context, still functioned as strident pieces of cinema in their own right.

In this respect, *The Savage Voyage* is a mind-blowing film to experience some forty-plus years after its making, and outside its profoundly pharmaceutical context. For a start, it never would have made it past the censor if put out on general release. The imagery is extremely graphic, but more than that it is disturbing, and dwells extensively on mental suffering. A female character, played by several different actors, appears as a baby, a young girl, an adult, and as an elderly woman, and always profoundly unsettled and anxious. By way of its considerable experimental montage, the film seems to embody her various mental states, simultaneously illustrating, enacting and even causing her distress.

Animated solarized images of sperm, volcanic lava and a protracted bloody birth, all accompanied by discordant electronic music by Tristram Cary, turn the processes of humans entering the world into a troubling, anxiety-ridden, psychedelic hell. In a kind of twisted reversal of the birth and evolution imagery as seen in *2001: A Space Odyssey* (1968), the growing baby appears alongside lurid images of fighting bears and fleeing and howling animals. The film returns to the woman at various points, zooming into and almost entering her eye at each pass. At one point, she stands naked in the dark, petrified by the camera's gaze.

'I came out of a kind of violence. A million years of genetic memory may have crippled me from conception – programmed my growing cells struggling to expand my mother's virgin uterus. After nine centuries of growth and adaptation, "they" made the first vicious assault upon my total security; made me make a bloody, savage voyage down the birth canal; thrust and crushed me out through the strangulating way whence half myself had come with such lubricious ease'.

It's incredibly dark, and yet like *Time Out of Mind* it was intended to illustrate and illuminate social issues and people's feelings of anxiety and distress, whilst simultaneously promoting a new psychoactive drug as a pathway to internal emotional equilibrium. The film goes to profoundly uncomfortable places as a way of stressing the importance of the pharmaceutical development. This was the context in which vivisection imagery, with exposed cat's brains being stimulated with an anaesthetized probe, primates being experimented on, and multiple lab-rats being sliced open, plus scenes of palpable human distress and suffering, and disturbing montage sequences, could be formally legitimized as a cinematic experience.

Context is of course everything and the hard montage presented as the woman has her mind scanned recalls the experimental cinema of the period, notably that of the American avant-gardist Hollis Frampton, a major early influence on Peter Greenaway, plus the psychological de/re-programming scenes contained in *A Clockwork Orange* (1971), when Alex is exposed to relentless outré material, with his eyes pinned-open. New thinking about imagery, programming and consciousness, partly influenced by Rorschach testing and psychedelia, were in the ascendant, and indeed at one point the woman's face morphs into a Rorschach test in *The Savage Voyage*. Many wanted to the see brain as a computer that could be stimulated, programmed and wiped, or at least selectively drained of emotional charge. This was the thinking behind Scientology (see this book's entry on *Secrets of Sex*).

For Marquis, the use of high-speed associative montage, consisting of heavily loaded imagery, became a way of illustrating the woman's internal thought processes, and her states of distress. 'Such fears cannot be measured. They can, however, be projected into ambiguous, meaningless targets. Patients can be asked to interpret deliberately vague pictures. The stories they weave around those situations are a useful indicator of their inner turmoil,' says the narrator. The first images consist of couples in different domestic situations, all painted. A little later we see an actual wrist being sliced, a man and a woman thrusting into each other and a probe penetrating an eye-ball, all in quick succession.

Variants of this experimental, underground quick-fire film technique, usually used to highlight and explore language, would later appear in other types of films and TV. It was dropped wholesale into *After Image*, an episode of paranormal investigative conspiracy drama series *The Omega Factor* (13/06 – 15/08/1979), a kind of 1970s BBC version of *The X-Files* (1993-2002 & 2016-). And in 1974, Mary Whitehouse complained to the BBC that a montage sequence in an edition of the long running documentary series *Panorama* (1953-) had been cut too fast and was overwhelming. Subliminal images, with single frames inserted into films and TV, would also be experimentally toyed with in later decades, in programmes including *The Young Ones* (1982-84) and *Brass Eye* (1997-2001). Most of these techniques were in fact developed as far back as the 1950s and 60s by Isidore Isou, Kurt Kren, Tony Conrad, Stan Brakhage, Jeff Keen, Antony Balch, Stuart Pound, Carolee Schneemann and Paul Sharits – who would make the bracing *Epileptic Seizure Comparison* (1976). 'Beauty shall be convulsive' said surrealist, André Breton.

Curiously, Marquis combined this kind of editing with the vivisection sequences, and by way of cutting back to the woman of the film, implied that the primates being manipulated and tested-on somehow illustrated or reflected the horrors in her mind, as well as demonstrating how the antipsychotic benzodiazepine drugs had been developed, and implicitly

'IDEALLY WE SHALL CONVEY A
SUBJECTIVE IMPRESSION OF THE
TUMULT THAT GOES ON IN THE
ANXIOUS MIND'

There are moments in 'The
Savage Voyage' which must truly
be seen to be judged. A technique
was devised to present a series
of images, each of which had some
threatening or possibly phobic
quality, in a way which leaves no
clear 'every-picture-tells-a-
story' impression on the mind of
the observer but, instead,
re-creates in the audience the
experience suffered by the
anxious patient.

These sequences involved
collecting almost one thousand
separate pictures and filming
them by experimental methods and
techniques which are very seldom
used in documentary films and
which have certainly never before
been attempted in a medical film

In a style unprecendented in the
medical field 'The Savage Voyage'
creates an impression of how, in
moments of acute anxiety, a blur
of fear-provoking images and
impressions attack the eye and
the mind of the patient

'One thousand separate pictures': but no amount of words could truly evoke the
unforgettable experience that is *The Savage Voyage* (1971).

how important it was to test on animals, according to the arguments of the piece. Men watching alarming footage of a construction worker falling out of a building were also included as a way of showing how different personality types might respond to anxiety-inducing material, and how they might be medicated. The film may include dynamic editing and a highly imaginative structure but for the purposes of a perceived greater good, everyone is essentially a lab-rat here. (Whilst the people were presumably actors, the animals were not so lucky.)

It all sounds wilfully transgressive and shocking but it was almost certainly extremely effective at getting doctors to recognize and take seriously debilitating mental anxiety and ill-health, whilst also pushing the politically controversial response of medication, presented here as the cure-all and only real solution. Marquis's work was unflinching when it came to evoking sensation and drawing the viewer into empathetic experiences. It was commissioned by the Swiss pharmaceutical giant Hoffman-La Roche who, having worked with Marquis before, knew he could deliver on the imperatives of their company, and it later won numerous awards. He was credited as producer, director and writer. (Peter Goodman receives a narration co-writing credit.)

At one level, we know what *The Savage Voyage* is, but at another it's quite bewildering. Extreme alienation has rarely been so clearly and disturbingly presented on screen. (Another example would arguably be Bergman's *Persona* (1966), which uses a lot of the same visual language.) Industrial films and public information films for the most part serve the status quo and reaffirm desired truths about society, but as Marquis's work attests they could also be ways of approaching difficult subject matter, unsettling and opening up the dark viscera of life, their brutal images sometimes assigning significantly more space and volume than their overall message, actually introducing violence, darkness and aggression by way of image combinations that, in terms of their explosive meaning and ultimate and continuing effect, cannot always be easily understood, or explained away. Another case in point would be John Krish's notoriously audacious public safety film *The Finishing Line* (1977), in which a children's sports day on a railway line leads to a litany of horrific accidents. Many of a certain age will remember it clearly. It was shown on TV several times and then, amidst rising concerns about copycat incidents and a debate on *Nationwide* (1969-84), was pulled and replaced by the much softer *Robbie* (1979).

Marquis's films were never banned or intentionally withheld from public view, but because of the context in which they were made, held back they in effect were. They're not documentaries, but would be classified in that way in a DVD collection, and they're not part of any canons – though maybe that'll change. (They may now really be cult films in waiting.) They were made to have specific, direct influence, not document the past or present. And now that future they proffered, with all its truth or lack of, has also passed. These films are out of time. What they perhaps do is document an attitude, and an institutional approach to life, work and power – and a world view, a kind of fictional place in our collective mind's eye, but one that, by way of each film's special and exclusive purpose, the absolute vast majority of people have never seen or experienced. Ultimately, we could say they were custom-made adverts. But whichever way we slice it, these visionary, purpose-laden, out-of-time films, made by Marquis and others like him, are very strange cinematic artefacts indeed. For several decades now, his films have screamed loudly in a soundproofed room. *WF*

The concept of controlled, contraband images and information, manipulated by larger powers for uncertain ends, also lay at the heart of this truly transgressive piece...

Skinflicker

UK Film | 1973 | black and white | 41mins
Director Tony Bicât
Script Howard Brenton
Production Company British Film Institute Production Board
Cast Hilary Charlton, Will Knightly, Henry Woolf, William Hoyland

'Should such a film be shown at this time? Should it even be made? More particularly, should it be made by a production group financed by a Department of Her Majesty's Government?' asked Alexander Walker in the *Evening Standard* about an unusual, extreme film that utilized documentary

Grey roads to a grim place: terrorists en route to kidnap a cabinet minister in *Skinflicker* (1973).

codes. Although produced by the BFI Production Board, *Skinflicker* came to close to existing, shockingly, in the same filmic universe as *Cannibal Holocaust* (1980).

The piece was full-on; it presented the results of a fictional terrorist action. Three dissidents – a teacher, a nurse and a thug – plan to commit a revolutionary act on film, the film we are watching. They kidnap a government minister, leaving his wife and son unconscious or possibly dead, and then threaten their prisoner with extreme violence while reading out prepared indictments of the society that he represents.

Henry, the 'grunt' of the gang, appears at first loud and clownish but after he clubs the said child and mother, knocking them to the ground, and later takes a blowtorch to the politician's face, that foolishness dissipates and everything turns upside down. The sexploitation director hired to operate the 16mm camera (in the film's narrative) can't believe that the politician is 'the famous one off TV', and when he does, he scarpers. The dissidents then take over the operation of the camera and everything gets worse. And we keep watching. *Skinflicker* wasn't pitched as a horror movie, but it was 'true horror'.

The idea of shock and explosive impact was something that many of the advertising campaigns for horror films of the same period actively cultivated. Films were sold as torturous, and exceeded the usual boundary points between horror, fact and fiction. The much-copied cinema poster for *The Last House on the Left* (1972) stated 'to avoid fainting, keep telling yourself – it's only a movie, only a movie…'; whilst riffing on ideas about truth, *The Texas Chainsaw Massacre* (1974) began: 'The film which you are about to see is an account of the tragedy which befell a group of five youths'; and the aforementioned *Cannibal Holocaust* was shot, for the most part, like an investigative, if corrupt, ethnographic documentary, incorporating horrific fake human, and real animal, death footage. It was a time of censorship, impeachment and post-Hippy nihilism. These films were like magic, trying to change and comment on the fabric of reality and fuse, or at least complicate, the viewers' relationship to that which was happening on screen.

Skinflicker's sexploitation cameraman character suggested that the scriptwriter Howard Brenton was at least partially familiar with this developing horror scene, but as a member of the experimental Portable Theatre group, his creative background was very different. Fellow playwright and PT member David Hare: 'we thought that Britain's assumption of a non-existent world role was ludicrous, and we also thought that its economic vitality was so sapped that it wouldn't last long. So we wanted to bundle into a van and go round the country performing short, nasty little plays which would alert an otherwise dormant population to this news.'

In the late 1960s, theatre moved away from social realism and the angry young men of the Royal Court Theatre and instead drew on political provocation and the live, unbound tension of the happening. In this tradition, Brenton wanted to proactively disrupt the conventional fabric of communication and he was inspired by the French avant-garde group 'the situationist international'. About Guy Debord's *The Society of The Spectacle*, he later said to *The Guardian*: 'it argued that society was like a printed circuit board that operates along certain channels, without which the economy won't work. Public life is a massive spectacle that everyone pretends to be part of, but no one is. I thought that this was a brilliant analysis, and very interesting for a playwright – after all, what do entertainments do but disrupt the spectacle?'

To this end he pitched *Skinflicker* to the BBC as a *Play For Today*, an incredibly bold move that, had it gone ahead, would have led to the broadcasting of a fake snuff movie to the nation, increasing the Portable Theatre's outreach many multiple times over. The gesture paradoxically both drew on and overlooked the controversy that had surrounded *The War Game* (1965), the fake documentary that presented the story of a potential nuclear strike as if it were a news report (see this book's entry on the film). The BBC pulled the broadcast of this seminal film and thereafter stayed away from the docudrama form when it moved into even remotely edgy terrain.

Brenton wanted to 'blow a hole in the evening television' and *Skinflicker* was clearly controversial. As well as taking the form of a situationist intervention, it drew on terrorist associated literature, paraphrasing Herbert Marcuse's *One Dimensional Man*, a book that critiqued the repressive forces behind both capitalism and Soviet Union communism, inspiring several European guerrilla terrorist groups, including the Angry Brigade who had planted a series of small bombs in London between 1970 and 1972. It was this latter connection, regarding the film, that riled elements of the press though the linking of sex and violence, by way of the porn director cameraman character, was also considered troubling.

It was racy stuff but apparently not enough to prevent the British Film Institute from stepping into the breach. The BFI Production Board took on a broad slate of projects in the 1970s, gradually becoming more radical as the decade wore on. In some senses, however, this alteration in platform and producer changed the whole context of *Skinflicker*. Unlike the aforementioned 70s horror films, titles that would in the 1980s became video nasties and were aimed at hardcore genre fans – whilst kicking-up as much of a fuss as possible, *Skinflicker* had been intended for a mass, general audience and the BFI's handling of this strange new film ultimately denied it that type, and level, of exposure. Later the BFI would try to actively address their problems with licensing and distribution, but in 1972 it failed badly at getting work out into the world. Tony Bicât, the film's director, registered his very reasonable dissatisfaction in a 1976 booklet about the

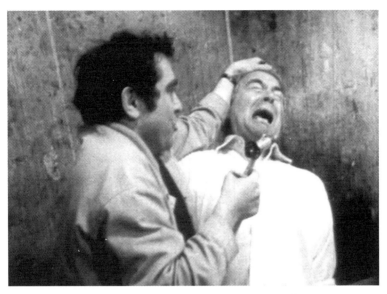

Unwavering resolve: Henry Woolf and Brendan Barry (top), and Hilary Charlton, Will Knightly and Henry Woolf (below), in *Skinflicker* (1973).

Production Board, suggesting: 'there must be someone appointed whose only job is to make sure the films are shown.'

The fake, shock documentary, virtually a genre today, was in 1972, exceedingly unfamiliar and had the aura of the avant-garde. *Skinflicker* went beyond simply being a terrorist film, shot by terrorists, however; by way of its opening titles, it became that movie reclaimed by the government for anti-terrorist training (but again faked) – a found, found object if you like – the equivalent of a municipal government using *The Blair Witch Project* (1999) to advise on camping safety. Seen in the cinema back in the 1970s, this unusual framing technique would have also highlighted the status of the film as an object – its physicality as a reel of celluloid, the true snuff movie artefact, found and projected – whilst also riffing on the recuperation of the transgressive gesture. It was all very troubling. Particularly as an actual government agency – the BFI – had supported the production.

For the characters within the piece, it meant upscaling a series of personal, arguably basic frustrations and upsets to the point of a political action; and, in this sense, they were not unlike its cast and crew, most of whom, not just Brenton, were part of Portable Theatre… The folds of self-reflection and links between the production and its content were really quite overwhelming, if one chose to think about. Was it in fact a documentary – not a fake one? It certainly documented something. Curiously, however, for all of Brenton's political literacy, left-wing specifics and demands, including references to the class system, were notably absent, despite the terrorists identifying themselves as 'soldiers fighting for a better world' (again, like Portable Theatre?).

Instead it became deliberately confusing, and absurd. The nurse in *Skinflicker* complains about the men who hassle her on the geriatric ward, making repeated references to their 'gropey hands and their bad arses' – 'why are their arses so very bad?' The grotesque humour recalled, in admittedly less strong terms, Brenton's 1969 play *Christie in Love* in which serial killer John Christie masturbates in the garden where he buries his victims. (The personal indignities suffered and confused political ideas more broadly connected it to Brenton's 1973 terrorist stage-play *Magnificence* – a significantly more well-known work than *Skinflicker*.)

The teacher, meanwhile, talks about a boy from his class, and at this point actor William Knightly becomes his most alive and convincing:

'I suppose what I want you to give me is peace of mind, freedom of guilt because of little Larry Smith. Larry Smith! A kid at the school where I taught once, a kid with glasses. He couldn't read. They said he was thick and a little bastard. Only eight years old and already was down for a life of crime in the teachers' books; an illiterate little lout. But it was his glasses you see. He had an eye cast over one eye. That was why he couldn't read.'

Was the above Brenton speaking directly – not abstractly – through Knightly's character? Brenton's sympathies ultimately lay with these kind of domestic situations, everyday people struggling against the larger forces of the world. His TV play *The Paradise Run* (transmitted 06/04/1976) presented the story of an English soldier in Ireland with learning difficulties who wants to go to 'paradise'. By the end, however, he has been used by both sides in the conflict and, tragically, ends up a damaged cynical alcoholic in an institution in Denmark. Brenton's desire to poke and upset appeared to be a way of getting beneath the skin.

But, of course, in keeping with Brenton's myriad other refusals, *Skinflicker* turned this kind of potential for empathy on its head. Again, the work won't be rationalized. The second of its three very clearly delineated 'acts' pushed the absurdism and claustrophobic theatricality to the back seat. We see only a point of view camera, Super 8, filming the road ahead, passing into country lanes and looking over at fields. The terrorists are hunting the politician. Director Bicât, in cahoots with Brenton, maps the physical and emotional distance that must be travelled for the horror to take place. Could we go down that road, and if not how do we feel about doing it in the cinema, or watching it at home on a DVD? Hitchcock would frequently attempt to merge the subjectivity of his characters with that of the audience, but not with this kind of provocation in mind.

The film jars productively and, unfortunately, sometimes accidentally, not least because of the Portable Theatre move from theatre to film. The actors were used to playing to the back row, not a camera placed directly in front of them. When they do perform directly to the camera, however, things change. Henry Woolf is particularly notable in this regard. The part-little-man comedian, part-thug looks at the machine almost continually and in a sense at us, decades later, trying to understand what's going on. When he goofs around, blowing raspberries and winding up his fellow insurgents, he's drawing what feels like a very thin skin over an inner

New Cinema Club
122 Wardour Street
London W1

Office hours
Monday–Friday 10–6
or 01-734 5888 any time

January–March 1969

new
cinema
club

Muscular presentation: Derek Hill's New Cinema Club projected the art-horror piece *Skinflicker* (1973) in January 1973.

anarchy and violence. 'Ain't it marvellous making a movie? All that power!' he guffaws. Later, he attacks the politician's wife and child. The film's rough aesthetic gave it, in George Melly's words, 'all the horrible authenticity of the moors' murderers' tape recordings and, in the case of the psychopath [Henry Woolf's character], the same hellish jocularity.' ('The thing that really shocked people was the degrading of the image', remembered Bicât.)

Embodying the complex mixed registers of politics and power, *Skinflicker* and the whole Portable Theatre gang had their roots in the theatrical literary traditions of Oxbridge and inevitably, in almost all cases, went on to traditional stage and TV roles in later years. The fever pitch, apocalyptic air of the early 1970s, which can still be experienced vicariously via other experimental theatre and film groups such as The Welfare State and the London Film-Makers' Co-op, could only last so long, but equally the system and the spectacle, as in the film itself, was adept at reincorporating its subversive personnel as the pressures of age and finance exerted themselves. (Maybe it symbolically began by working with the BFI, but equally Brenton wanted to intervene in the spectacle.) Of the cast, Henry Woolf, the aforementioned thug, memorably ended up as a presenter on children's television. Tragically, Hilary Charlton, the nurse, passed away after an impressive run of Portable Theatre productions. William Knightly occasionally appeared in long running evening TV shows such as *EastEnders* (1985-), *Heartbeat* (1992-2010) and *Midsomer Murders* (1997-), but mainly stuck to the stage. In 1985, he became the father of Keira Knightly. Some would be shocked I'm sure to see what her father once did.

But back in the early 1970s, *Skinflicker* opened at Derek Hill's New Cinema Club, a venture that operated as a private club and profiled films that had been refused a certificate, or had not received the exposure that Hill felt they deserved. Hill was able to avoid censorship laws and in 1967 launched the Forbidden Film Festival, partly as a way of humiliating and protesting against the British Board of Film Censors. It was all a bit proto-video nasty, sort of. It was weird that a film produced by the BFI should go this route. Some in the press tried to whip-up a modicum of outrage that the film had been made at all, in light of recent terrorist attacks. Others pointed out that it had been commissioned before the 1971 bombing of the house of Employment Minister Robert Carr. Cinema-going went into decline in the 1970s, primarily because of TV, and the BFI experimented with what it meant to support alternative film. Decisions could be controversial, inside the organisation as well as out; Tony Bicât recalls overhearing one outraged BFI Production Board member demand that the *Skinflicker* negative be destroyed. Denis Forman, once BFI director, then chair of the board of governors, said 'this is what we're here to do'. It was its counter-cultural, but also Oxford credentials that ultimately 'saved' it, depriving it of both an outright banning, and the wider audience that its creators sought. It went totally went under the radar, despite Derek Hill's support. It later screened at the Academy Cinema on Oxford Street (now a Marks & Spencer) with the Bill Douglas film *My Childhood* (1972). 'The person who might like one, wouldn't like the other', reflected Bicât, not unreasonably.

If your feathers are at all ruffled by the film's lack of clear political position, or by the BFI's involvement, be reassured by the Bicât scripted 1977 ITV play *It's Only Rock 'N' Roll* (28/06/1977). Again, a man is kidnapped but this time he's a troubled, drug-addled glam rock star, played by a brilliantly vacant, twitchy Richard O'Brien. None of the characters are wholly likeable – again – but the lines of power and sympathy are more clearly drawn. Doing their sums, record company executives decide that a dead rock star is more bankable than a live one and refuse the ransom. O'Brien's character is fished out of the Thames, like an old tyre. But before his murder, the camera peers at him through a veneer of mesh fencing. Wearing a white, bright fur coat, he wearily speaks with the gang about his life and the political contradictions in theirs, and they all look like rabbits, trapped in the mechanisms of capital.

A similar peering through takes place in *Skinflicker*, the double-framing of the reclaimed snuff movie creating texture and fog in front of the viewer's eyes. But *Skinflicker* is so much rawer than *It's Only Rock 'N' Roll*. It embodies its underground connections and contradictions in its very materiality and in the way in which it was made, even with, ironically, the support of the BFI. It's filmmaking with no recourse to another model, the aesthetic much more jarring then than it appears today.

Skinflicker was no video nasty – we'd know about it if it were. But it engaged with concepts of the forbidden, in slippery fashion. Truth and obfuscation rolled on top of each other as the characters make continual references to the illusions of cinema and the film's home-movie moments turn the gang into real people; they fill a kettle, eat baked beans and shave. 'Many families own such cameras', notes the narrator about the terrorists' handheld 8mm machine.

The picture is what you might call 'skuzzy' and the camera-work rough and ready. It lurches between black and white 16mm and fuzzy colour Super 8. Seen today the film can feel extremely curious, and surprising, in terms of how terrorists are presented in the age of ISIS / Daesh and their slick, glossy beheading videos. Put next to other films, the theatrical aspects shine out more overtly. But there's no doubting that this strange, forgotten bombshell from the early 1970s is a singular piece of work and, in that sense, it is best watched in isolation. The inconsistencies, the arrival at the minister's house, the brutal violence, as well as its confidence and sense of evocative fragmentation; they all pack a true punch in that scenario. Utilising the codes of actuality and documentary, paralleling a growing tendency within horror films and elsewhere, and combined with its terrorist storyline, plus its very final, brutal end – where everyone dies, horribly – for those that actually saw this film back in the day, it must have been a real blow to the head. *WF*

THE WAR ROOM

'Don't mention the war.' It's an iconic line from the iconic TV comedy series *Fawlty Towers* (1975-1979); but just like Basil Fawlty, 'mentioning the war' is something that as a nation we can't help but do. Screaming about it, shouting about it, endlessly replaying, re-enacting, venerating or vilifying British involvement in the big conflicts of the twentieth century, we endlessly remind ourselves of war's endless effect on the national psyche.

The many acknowledged studio 'classics' of British war cinema, from *In Which We Serve* (1942), via *The Dam Busters* (1955) onwards across *The Bridge On the River Kwai* (1957), constitute just the tip of an enormous martial mountain. There's been a plethora of television dramas, from *Colditz* (1972-1974) to *Secret Army* (1977-1979) to name just two especially cracking examples. There's no doubt about it, we're obsessed, whether we like it or not. Now get your hair cut, you 'orrible little man.

Ken Russell's *Elgar* (11/11/1962) critiqued World War One and the corruption of Elgar's *Pomp and Circumstance March No. 1* into *Land of Hope and Glory.* Considered by some Russell's greatest contribution to BBC art series *Monitor*, it knitted together reconstruction with archival footage – to the considerable displeasure of series producer Huw Wheldon.

‹ **Abject expressionism:** artist Stuart Brisley submerged in fetid water and rotting meat in the 1972 performance piece *And For Today... Nothing*, as documented in his film *Arbeit Macht Frei* (1973).

Actually one of Russell's most restrained pieces, it was far from being his best; but its controversial fusion of materials and refined classicism has ensured its place in the history books. Another approach to cinematic discourse upon war has been to put aside politics and revel instead in the high drama of the crisis moment; *Dunkirk* (2017) being a recent example. In a scenario of this kind, there is perhaps no great need to develop context, just a shared will that everyone involved – cast, crew, audience – will get through it and prove the rugged resilience of British character, despite there being few actual characters, or problematic ideological questions, on show.

Other references to war, and its effects and traumas, have been darker and much more oblique. It inhabits the work of the Goons: Sellers, Milligan, Bentine and Secombe; and is thoroughly embedded not only in post-war comedy but more broadly in the lives, outlook and work of all those that served in the forces, the people that actually lived through it, and got out the other end; and many of those that came afterwards, and very much lived with the ongoing after-effects of war in the decades that followed.

Of those that came after, one was extreme performance artist Stuart Brisley, who went through National Service, and had been traumatised by footage of the liberation of the camps. In 1972, he began an art action in a contained gallery space entitled *And For Today… Nothing*, in which he submerged his body, two hours at a time, daily, for two weeks, in a bath full of fetid water and rotting offal, temperature controlled to veer from as hot as he could bear to as cold as he could stand. The action – including the vomiting this induced in the artist – was visually documented in his film *Arbeit Macht Frei* (1973). The title, of course, referred to the grim text cast above the gates to Auschwitz, and other concentration camps: 'Work Makes You Free'. Absolutely nothing to laugh at here, assuredly, yet somehow the worlds of radical counter-cultural art and weird absurdist humour find a common ground through the horrors of war. For well over fifty-years now, Brisley has explored ritualistic ways of marking and highlighting time and structuring and institutional power, through feats of bodily endurance; and also through his paintings, collages and films.

Absurdist Goon Spike Milligan, who served in the forces, as documented in various splendid volumes of war memoirs, was later a peace and anti-nuclear war arms campaigner. In such strange TV programmes as *A Show Called Fred* (02/05 – 30/05/1956) (made with friend and fellow Goon Peter Sellers) and the later weird comedy extravaganza series *Q* (24/03 – 05/05/1969) he made direct upfront references to the H-bomb and mocked political authority in a way that those who followed could only mimic – unable to access the deep-rooted venom and underlying sadness that had grown out of his involvement in World War. Milligan's bizarre riffs and jokes weren't always entirely funny: sometimes, you could argue, they were just weird, or confusing. He was increasingly bewildered by the world and what he had gone through, his absurdity barely masking a bleak, melancholic nihilism as it bled out into view.

The Goons' fusion of zany playfulness with absurd, barely camouflaged mocking of decorum and authority filtered through to the sixties counter-culture and the whole next generation, such was its subversive power. The Beatles had grown up listening to their ground-breaking radio show. Despite its shiny surface, and its psychedelic, colourful frivolities, their hit 1967 album *Sgt Pepper's Lonely Hearts Club Band* musically and lyrically looked back in many ways to a greyer, more depressive post-war Britain. It drew on older forms of musical and community culture by way of the traditional 'bandstand' on its cover, as revitalised in the pop-art idiom by former National Serviceman Peter Blake. Many of its most famous songs – despite their formal experimentation – reflected not upon a fab psychedelic future, but upon everyday life and experience in a disappearing working-class world. These British nostalgia-futurist themes percolated into the art, films and visual culture of the age; and developed into a distinctively rose-coloured yet frequently melancholic – if not outright depressive – lens for a movement that was for the greater part otherwise in thrall to America. The psychedelic trip had a complicated, sometimes even torturous relationship to the shadows of blitzkrieg trauma.

Riffing on the decline of the British Empire and a heartfelt fear of the atomic bomb age, Professor Bruce Lacey and the anarcho-comedy troupe The Alberts, who had developed in parallel with the Goons, launched TV station BBC2 in 1967 with a special anti-establishment comedy programme; and collaborated with the boundary-pushing animator and filmmaker Bob Godfrey. Their stiff Edwardian attire and protruding olde-worlde facial hair directly or indirectly fuelled the *Lord Kitchener's Valet*

It's rubbish, but by jingo it's British rubbish: The Massed Alberts led by Douglas and Tony Gray and featuring Jill Smith and Bruce Lacey.

fashions of the psychedelic era (latterly revived in the twenty-first century); trends which both apparently semi-celebrated but concurrently mocked stuffy old ideas of Empire and Britishness. They were determinedly anti-war, and part of the CND movement, all having been in the military.

For Bruce Lacey, art became his therapy, which included making a series of 16mm films. A fascination with Empire movies, such as *Beau Geste* (1939) and *The Four Feathers* (1939) created a curious tension in his works, however. In his films, he and the Alberts dressed-up as if appearing as extras in these movies, whilst simultaneously they mocked the politics. Their use of the Union Jack was ultimately subsumed into the soft jingoism of Swinging London, perhaps because of an occasional perceived ambiguity in a stance that seemed both to critique and celebrate the old ways simultaneously. But watch Lacey's films made with Bob Godfrey, *The Battle of New Orleans*

(1960) and *Bang!* (1967), plus his collaboration with The Alberts, *The Flying Alberts* (1965), and the politics become crystal clear: flags are muddied, and everything fails.

These films existed as a part of a post-war so-called 'amateur' and experimental film scene, that involved numerous National Servicemen, and also women. Margaret Tait, having trained in medicine, was called up in 1943 by the Royal Army Medical Corps. On her return to her native Scotland, she began making poetic, observational 16mm films that frequently meditated on the environment and on its social, physiological and political histories. In *Colour Poems* (1974), she juxtaposed an Armistice Day parade with a sunny poppy field, a Royal visit, and a large-scale industrial quarry site, with giant vehicles and machinery passing through the torn-up landscape. Tellingly, one title reads 'Brave New World'.

Creative responses to war vary in scale – the larger they are the louder they tend to shout – and yet Tait's deceptively modest work enabled a type of thinking through film that was personal, exploratory and deeply layered. Many such films have been made, by Tait and others; small in scale but concerned with the larger viscera of life.

According to a recent BFI statistical investigation, 'war' is the most often-used word in all British film plot synopses. In this section, then, despite Mr Fawlty's valuable advice, we shall repeatedly mention that most inescapable of realities, which stands ominously alongside age and death: war.

Our first dangerous entry in this section dropped the viewer right in the heart of the action and asked difficult and probing questions about the fabric of British society, so difficult that the powers that be refused to allow it to be broadcast...

The War Game

UK TV | 1965 | black and white | 47mins
Director Peter Watkins
Script Peter Watkins
Production Company BBC
Cast Dick Graham, Michael Aspel (narrators)

The War Game was made to give an image to something that didn't as yet exist, something terrifying, cataclysmic and potentially very real indeed. It was commissioned by the BBC documentary department and was to have been the second TV film written and directed by Peter Watkins. Shooting began in April 1965 and a rough cut was completed in June. In September, however, the BBC began to have serious concerns and, as has been revealed in recent years, spoke to the Cabinet Secretary and other Home Office officials. The ministers intervened and the film was pulled from broadcast. The official line was that the public would be too startled and unable to take what they were seeing, were it to be relayed in the comfort of their own living room. *The War Game* was a carefully researched and brilliantly directed film about what would in all likelihood occur should just a single one-megaton nuclear weapon be dropped on the county of Kent.

Peter Watkins had begun in the amateur filmmaking scene of the 1950s and 60s, counting amongst his contemporaries John Schlesinger, Ken Russell and Kevin Brownlow. He shared with Brownlow, plus his co-director friend Andrew Mollo, an almost obsessive interest in detailed reenactment and worked on their debut feature *It Happened Here* (1964). That film presented a shocking alternative UK where the Nazis had in fact won the War and featured fake archival footage shot on different film stocks plus a rich array of different historical military uniforms, all carefully researched and sourced.

Brownlow would speak of his admiration for the director Erich von Stroheim who insisted actors playing soldiers wore historically accurate undershirts in his epic film *Greed* (1924), even when the garments might never be seen on screen. It was as though the very wearing of specific clothes brought the actor into a greater contact with the past, a bodily contact enabling them to channel other times. Detail and accuracy were important.

Watkins' early films were also very carefully made. *The Diary of An Unknown Soldier* (1959) told the story of a World War One soldier in the trenches whilst *The Forgotten Faces* (1961) transposed the Hungarian revolution of 1956 to the wet and grubby streets of Canterbury; both films being shot handheld and ground in rain and dirt, bringing two specific historical moments to life with powerful, visceral directness.

It won the 1966 Oscar for Best Documentary Feature and was published as a book: Peter Watkins' *The War Game* (1965). ›

AVON / NS23 / 95¢

The War Game

by Peter Watkins

The controversial
Academy Award-winning film.
"It may be the most
important film ever made."
KENNETH TYNAN

His first BBC production *Culloden* (transmitted 15/12/1964), by way of contrast, deliberately confused timestreams and realities. It presented the story of the eponymous battle of 1746 in Scotland as if it were a contemporary news event. A reporter with a microphone speaks from the frontline, and the camera lunges to one side when a cannonball crashes down, smashing the terrain. As in *The Forgotten Faces*, the film highlighted the visages and roles of individual participants whilst now also calling time on the injustices of history and the culpability of the English officers. A very similar agenda would come to bear when it came to the script for *The War Game*, a film that would place the viewer right in the heart of the action whilst asking difficult and probing questions about the fabric of British society.

'Britain's present nuclear deterrent policy threatens a would-be aggressor with devastation from thermonuclear bombs to be delivered by Victor and Vulcan Mark II aircraft of British V-Bomber force. In a time of international crisis, it is at present planned to disperse a part of this V-bomber force to certain RAF and civilian airfields spread throughout Britain.'

Russia would in all likelihood have allocated a number of thermonuclear weapons aimed at precisely these locations, plus the surrounding twenty-five major cities, the film continues to report. In less than a minute and a half the potential for swift and utter nuclear devastation has already been clearly unpacked.

A specific fictional – but plausible – narrative then develops. The Russian and Eastern German authorities have sealed all access to East Berlin, indicating their desire to occupy the Western part of the city, if the American military does not withdraw its threat of a nuclear strike against the Chinese forces invading Vietnam.

The drama then begins, sucking us into this very real-feeling tale about nuclear addiction, in part by parroting the traditional authoritative voice of the BBC, and by having a cameraman drive down a street on the back of a policeman's motorbike, and by following the rider into and up the stairs of a municipal building where an emergency meeting is taking place – all in one continuous shot. Even at this early stage when an attack is only a possibility, power, or a form of power, goes into effect, and the viewer is thrown into the heart of the action. The escalation is terrifying.

The story is fictional but the film is grounded in verisimilitude; quotes from high-ranking officials are included and people (actors) talk 'vox pops' style directly to the camera. It's relentlessly hard and convincing. From the extraordinary performances – people ground down and weary – to the minimal but extremely evocative action sequences – devastation sequences might be more accurate – it's an astonishing piece, quite separate from any political and sociological concerns or messages. Frankly, it's terrifying. When the buildings burn, and the firestorm rages, the cameraman, Peter Bartlett, simply stares with disbelief at the destruction, shaking violently from the shock and the collapsing material infrastructure and exploding bricks. Russia strikes.

The images are violent and dramatic but silence is also used to convey the horror, and to great effect. The sick traumatized bodies of children and old women flick their empty eyes up to the camera; one woman clawing at her blackened throat as if to swallow down the pain, or to draw up some words of anguish, anything, from within. The image is then repeated without sound, only adding to its power; silence from institutional structures to be replaced by a far greater silence and eventually an agony so unfathomable as to be beyond the scope of even this film. We can only imagine what life would be like years after the blast. And yet as Jon Savage has written, *The War Game* 'told a terrifying and unpalatable truth'.

The Mirror said this was 'one ban the BBC need not have defended. The real horror is the stark documentary quality of the film. It reproduces with sickening realism charred limbs, crushed faces and eyes melting in their sockets. This, as the BBC rightly decided, could not have been borne by the millions of viewers sitting at home,' a view the BBC Director General Hugh Carleton Greene publicly concurred with. Fearing a situation similar to when Orson Welles told America that the Martians had invaded during his controversial *The War of the Worlds* radio adaptation (USA transmission, 30/10/1938), Greene said that pensioners and certain viewers would find it too confusing and overwhelming, thinking that the bombs had really dropped. It would be unpalatable.

But who was this truth ultimately 'unpalatable' to, to use Jon Savage's words? Taken at face value, the film asks a lot more than what would the UK do and what would happen if a nuclear bomb was dropped by a foreign power. How is power given and how is it used, it asks? Do those in charge really think about what they are doing? And do they really care about the populace that they control through the deployment of resources and military

Foreword

If the country were ever faced with an immediate threat of nuclear war, a copy of this booklet would be distributed to every household as part of a public information campaign which would include announcements on television and radio and in the press. The booklet has been designed for free and general distribution in that event. It is being placed on sale now for those who wish to know what they would be advised to do at such a time.

May 1980

If Britain is attacked by nuclear bombs or by missiles, we do not know what targets will be chosen or how severe the assault will be.

If nuclear weapons are used on a large scale, those of us living in the country areas might be exposed to as great a risk as those in the towns. The radioactive dust, falling where the wind blows it, will bring the most widespread dangers of all. No part of the United Kingdom can be considered safe from both the direct effects of the weapons and the resultant fall-out.

The dangers which you and your family will face in this situation can be reduced if you do as this booklet describes.

Endless horror: pages from a UK nuclear attack warning and information booklet, 1980.

force? The shocking lack of provision made by the government and the actually very thin ties that bind society together are both highlighted in this film, and drawing these questions to the public's attention was perhaps the real 'unpalatable truth', at least to those in control of the BBC, from the stationmaster right up to the government itself. The government's incredible lack of provision was as much revealed as the human price of a nuclear strike. No wonder Whitehall called it a film with 'serious political implications.'

How did the film get the go ahead? Surely the BBC read the script, which not only contained the statistical information but the suggestions about absent governmental provision as well as the implicit critique of institutional power. One can only assume they didn't count on the film being so well made. It is certainly more condensed and driven than *Culloden* and Watkins' amateur works made before he joined the BBC, though these are also direct and distinctly engaging.

The War Game, plus these other films, bring military conflicts home, forcing the viewer in the UK to consider not just the background to war but also questions about responsibility and what he or she would do, what it would be like for us, in each given situation. *The War Game*, for example, derived a substantial amount of its information from the atomic bombing of Hiroshima and Nagasaki, plus the assault on Dresden in World War Two. And in *The Forgotten Faces*, when soldiers fight back and suppress the Hungarian rioters, Watkins, as narrator, asks: what would the oppressed do in the shoes of the oppressors, were the situation to be reversed? We are all potentially culpable.

Watkins, like nearly all men his age, had been in National Service. (It was obligatory after the War until 1963.) These works feel like he was trying to purge his experience, maybe even a specific experience, bringing the war home and reminding or even telling people what military conflict means on the ground, with all its devastation, mess and lack of respect for individual human life, no matter what the nationality. The news reportage style of presentation in *Culloden* did this and Watkins hoped audiences would make a link to the Vietnam War then being broadcast on television. Such concerns run through almost all of Watkins' films. In *The War Game*, he implicitly asks the audience to identify with the victims of Dresden, which was daring so soon after the War.

He wanted to meet and engage with trauma. In his 1965 TV film, we are told that 'at a meeting at the Vatican an English and an American bishop expressed the view that "the church must tell the faithful that they should learn to live with, though need not love, the nuclear bomb, provided that is it "clean" and of a good family."' And then a toddler, playing in a large garden, screams because the retinas in his eyes have been burnt by the light-flash after the blast. His well-spoken parents rush from their large house to console the child and, like many faces, we see them again later, smeared in soot and dust, unable to process what has happened. Like the victims of war, the bomb shows no respect for class or privilege. It is also a warning; the family had clearly ignored the alarm.

The BBC was still at this point very much operating in the class conscious, status driven, paternalistic mode laid down by Lord Reith (note Lord), its first director general. *The War Game* in a sense refuted that privilege and challenged the concept of post-war consensus. It highlighted class structure and the deployment of power, and also the different values and sociological context between country and city. Again, it was perhaps for this reason that Whitehall said screening the film on TV would have 'political repercussions'.

Paradoxically, *The War Game* also assumed and played with notions of authority through the very manner of its construction; this was another one of its challenges. It used and exploited the documentary form, incorporating and even extending the new technological and stylistic conventions made possible by new mobile synch-sound 16mm photography. The form allowed space for vox pops style interviews that often confused and challenged the viewer as to their veracity, notably early on when views are sought on the impending possible situation. The opinions are varied and sometimes racist, but more often than not they showed how ill-informed the public would be, and effectively how public opinion could be steered and manipulated according to the designs of the ruling government.

The film went on to win best documentary at the 1966 Oscars but for all the reasons discussed above, the BBC would thereafter avoid combining the docudrama form with themes of attack and disaster. The apocalyptic or post-apocalyptic TV dramas that were made in the 1970s all notably stuck within the confines of both traditional narrative structures, and conventional production styles. *The Guardians* (10/07–02/10/1971) imagined a future fascist UK whilst an overly officious and authoritarian father hoards food and goods in the face of social collapse in weird kids' drama *Noah's Castle* (02/04 – 14/05/1980).

Survivors (1975–1977) follows a small group of people as they deal with the aftermath of deadly, apocalyptic mass contagion. Once things settle down, their world is a little like that imagined by the socialist William Morris, a kind of medieval return to the land with no property delineations and with work performed as activity for its own sake, with its immediate rewards, and disappointments. Finally faced with the option of turning back on the National Grid, the characters do it, symbolizing a disappointing return to the old ways – the recent old ways – and presumably a form of national government.

But even outright fantasies on TV have power, with location shooting used to make things seem somehow 'real' in the mind's eye. In 1981, *Time Out* discovered that, because, in part, America was now storing nuclear weapons in the UK, large swathes of the UK population thought they would see a nuclear war in their lifetime, and that the aftermath would look like *Survivors*, which was frankly optimistic.

Threads (23/09/1984) was a more obvious TV follow-up or 'successor' to *The War Game*, though it too avoided the documentary form that had been used to palpable effect elsewhere. The most notable example was the classic single mother drama *Cathy Come Home* (16/11/1966), which had led to changes in housing regulations.

Threads picked up on and updated much of the information in *The War Game*, whilst also showing, in speculative fashion, the barren life of the next generation. Like *The War Game* its socio-political scope went beyond the already overwhelming portrait of thermo-nuclear war, and it used the analogy of a spider's web to show how if just one thread in the structures that bind us together should break, everything would collapse, chaos and societal breakdown enveloping us all. At the end, a perpetually sick, animalistic girl, born after the blast, roams the countryside, barking some new form of guttural language, knowing nothing of her parents, or what had come before. In this respect, it mined the conceit behind Humphrey Jennings' *A Diary For Timothy* (1945), asking what would life what be like for the generation after World War Two, by way of a new-born child. *Threads* issued a speculative warning, however, not an open question.

Terrifyingly, actual governmental information films made for screening in light of a nuclear attack are seen broadcast on a TV. The films advised how to conserve water and what to do with dead bodies. But the most tangible, abject sequence comes when a woman pisses herself during the bomb-blast, the urine running out of her trouser leg. (Many remember this, and artist, Mark Leckey, cut it into his *Dream English Kid (1964 – 1999 AD)* (2015).)

Unlike *Threads*, *The War Game* did not dare to imagine and create images of what life would be like in the years after the devastating explosion. The image of the woman clawing at her throat, repeated at the end, is enough. It's like something drawn from Dante's *Inferno*, the figures suffering for eternity.

The War Game stayed well clear of narrative resolution and even included strange potent imagery that took the appalling horror to unexpected places. At one point soldiers in gas masks stand casually in a peaceful muddy country lane, inadvertently creating their own science fiction universe. Glimpsed through a mesh of wire, they look totally out of place. But more typically shots were intimate and immediate; faces speak directly to the camera, creating personal relationships to the enveloping chaos and destruction.

For all its future image making and speculation – based on careful historical research – it was an extremely creative piece of work. The final scene draws many of the film's different tendencies together: a group of refugees celebrate Christmas by listening to a record of *Stille Nacht* (a.k.a. *Silent Night*), a man at the front rotating the cracked gramophone disc with his hand. Absurdity, loss, universal humanity, community, the death of religion and ultimately silence – the silence of government and the silence of death; all these things whirl around the stylus and play out as the credits finally roll. For all its darkness and political repercussions, the film is ultimately humanistic, and talismanic. It reaches out to the viewer, drawing the personal and political together with powerful directness. The characters deal with the situation as ultimately many of us would, which is partly why it's so terrifying. The film is fifty years old and yet all this feels like it could still happen, and at the blink of an eye – or rather the flick of a switch.

Peter Watkins, now in his 80s, has continued to make direct, multi-layered, experimental, critical films and investigations into different forms of governmental power and media control. The fourteen-hour, episodic, discursive package, *The Journey* (1983-87) simultaneously updated much of the information contained in *The War Game*, critiqued the manipulative and heavily-edited mainstream media practice, and initiated and documented a dialogue between several families separated by ideology and considerable expanses of geography. Governments have continued to make bombs. *WF*

For some, the bombs that have already blasted still resonate, the fall-out rippling right through their whole life, post-traumatic stress of sorts derived from war triggering and signalling powerful creative decisions and unusual ways of being…

White Dust

UK Film | 1970-72 | colour | 33mins
Director Jeff Keen
Cast Steve Wynter, Dexter Duke, Jackie Keen, Tony Sinden, Stella Keen

Jeff Keen served his country but did the country serve him? We're not trying to evoke some strange patriotic fervour or nationalistic conservativism. After all, those who'd subscribe to those feelings would deeply dislike and even object to Keen's work. And Keen himself was, not virtually, but actually, communist for much of his life. He grew up in Trowbridge, Kent, near a manor house where his father worked, and felt profound class anger and resentment, feeling held back from art and creativity after seeing a piece of incredible, magical art which inspired him to paint his bedroom red. The art was the movie *Fantasia* (1940).

Like most people, Keen could embody contradictions. But importantly it didn't stop him. His own films were a far cry from *Fantasia*, not so much in terms of content and ideas, but scale. Countless individual artists toiled over that famous, actually rather overwhelming Disney movie. Keen's films, by way of contrast, were short, explosive, vigorous and visceral.

The cryptic, experimental plot for *White Dust* begins:

Water washes over the image, as though we were entering a dream. And Keen's street, dotted with a few cars, is presented.
Fades in and out create further dreamlike evocations. Refers back to the gentle romanticism of classic cinema.
Inside the house, a young Stella Keen sleeps quietly with her doll, her eyes closed too. Perhaps dreaming. Is this her dream?
The film proper begins – breaking absolutely with experimental filmmaking convention at the time, which was vehemently anti – narrative – with an intertitle 'the story so far....' Piano music and library music emerges, with the crackling of a record. Creating drama and evoking the period and a kind of self-reflexive knowingness, much like Balch did in Secrets of Sex *(1970).*

Why should the country care? Well, Keen's work might seem superficially detached from his experiences in World War Two – in which he served, experimenting with and developing new tanks – and more in tune with bright, lurid, psychedelic, counter-cultural art, but like many artists who'd been in National Service, his experiences and work didn't entirely map over to the sunny optimism of 1967.

Peter Blake had been in National Service, meaning he had been obligated by law to serve in the army, and Richard Hamilton, another British pop artist, had also had military experience. And he designed the Beatles' *White Album* cover and photographic collage interior. Younger artists and musicians were able to avoid such press-ganging into service; conscription was done away with in 1963. This meant there were individuals who felt connected to the counter-culture but unlike their younger brethren had had direct experiences of conflict, war and death.

The cryptic, experimental plot for *White Dust* continues:

> *Kick of splicing tape.*
> *'…while Silverhead lay trapped in the lair of the Spiderwoman –*
> *Naturalman disappeared, believed victim of Prof. Volta and his assistant,*
> *the beautiful Vulvana – meanwhile in the Slums of a certain well-known*
> *seaside resort…'*

There was a strange dissonance. Jeff Keen, the artist and filmmaker based in Brighton, a city symbolically detached from but close to Swinging London, was another former soldier. But unlike these other artists, he never designed a cover for the Beatles, or found other forms of above ground recognition, or indeed money. Rather he worked incessantly in his small flat with his wife and young child, and piled-up the art works. Paintings vied for attention alongside melted dolls' heads, children's army toys, numerous plastic robots and guns, strips of film dangling from doorways and bookshelves and a large Cadbury's chocolate éclair sweet jar filled with tall dolls and labelled 'The Brides of Frankenstein'. There were also old U-matic video decks, super 8 cameras and sound machines. (By the end of his life he had a wardrobe entirely filled up with sketchbooks all made in his later years, when his mobility and energies had become reduced.)

Keen, at one level, had a lot in common with the likes of Peter Blake, who loved comics and wrestling. But he reflected, defiantly, 'people say I'm a pop artist. But I'm not a pop artist'. Certainly, he never went to that grand, highly regarded London art school, the Royal College of Art. Blake and Hockney went there and so did Derek Boshier, all of whom subsequently appeared in Ken Russell's *Monitor* documentary *Pop Goes the Easel* (transmitted 25/03/1962). Keen briefly attended a drawing course at the Chelsea School of Art but was largely self-taught.

White Dust runs on:

> *Howling wind and dramatic music play over brief tableau shots of the players to be seen over the next thirty-one minutes. Dolls, mannequins and faces all mix in and out of each other as hand-held shots and double-exposures create a pool of fluid, interacting imagery. The viewer has to personally decide on what image to focus on. It's actually not narrative in the traditional sense. But certain images punctuate or rupture the mix, often when the players look at the camera – a gruff, hardened criminal slicing off his own large (plastic) ear, Jackie Keen adopting/copying the pose of the naked woman in the wood in Manet painting* Le déjeuner sur l'herbe, *also naked, next to men in dark raincoats.*

His primary medium being film, of course, also went against him. Being an underground filmmaker was a thankless occupation in the UK, much less so than in the States where the likes of Andy Warhol rubbed shoulders with organiser and practitioner, Jonas Mekas, and Jack Smith and Kenneth Anger. These filmmakers had shock and sexiness on their side, plus a forceful desire to get their work seen – as well as an international tour called 'The New American Cinema' to promote it all. American creatives were cleaning-up, reputation wise, in the 1950s and 60s.

Curiously Keen's work looked the most like the Americans of all the British filmmakers, and he was one of the few practitioners (James Scott being another) to catch the New American Cinema tour when it came to the ICA in London in 1962. His films were unusual in the UK for actually including people, and they were dressed like members of a provincial, seaside version of Warhol's Factory. As Australian poet Jas Duke recalled, Jeff 'said to me "We're making a movie tomorrow would you like to be in it?" or words to that effect and in no time I was dressed in yellow tights and wrapped in a purple cape and tee-shirt with MARZMAN on the front and I AM BRIAN DONLEVY on the back, striking attitudes in the middle of

Masks and make-up: Jackie Keen in *White Dust* (1972).

the Brighton municipal garbage dump – a Martian desert littered with the remains of lost civilisations and thus very suitable for titanic epix movies.'

White Dust:
In classic Keen style, painted cardboard prop hats, badges, labels and guns all populate the film and contribute to the myriad costumes and archetypal referencing. Figures sleep and are covered with polystyrene and plastic sheeting. It's a thick weave of psycho-sexual imagery, all rendered through the aesthetics of early Hollywood and classic B movie serials. James Whale, the director of the earliest Universal Frankenstein films and The Old Dark House *(1932), would be proud. It's 'dream factory' stuff but of a different register, Keen revelling in its magic and the possibilities of incomplete narrative and play with friends and family. The same faces*

appear, in different guises, in different wigs, in different locations, over and over. Friends Nadine (one of Jackie Keen's – Jeff's wife's – many 'stage names'), Steve Wynter, Dexter Duke and Mortune Duane receive credit, but others such as the artist and experimental filmmaker Tony Sinden, who was clearly extremely influenced by Keen early on, also appear. They're like the studio stars of old, relocated to 'a certain well-known seaside resort', Brighton. Objects also reappear, refashioned and re-contextualised. The ear is presented as a dish – a culinary invitation worthy of the surrealists.

Other UK filmmakers, for the most part, instead used found material, literally film strips found in the rubbish bins of Soho. It must have been strange for Keen, not only being significantly older than other filmmakers on the scene – Keen was 37 when he made his first efforts, the black and white 8mm works *Wail* (1960) and *Like the Time is Now* (1961), which later

Psychedelic happenings on the Brighton coast: Jackie Keen, Jas Duke and Steve Wynter in *White Dust* (1972).

found write-ups in the amateur film press. Weirdly he still found indirect connections to the USA scene by way of the holidaying American poet Piero Heliczer who appeared in Warhol's films, and the two eccentric multimedia artists made *The Autumn Feast* (1961) together. Strange terminologies and names derived from a calendar made by Angus MacLise, the first Velvet Underground drummer, found their way into Keen's work via Heliczer too, one example being *Day of the Arcane Light* (1969).

Keen seemed to channel all sorts of influences and connections, bottling them like lightning. It's a suitable analogy, speed is of the essence in Keen's films. Cutting virtually takes over the films at times, sequences sliced-up like a plate of tripe ready for shovelling down. Explosive terminology derived from American comics that he and many other ex-servicemen apparently enjoyed also found a place. Keen painted on films, and painted in them, introducing strange thought bubbles and quotes – 'Samuel T. Coleridge on the melting brain wave' being one. He loved Marvel comics

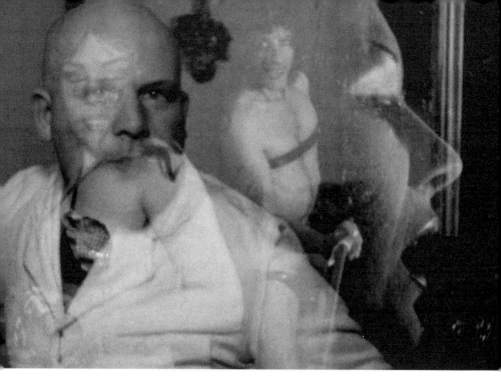

giant Jack Kirby, and loved characters like *The Punisher*, with his military background and perpetual references to war.

Keen films pulled on so many influences and connections and yet they still feel utterly personal and unique. The war allusions were important and singled him out from other filmmakers, and also other pop artists, afraid to reference their pasts, even obliquely. Keen would insert the sounds of bombers over six-part film montage *Meatdaze* (1968), and refer to Blatz in *Cineblatz* (1967) and *Blatzom* (1968) and many other derivatives. The word refers to 'Blitz' or 'Blitzkrieg' – Hitler's total war. Cine-blitzkrieg, but with a comic book edge – 'POW'. His sense of playful nihilism bellied a seriousness and a dark melancholy. When presenting shows into the 1970s and later, he'd wear a white boiler-suit with 'Born to Kill' spray-painted on the back. Keen was a complex character but statements such as these suggested war defined him, or was an ever-present reference; and in the worlds of British experimental film, he came from another planet.

His formal interests included homemade multi-layering, matts, scratching and painting the film, multiple superimpositions, collage and random editing. He was *au fait* with all the art ideas. But these abrasive textures suggest tension and the presence of his personality within the very materiality of the film. Unlike his friends and family, including his muse, wife Jackie, he never – or only very rarely – appeared in his films in the 1960s and 70s. Rather, his presence and personality were suggested more abstractly.

For all his distance from the capital, and his difference to the current vogues in British experimental film, he did get support from the Arts Council film department. One might wonder if this kind of occasional help actually encouraged him to make more films, and meant that more light was shone on his films than his paintings, writing and other forms. *White Dust* was one such film, shot on 16mm and combining multiple and double exposures, shot over several years. If Keen wasn't a pop artist then he was definitely interested in and evocative of the Surrealists, the group who loved pop and trash culture, evolving after World War One. Tidal water washes over the entirety of *White Dust*, evoking a dream-like narrative whilst numerous small individual scenes representative of B movie genre cinemas – crime, horror, monster movies – are played out by way of individual moments, telling their archetypal stories by way of simple familiar dramatic scenarios.

> *Kick of splicing tape.*
> '*…while Silverhead lay trapped in the lair of the Spiderwoman – Naturalman disappeared – believed victim of Prof. Volta and his assistant, the beautiful Vulvana – meanwhile in the Slums of a certain well-known seaside resort…*'

Sequences were shot in 100 foot lengths and rewound in the camera. Other actions were performed, engaging in chance as to how the two sequences might interact and interrelate. Keen did something similar when he combined films through performance, projecting multiple films simultaneously, often burning something at the same time. The sea and fire were recurring alchemical images in his films and art.

Some sequences appear as if they were stills. Their narrative is so archetypal, immediate and familiar that no other actions are required. They're like cinema lobby cards pressed into time. Some scenes look as if they have been constructed with considerable effort, the set-up and make-up appearing ornate and almost baroque and ritualistic, actors appearing slightly stiff, doing what they are told. Other moments are like family home movies, completely free form and the camera responding solely to the action. These usually involve Jeff and Jackie Keen's daughter Stella. But whatever, the music waxes and wanes and yet the sounds of crashing waves hold the dream together…

Japanese monster films sneak into the melting pot by way of a brief Mothra and Silverhead face-off. In some cases characters evoke pre-existing archetypes. In others, they become part of a lexicon of new characters, pressed from the moulds of comics and B movies but still very much Keen's. Silverhead populates several movies, his visage – looking like the robot monster from a 1940s serial – is a prop, a tall, stiff, silver photography bag turned inside out. He got his own movie in 1982 – The Return of Silverhead, *the robot like ambiguous anti-hero being serenaded by Wagner. Other later characters include the 90s Keen avatar Omozap, a homo sapien death machine writ from the same seeds as* Predator *(1987),* Punisher *and* Robocop *(1987).*

Characters in *White Dust* penetrate paper and mix with moments of animation, often performing out on the tip, a site of creation and destruction that appears right throughout Keen's oeuvre, and very prominently in the *Doctor Who* story *The War Games* (19/04 – 21/06/1969), where it doubles for World War One trenches. Keen would approve. In Keen's story the natural light has a silvery, water colour look; his ghosts seem to move like shadows in a special play, the story of which we don't and can't fully know or understand.

Mad professors, spies, soldiers, spivs, strongmen, masked heroes, masked villains, explorers and vamps all feature.

Briefly Keen presents his mythic birth narrative for the camera. He was born from blitz/blatz and a graffiti like monochrome picture painted on a bed sheet and held aloft by friends shows tanks on the sea and bombers flying overhead. A line of fire tears the sheet in two and a man wrapped in a cocoon like sheet, it could almost be a straight-jacket, walks stoically from the bisected membrane. Keen said he only knew World War Two was over when he and his servicemen friends saw bombers flying over-head.

It's a rich, continuous flow of characters and costumes and the colours go from watery white to lurid and saturated. Red blood or blood red appears in rhythmic bursts whilst the music swells and begins again, renewing the sense of where we're at and where the images are going. Cut outs like 'the missing bride' create further associations and intimations of story, and milk poured from a glass onto a woman's topless upper half evokes Kenneth Anger's psychodrama dream film Fireworks *(1947). The moment is repeated with blood fluid later on, exactly matching Anger's shot. (Breasts and blood together – a big no-no for the British Board of Film Censors. But although the work was funded by the Arts Council of Great Britain, the BBFC would never have seen it.) And then again with Steve Wynter, the strongman. Keen himself appears briefly, looking like the phantom of the opera, his nose stuck-up flat like a pig, mimicking Lon Chaney. Keen's costume includes a toy bomber pinned to his chest – of course.*

Secrets, lost love, rescues, magic, monsters and resuscitation and revelation all interweave and it concludes back where it started, on a quiet street 'in a certain well-known seaside resort'. The monster rescues the bride and the evil Doctor Volta is press-ganged into cleaning the street.

Turn-off the sound – or the noise, if you like – when watching *White Dust* and a brutal, harder experience seems to emerge, and in a way you couldn't possibly expect. Its intention, its visual rhythms, the actual content of the images, punch the viewer. Bright lurid colours, parallel edits and the speed of its lyricism seem hard and unrelenting then. An occult symbolism written in the language of early cinema seems more overt, like the whole film is a magic spell. The Kenneth Anger connections feel stronger with the sound down too. It's not a mixture of random elements constructed from playful Sunday afternoons, when work is done and playtime begins. It's an intense, insistent, restless collage, built by a man who must keep going, and never stop, always creating and doing something with his mind.

Stella Keen, Jeff Keen's daughter, who appeared in and helped to shoot several of his films:

'In Jeff's universe, the quest for creative fulfilment is always elusive – the artist is always striving to reach a goal he never fully attains; hence the quest will always continue. The creative process reiterates the cycle of life, death and renewal. As Jeff wrote across one of his paintings in the 1990s, "All life is war and the long voyage home."'

His costume play, collage and abrasive markings were an expressive mask for something truly dark and deeply felt. Keen's films are like gateways to another world – and it's a world shaped by war. *WF*

A whole generation of comedians had their perspectives shaped by memories of the War, and wartime service. Among them were the Goons – Spike Milligan, Harry Secombe, Michael Bentine and Peter Sellers – and the War is writ large across their careers...

The Blockhouse

USA/UK Film | 1973 | colour | 92mins
Director Clive Rees
Script John Gould, Clive Rees
Production Company Galactacus Productions
Cast Peter Sellers, Charles Aznavour, Jeremy Kemp, Peter Vaughan

Success on the wireless as a Goon, and subsequent worldwide acclaim as a film funny man, was not enough. Peter Sellers still hankered after serious roles that would prove his scope and sophistication as a 'proper' actor. Certainly he had the talent for it; he just needed the opportunities; often what he lacked, perhaps, was the self-discipline to keep himself in check on set, or someone tough enough to make him toe the line (The Boulting Brothers could manage it, as could Blake Edwards). From the early days on, he invested his comic characters with more depth than was necessary to the viewer, perhaps. But it was assuredly necessary to him. Everything had to be right.

Even in his first real feature, the low-budget Brighton-set Adelphi Films comedy *Penny Points to Paradise* (1951), Sellers imbues his underwritten Major (an extension of his radio roles, for let us not forget he began as a 'voice man') with something extra. There is the distinct sense that there may be something more going on beneath the surface; and by the time of his character comedy heyday, at the end of the decade, he was an expert, as in the case of the immortal union shop steward Fred Kite of the Boulting Brothers' *I'm All Right Jack* (1959). You could believe that the character continued to live, even out of camera shot. Sometimes, though, these superb character parts were perfected to the detriment of the humour – as with his self-directed tale of a small-town French school teacher turned gangster, the long-neglected *Mr Topaze* (1961). The titular Topaze was, typically for Sellers, a brilliantly realized role; but the living, breathing potent ordinariness of his meek, mediocre tweedy schoolmaster unfortunately all but cancelled out many possible laughs inherent in this engaging, engrossing but intermittently mirth-free 'comedy' film. A series of fine comic characterisations by a superb cast – including Herbert Lom and Nadia Gray – are weightily perched upon a script sometimes precariously lacking punchlines.

He endeavoured to play it absolutely straight as a brutal gangster in John Guillermin's excellent *Never Let Go* (1960) – mercilessly scrunching a disobedient young thug's fingers (played by a boyish *Beat Girl*-era Adam Faith) beneath a radiogram lid – but the critics were not prepared to engage with Sellers sinister and straight. Though he scooped up an Oscar nomination for *Dr. Strangelove* (1964) and was hot box office stuff thanks to *The Pink Panther* (1963), the straighter stuff seemed always to lead back to the doldrums – and though Sellers could be a big draw when he did the funny stuff, he didn't help himself, either, becoming renowned for being difficult on set, and off it.

By the latter half of the 1960s he'd thoroughly blotted his copybook. Increasingly difficult to handle, paranoid, unpredictable, and becoming obsessed with astrology, he'd been an architect of destruction on the bloated James Bond spoof *Casino Royale* (1967), derailing the already shaky production train by refusing to appear on screen with co-star Orson Welles, despite the fact that they were to share a big scene at a card table. This was apparently because Sellers was dismayed to find that his co-star already knew his chum Princess Margaret, so he couldn't introduce her to him, and when she spoke to Welles first instead of Sellers at an on-set luncheon, poor petulant Peter was crushed. Scenes featuring Sellers and Welles had to be

Going underground: dust jacket design for Jean-Paul Clébert's 1955 novel *The Blockhouse*. ›

trick-shot using mirrors, to create the illusion they were on screen together. He also made things interesting by having a punch up with Joe McGrath (just one of the directors on this troubled production) and by doing a bunk before all his scenes were finished. So upset were Columbia, notes Michael Starr, in his thoroughly splendid *Peter Sellers: A Film History*, that they promised he'd never work for them again. This was, Starr persuasively suggests, Sellers' lost decade, in which the actor's reputation hit rock bottom. He played a matador painted blue in the bewildering *The Bobo* (1967), and such had his value diminished that even the mostly-funny *The Party* (1968), which reunited Sellers with Blake Edwards, couldn't help, and it was released to little immediate interest.

Bizarre misfires and uncommercial oddities abounded in this uncertain era of the star's career, and the laughs were sometimes few and far between; sometimes, you couldn't quite figure out whether a Sellers vehicle was intended as a comedy or not. Take, for example, the star's almost eerily solemn turn as the odd *Hoffman* (1970), a bewildering role choice that sees the titular frustrated, misogynistic office executive blackmailing an attractive young female secretary into moving in with him for a week. Sellers is astonishing in the role, in an eerie film which – some argue – mirrors episodes in his own life. Whatever the case, it wasn't box office gold. Sellers, Starr notes, pleaded for the completed film to be destroyed. Perhaps it may have mattered more if anybody had wanted to come to see it; but they hadn't anyway.

Flops, poor choices, and acting like a prima donna had left Sellers beached on a cinematic sandbank and in sore need of a hit. But occasionally, Sellers could still behave himself. And so keen was Sellers to get to work on his most solemn screen role of all, *The Blockhouse*, a film he believed would surely prove his worth as a serious thespian, it would seem that he even forgot to be difficult – despite the fact he was working on a small-scale picture for a wet-behind-the-ears first time feature director.

He had, apparently, been aware of the project for some time. 'I first read a script a long time ago, two or three years, and before that the book,' he told the *Daily Telegraph Magazine* in 1972, as shooting began. 'I felt straight away I would like to do it…it'll be a bloody marvellous film if it works.'

Marvellous it is, but also exceptionally miserable, one of the most morose cinematic monuments mulled over in this book. Set in the latter days of World War Two, *The Blockhouse* was based on the true story of a group of prisoners of war entombed by allied bombing in a huge German underground bunker. Trapped with bounteous amounts of food, whisky and wine, but no water, they were compelled to eke out a strange subterranean life for seven years, until help came – by which time only two of their number still remained alive. It actually happened in Russia – but the fictional version took place in Normandy, as you'll read in the bleakly brilliant source novel by Frenchman Jean-Paul Clébert.

The book was a success across Europe and was adapted by John Gould into a screenplay – but it was turned down by various producers. It did eventually find a home with two young filmmakers, Anthony Rufus Isaacs and Clive Rees. Having made their money in films shot for corporate clients – including Esso and Natural Gas – Isaacs and Rees poured their own money into their venture, eventually building a modest but respectable budget of £150,000. The film was austerely shot in what publicity described as 'grimly real surroundings': a genuine underground complex built by the Nazis in Guernsey.

Bravely gambling their capital on this decidedly risky project, and despite their inexperience, they lured a superb international cast to the production, including Jeremy Kemp, Peter Vaughan, Per Oscarsson and Charles Aznavour, alongside the notoriously difficult-to-handle Sellers. 'I was not affected by all the big stars being in my first film,' Rees claimed coolly in press material at the time. 'That meant nothing to me at all. Many people said that trying to handle Sellers was like trying to control a volcano. With us it was nothing like that.'

Looking at the novel you can certainly see the elements that might have appealed to Sellers, and perhaps begin to imagine why he decided, on this occasion, to behave. Years after *Topaze*, here was a still-meeker schoolmaster character, the bookish Rouquet, for him to create: surely this was the ideal opportunity for him both to reassert his reputation as a serious actor, by building a complex, characterisation just the way he liked to do it – from the inside out.

In the book, interior monologues slowly and subtly establish, then differentiate, the characters of a small band of extremely unexceptional and average 'little men' – the kind of men, like Topaze, or Kite, that

Solemn Sellers: the great man behaving himself on location for *The Blockhouse* (1973).

Sellers loved to portray: he surely delighted in the construction of delicately nuanced depictions of minor men. And this fascination extended until the very end of his career: contrast the melancholy Nayland Smith of *The Fiendish Plot of Dr Fu Manchu* (1980) with his hammy and ridiculous Fu. Fu may be (supposedly) funnier; his Nayland Smith is certainly more fascinating.

Might we conjecture then that he found significant artistic contentment in carefully conveying the multitudinous minutiae of what you might call mundanity: ordinary men thrown into a position of drama, right through from meek army man Tully of *The Mouse that Roared* (1959) via the Welsh librarian of *Only Two Can Play* (1962), onwards down the line to Chance in *Being There* (1979).

We know, certainly, that Sellers loved to build his character from within, in the way he had with Fred Kite, attesting that until he fully 'knew' the man from the inside out, he couldn't play the role. With *The Blockhouse*, amidst a similarly powerful cast of his international peers, Sellers had the opportunity of a lifetime. Here he would attempt to give external expression to the internal monologue of the most closely confined and least theatrically 'made up' character he would ever play – without any opportunity for flamboyant behaviour, or fancy dialogue. And, although not every critic could resist looking for Clouseau somewhere in there, he succeeded. More than that; he's masterly. Bloody marvellous, in fact.

Sellers' bearded schoolmaster reads, writes on the walls, and comes up with things to do to try and maintain his mental faculties in the underground prison that is *The Blockhouse.* He and his fellow prisoners slowly unravel, in their bleak underground tomb, and amidst homosexual fumblings by a couple of the other inmates, they must attempt to cope with power struggles, isolation, creeping madness, and death, seen only by candlelight. In fact, much of what he does – and what the other players do – is indistinct. A muffled soundtrack adds an air of oppressive claustrophobia to the proceedings; eventually, narrative seems to stop altogether; all that is left are the last two men alive, lying about, exhausted, mole-like, with their wine bottles, stumps of candle, and last few precious matches. Not much happens. For all of these reasons, *The Blockhouse* may not be an easy film to enjoy, and still harder to like. But also for all of these reasons you might well find it fascinating.

As you might already have surmised, the completed film was not, alas, heralded as 'bloody marvellous'. Furthermore, before it could even be released, Rees fell out with his production company, Hemdale, who complained about it running over budget, and, thoroughly dismayed by its glumness, insisted on removing a caption card at the end – uncharitably described by Hemdale director Donald Langdon as 'a gimmick' – that would have revealed the death of the last two remaining protagonists shortly after they were released. Rees raged at the removal, saying that it cancelled out 'a tragic irony in this denouement'.

Even after fiddling with the ending, Hemdale weren't much disposed to distribute. Aside from a screening at the Berlin Festival in 1973, it sat on the shelf. Attempts were made to reinvigorate interest in the film by Isaacs, in an article in the *Evening News* (accompanied by a somewhat Bergman-esque shot of a bewhiskered Sellers sitting in character at a chessboard) after Sellers' death, and, tellingly, after *Being There* had convinced the public to accept Sellers as something other than Clouseau.

'The picture never found favour with distributors because of its traumatic setting of a Nazi slave labour camp,' claimed the paper, bringing to mind another serious film featuring a would-be serious actor only really ever accepted as a comedian, the great Jerry Lewis, and his still unreleased holocaust drama *The Day the Clown Cried* (1972). But unlike Lewis, Isaacs, by now a Lord, was keen that people should see his film. 'It was one of the few films which Sellers made which he actually believed in,' he argued. 'It's a very serious film and one of the best things he ever did...his Macbeth if you like.' He hoped the film would become 'a posthumous cult success'. It never did. But it eventually made its way on to DVD, emerging as part of an odd-bedfellows DVD box set, which bewilderingly packaged it alongside the early British Sellers service comedy *Orders are Orders* (1954) and the hypnotically awful US medical comedy flopperoo *Where Does It Hurt?* (1972). Undignified company for *The Blockhouse*; but worse than that is that it made its DVD debut in a cropped, grimy-looking, muffled sounding form, which really didn't do it justice at all.

The aforementioned Michael Starr doesn't like *The Blockhouse*. Rees' direction is 'stultifying', and the cast are 'terribly wasted', he declares. He argues a persuasive case, and debate is the stuff of film criticism assuredly, but maybe stultification and waste were what they were after. Besides, unremittingly bleak though Rees' film is – eerily ending with the flickering out of the last candle – compared to the source novel, it's remarkably chipper. The last few chapters therein are played out in absolute darkness, when, after some drunkenness, the matches for the candles get lost.

Glum stuff, certainly, the film was too much for distributors to swallow, and after a preview in Berlin in June 1973, it barely saw release. It finally picked up a review in *Monthly Film Bulletin* in 1977, where critic Richard Combs seemed thoroughly unimpressed by it all, accusing Sellers (by this time wholly re-entwined with his *Pink Panther* cash-cows) of 'emerging from the shadows to play Inspector Clouseau', then putting the boot in further, bemoaning the lack of clear character delineation, the film's 'minimal dramatic means' and how it 'piously refuses to detach itself from their experience, and to offer any kind of reflection on the situation which would enable the viewer to apprehend it as anything other than an uncomfortable way to spend an hour and a half'. He may well be right about that last bit; but that was precisely the idea, wasn't it? Escapism, this – patently – was not.

Populated with micro-characters, this is a micro-drama uncomfortably unflinching in its inward-looking aspect; made striking by its claustrophobic zooming in on the disintegration of a set of extremely unexceptional characters; made special precisely by the fact that these characters are resolutely *not* special. This indistinct group of disparate souls could have been anybody at all; a shadowy selection of people as dim, dark and indistinct as the gloomy confines of the blockhouse they are trapped in.

After brief, brightly lit moments set outdoors at the very beginning, the unrelenting focus of the film quickly becomes the disintegration of the men and the day to day reality of their decline, rather than the men they were on the outside. And Sellers, here, as he would do again with Chance in *Being There*, was given the golden opportunity to mould characterisation out of nothingness. Sellers, so keen always to get everything right about his character, down to the tiniest detail, here perhaps faced his greatest challenge. Operating within the cramped confines of a concrete doll's house, unable to make a grand gesture, even if he wanted to, barely even able to move, he faces the challenge of performance on a tiny scale, the challenge of an entire absence of thespian gimmickry. All we as viewers have here to go on are those tiny character details, at which he excels, but owing to this setting even they are sometimes blunted, sometimes muddy, sometimes indistinct. Sellers sadly fiddling for a moment with a pair of grubby glasses; a momentarily intense, melancholy stare across a grimy chessboard; these were the kind of microcosmic acting tools he had to work with. It was, in fact, the supreme test for the master. And so, at the very least for that reason, if no other, he behaved himself. *VP*

MUSIC AND MOVEMENT

If anybody tries to tell you that British pop music only began with the Beatles, don't believe them – there were great things going on in Blighty, yeah, yeah, yeah, well before the four cheeky mop-tops took the world by storm – albeit on a smaller scale, and in the swaggering shadow of Presley and company across the Atlantic. Just as Elvis was showing everybody how rock 'n' roll was done, to the delight of that new breed of kid with cash, the teenager, here in England in the late 1950s we had our own homegrown rock and roll heroes.

Early examples included the impressively trousered Tommy Steele, swinging his momentous grey flannels impressively as he invited us to *Rock with the Caveman*, and tormented Terry Dene, another talented popster, who alas couldn't handle the heat when he got called up for National Service. There was soon an impressive army of domestic sneer-lipped heartthrobs, including gauntly groovy Billy Fury, *Expresso Bongo* breakthrough artiste Cliff Richard and big-quiffed Marty 'Bad Boy' Wilde, father of Kim.

Boys were supposed to want to emulate these hit-parade heroes; girls were supposed to fall for them. The middle-aged money men behind the scenes (they're always there somewhere, aren't they?) desperately hoped the kids would splash all their disposable cash on their waxings. And they

‹ **Hip to be square:** Aussie pop yodel-meister Frank Ifield tries and fails to relax, flanked by Annette Andre and Suzy Kendall, on the cover of the soundtrack LP *Up Jumped a Swagman* (1965).

did. The advent of more personal, almost introverted singer–songwriter material–another significant strand of the rock-music revolution, ushered in by the brilliant recordings of short-lived bespectacled hiccup-popster Buddy Holly, softened the soundscape somewhat - and what we may classify as his 'fop rock' found particular popularity with nerdy bespectacled types on this side of the Atlantic.

By the end of the decade, future movie score maestro John Barry was teaming up rough-edged but soon-to-be-fop-rocker Adam Faith, mixing up raw rock 'n' roll recordings like *Runk Bunk* with acting, in the aforementioned *Never Let Go* (1960) and, as a star, the hep classic *Beat Girl* (1960), were younger chaps hoping to carve themselves out a slice of an increasingly lucrative pop-pie. As the sixties began, marvellous but unhinged genius pop producer Joe Meek was propelling his protégés The Tornados to number one in the US charts with the incredible space-age instrumental sounds of *Telstar*. What's more, he was recording the records in his own flat, creating interstellar sounds in a tiny toilet, and banging dustbins on the staircase, above a leather shop in the Holloway Road. He would then flog the masters himself to the big labels. He was some dashed young jackanapes from the sticks who hadn't even gone to a good school. It was quite, quite unheard of, and not the done thing at all.

Film producers–mostly those old chaps we mentioned, sporting nice blazers, with shiny gold buttons–overcame their reservations and had rushed to clamber aboard this new teenage bandwagon, cranking out features designed to grab the shillings of the new generation of British pop music fans. Early effort *Rock You Sinners* (1958) mixed Brit rock with skiffle, the folk-based do-it-yourself coffee bar music made popular by Lonnie Donegan; by 1962, Billy Fury, velvet-voiced charismatic rock and roller of the first rank, was shyly showing the kids how to twist in Michael Winner's first feature film *Play it Cool*. The thing was, though, no matter how hard we twisted, sometimes those stiff upper lips we mentioned earlier on were still in evidence – somehow, when it came to rock and roll, we just weren't quite as effortlessly hep, or as free with our hip swinging, as those American originators. We found it hard to let ourselves go below the waist. A certain reserve had to be maintained.

Britain-based American Dick Lester shook things up somewhat when he shot pop musical *It's Trad, Dad* (1962) (and skiffle-king Lonnie wasn't in that one) and then, more famously, he made the Beatles' first feature *A Hard Day's Night* (1964). This came across something like a super-stylish hybrid of American ad campaign, pop musical, and very-visual Goon show (Dick had learnt his already superlative style chops shooting the Sellers/ Milligan TV comedy show *A Show Called Fred* (02/05 - 30/05/1956)). The coming of the Beatles – and the concept of a more bespoke pop film carefully built around them, celebrating them, rather than jerrybuilt just to cash in on them – signalled a shift in how 'pop personalities' would be positioned, packaged and sold in the years to come.

Of course, by the end of the decade, the new pop royalty, beginning to realise and get a hold on their own commercial importance, were more closely controlling how they were being represented on screen (Jagger was, for example, achingly cool in *Performance* (1970), and the Stones had never looked more raggedly elegant than in *Rock and Roll Circus* (1968)). But there were still those smaller players behind the curve, still being exploited by management, perhaps, or maybe just unable to adapt to the latest fads and fashions – like Frank Ifield, country-singin' super-square cut adrift in his own movie somewhere deep inside the oddly experimental *Up Jumped a Swagman* (1965), or early sixties silly-pop throwbacks Freddie and the Dreamers doing their best in the bewildering music and scout-movement misfire *The Cuckoo Patrol* (1967).

Despite efforts to keep pop music in the nursery, it had come to be perceived latterly as a counter-cultural force–almost adult; maybe art, even. By the end of the sixties, thanks to the pathways forged by Beatles, Bob Dylan, and other cerebrally creative forces within the music business, pop had become self-aware, self-reflexive, and–it must also be said–cynical. For filmmaker Peter Watkins, mentioned in a previous chapter, the pop star had become a prisoner of his own success, locked in a cage while the girls scream at him, perhaps the most spectacularly effective visual to be seen in his thoroughly splendid *Privilege* (1967).

By the dawning of the next decade, rock and roll was already looking back on itself with the jaded eye of experience and nostalgia in films like *That'll Be the Day* (1973), which focused on the early rise of the British rock n roll idol, and *Permissive* (1970), which dealt with the darker later days of the groupie culture.

It was all very knowing, but something clearly hadn't quite gone to plan. As the kids queued up to buy their tartan Bay City Rollers flares, and Little Jimmy Osmond sang about that *Long Haired Lover From Liverpool* there was definitely the sense that the big Technicolor takeover of straight society that Paul McCartney and the others had seemed to be pushing towards though the pot-smoke clouds had not come to pass. More ground-roots agitation was required.

With the coming of punk, Derek Jarman shook things up with *Jubilee* (1978), and the Sex Pistols were belatedly seen in cinemas in *The Great Rock and Roll Swindle* (1980). For the first time too, there were substantial and much-needed black and female perspectives sliding into the frame in part by way of the Super 8 camera, a DIY tool that allowed Don Letts' to make *The Punk Rock Movie* (1978), shooting all the great bands of the day, and, later, Jill Westwood's *The Wound* (1984), an extreme art film constructed when Westwood wasn't undertaking actions with Diana Rogerson in industrial music and performance outfit Fist Fuck. Film and independent video releases, such as *The Greatest Hits of Scratch Video* (1984), were embraced by the post-punk art and music scenes; but just as a glimpse of stocking was once something shocking, so the establishment gradually adopted, in watered down fashion, the garb of the outrageous and the counter-culture struggled to retain its aboveground coherence.

Fast forward to now. Music, style and technology is increasingly controlled, and capitalised upon–by the big corporations, of course, not by the artists. Money for music? That's a laugh. People pay now for the tech, not the tracks–they can steal those. Whatever became of the counter-culture, the over-the-counter-culture, it seems, has never failed; even through the eras of rave and the free party scene.

In this section, we zoom in on musical misfires from the heyday of the counter-culture, examine the latter-day exploits of one of the key cultural figures of that time, and explore the oft-peculiar and increasingly self-reflexive aspects of pop music and film as the 1970s beckoned. The peculiarly exposing kind of self-reflection that marked the era is not always looked back upon with fondness by those who participated in it; yet, awkwardly perhaps, the cultural artefacts of those times remain, outside the contexts that created them, for us to gawp at and draw conclusions from now.

Such of-their-time works may lack the proud gloss of polished consideration; but the roughly ephemeral edges can also be rather more revealing than well-turned works of later years. Indeed, the great Ray Davies asked us, with a slightly sour and suspicious air, when he came to a screening of *Star Maker* (1974) at BFI Southbank: 'Why are you showing *Star Maker* and not *Return to Waterloo*?' I'm sure he knew very well why. But here we attempt to answer.

But before all that: what to do, if you're a pre–Beatle UK pop heartthrob in a post–Beatle world, with a contract to shoot a feature? Frank Ifield was that man. Let's join him now, then, or never, starring in the post-modern pop musical time forgot…

Up Jumped a Swagman

UK Film | 1965 | colour | 88mins
Director Christopher Miles
Script Lewis Greifer
Producer Andrew Mitchell
Production Company Ivy Productions
Cast Frank Ifield, Annette Andre, Ronald Radd, Suzy Kendall

We are watching a film from the 'Swinging Sixties'. A young pop singer arrives for an audition at a gaudily-lit studio, filled with unwieldy sales-prediction computers and flashing lights. While he strums his guitar, he is measured up to see whether he will make it as a pop star – from his height and weight to the gradient of his cheekbones. A young girl – wearing a wired helmet, sitting in a chair marked 'TEENAGER' – is monitored to determine his appeal (she screams at the end of his number). His songs are deemed sufficiently puerile by an aged record company representative, and two pipe-smoking lackeys. He is considered to have star potential, providing he finds a 'new sound'. Self-referential and cynical in its take on the booming pop music industry, this could *almost* be a forgotten scene from a Richard Lester Fab Four movie, or even an outtake from Bob Rafelson's deconstruction of the Pre-Fab Four, The Monkees, *Head* (1968). But it isn't.

Socks and sandals: Frank goes fishing while his girlfriend tries to figure out how to convince him to buy some new threads, on this 1960s album sleeve.

It's from *Up Jumped a Swagman*, the ahead-of-its-time post-modern pop musical it will never be cool to like.

You can see why. One reason for its obscurity is that it features one of those unfortunate 1960s pop-stars who – regardless of the talent they may have possessed–will never get a revival. In this case it is the smooth-voiced, but forever-square Australian singer Frank Ifield, who had the misfortune of having his career as a pop-balladeer coincide with the onset of Beatlemania. Suddenly all the rules about being a pop-star were rewritten. Sex had reared its sweaty head. A neat haircut and a nice voice were no longer enough. Still worse for Frank was that his big hit – *Lovesick Blues*, and particularly its flipside, *She Taught Me How to Yodel*, revealed a particular propensity for alpine-style vocal theatrics. Not exactly cool. What's more, he was from Down Under, and so he also effortlessly churned out a stream of chirpy Aussie numbers, like *Waltzing Matilda*. Thus, despite a definite versatility, he was viewed with suspicion by hipper music fans, and was wrongly doomed by this record to sit in the 'novelty' section as a result. His image was wrong, too, especially post-Beatles and Stones. He was all fawn trousers, drip-dry nylon shirts, and looked just a bit otherworldly. His chiselled good looks, seemingly frozen in a half grin, his eyes hidden under their lids, with an unmoving neat-and-tidy blond short-back-and-sides at the top, harked back to the good looks of Adam Faith (who'd sung pretty, polished, pseudo-Buddy Holly pop after his early rock 'n' roll years, also beginning to flounder in the pop charts by the mid-sixties) and would surely have held more appeal to the teenage girls of Faith's more innocent 1961-62 heyday. But while Adam sometimes struggled to hit the high notes, Frank was actually a very decent singer, especially good at sad country ballads. Frank's voice expressed something that his face could not – and the production on his records – by the underrated Norrie Paramor–was always tip-top. But a Beatle or a Stone he could never be.

Frank was surely at the mercy of his management, and I imagine Frank may have signed up for this film at the height of his popularity long before it got made. By the time it was in the cinemas, in January 1966, though, *Day Tripper* was topping the charts and Frank, and his 'Waltzing Matilda', must already have seemed like dusty exhibits from the museum of pop-culture. Frank would only have one lower-regions chart hit in 1966. The world had changed. This gives the central narrative idea at the heart of *Swagman* – an aspiring pop singer in search of a 'new sound' – a strange poignancy. Though he plays the newcomer, Frank's pop career was, in effect, all over. The irony must surely have been apparent. To him, and to the filmmakers.

It was directed by Christopher Miles. His previous pop film *Rhythm and Greens* (1964) was a short but ambitious-sounding musical drama that had attempted to tell the story of mankind through the instrumental group, The Shadows. *Up Jumped a Swagman*, written by Lewis Greifer, is similarly ambitious, and has many clever touches; but the script seems ultimately dismissive of the star at its centre. Which makes the film a fascinating, confusing and ultimately paradoxical artefact. The flashy, knowing cine-literate touches that litter the script and fancy up the frame cannot entirely camouflage flat humour, half-baked ideas, and an undoubtedly slapdash story, possibly knocked up on the back of a fag packet.

A singer arrives from Australia, looking for a big break, auditions and is told to find a 'new sound'. He goes and moves in to a flat, and fantasises about a society girl he spots on a poster, Melissa Smythe-Fury (Suzy Kendall). Meanwhile, he meets a girl who works for the record company, Patsy (Annette Andre). Gorgeous though Patsy is, Melissa is the girl of Frank's dreams. Frank spends a lot of time sitting in his flat, singing his entertaining but vaguely anachronistic songs at inopportune moments, or wandering the streets of London with Patsy. They wander about at a market – presumably reflecting the down-to-earth quality of their relationship. And that's about it for most of the film. Meanwhile, there's a tedious sub-plot about a jewellery shop robbery, lamely spoofing *Rififi* (1955), with one of this tiresome assembly of burglars even commenting 'we could learn a lot from those European films.' Yes, perhaps they could. But does the scriptwriter need to point that out instead of improving his own script? The gang burrow through the floor of Frank's flat into the shop below, while he's out and about (singing a song, most probably). Frank, meanwhile, ends up at a society party, where he finally meets the elusive Melissa – whom he dances with all evening, though her dreary-deb dialogue is perhaps supposed to mark her as boring and less suitable than perky, earthy Patsy (who is seen seething in the background). After the party, Patsy (rightly) bawls out Frank, but this plot – and the jewel heist – is abruptly dispensed with for a bewildering finale, with Frank – for no reason at all – suddenly chased around the streets by a villain in dark glasses with an automatic pistol. Poor Frank even gets shot in the shoulder (for the rest of the film, his clean-cut image is rather damaged by the fact that he has to sing his sad songs with due decorum in a blood-spattered shirt). Stranger still, the film climaxes with a bizarre scene with Frank returning to the record company offices, but this time he's 'on trial' – with the rest of the cast sitting as jury to decide whether or not he's 'guilty'. Of what, exactly, is not entirely clear. But the next scene sees Frank in prison, though the door is not locked, for he goes out for a walk with Patsy, when she arrives suddenly. Then they're back in the market. Frank – looking relieved to escape from all that stream-

Clunk click, every trip: Frank borrows one of Elvis' stage outfits for the sleeve of this 1970s small-label waxing.

of-consciousness stuff – sings *Waltzin' Matilda* – thankfully now wearing a clean shirt – and the credits roll.

Trapped in a post-modern screenwriting exercise, Frank is jarringly incongruous throughout with his pleasant but out-of-date songs. No quarter is given him: no attempt is made to fuse song and image creatively. For example: the surprisingly catchy and upbeat *Cry Wolf* – surely a cue for some dancing – merely provides the soundtrack for Frank, casually clad in fawn slacks as usual, walking around his flat, looking at some dusty old pictures on the wall, while he blankly mouths the words. The camera jerks a bit every now and then, but life is not infused in the action. It is clear that Frank is no actor, but he can sing a bit; yet it seems that the production team are playing against their star's strengths and there is the sense that somebody upstairs is trying to sabotage Frank's songs. These are continually interrupted before the end, or their performance juxtaposed with Frank undergoing some kind of torment. As Frank attempts to sing another trad fave, *Botany Bay*, he is perilously hoisted high in the air on a crane by some mischievous workmen, while Patsy screams with laughter. Frank gamely attempts to invest the performance with feeling while he is pulled ever higher. If this isn't indignity enough, he is – for no reason at all – hosed with water before he can finish singing his song. Another track is visually sabotaged by concluding with a close up of Frank's socks – something for the ladies? – as he rubs his feet together before going to sleep fully dressed on a Saturday afternoon (we didn't know why, either). Frank suffers in this film. There is a sense that nobody likes him, on screen, or off; and almost that he – and all other pop-stars, come to that – don't deserve to star in films. On the occasions that Frank is allowed to get through a song, and he's allowed some dancers to spruce it up a little, they seem to come from some distant, bygone age of light entertainment – for one bargain basement number, a small troupe of men and women in natty ballroom-dancing style blue outfits high kick and twirl bowler hats politely whilst emerging from behind poor Frank's sofa to naughtily fiddle with his cushions (the only props to hand); while a later routine – as Frank, against the odds, sings about how he wants a woman for lovin', not for cookin', sees a troupe of dancers dressed in pseudo-Edwardian servant outfits prancing jauntily around a kitchen. It's all at least ten years out of date; post Rolling Stones, it must have seemed utterly absurd, and today makes for grimly compelling viewing.

We never get much of a sense what Frank's thinking – painted into the corner of his own film, forced to perform ludicrous tricks by the knowing production team, he spouts the banal non-sequitur dialogue he's been given (he's not alone in this). He does his best to give his songs some dignity, but the odds are stacked against him. The Frank of the film – jumping train fares, avoiding a 'proper job' – is depicted as shallow, cynical, and self-seeking. I have no doubt that the real Mr Ifield – who somehow, through it all, still seems like a nice chap – was hard-working and amiable by contrast.

'Thin and forced,' the *Monthly Film Bulletin* concluded, and they may have been right this time, but they neglected to mention that the film has a kind of dreadful beauty that makes it an irresistible watch. It combines old and new so awkwardly, so unexpectedly; and in so British a manner. Unrivalled in its empty, cynical exploitation of a pop star on the way out of the charts, it nonetheless constitutes one of the missing links between the playfully post-modern *A Hard Day's Night* and the destructively post-modern *Head*. With the strange trial scene at the end, there's also a touch of *The Prisoner* about it; indeed, its scriptwriter even went on to write an episode of that cult series – before he began a rather lengthier tenure on the soap opera *Crossroads*. Go figure. Fascinating but ghastly, it's hard to imagine that *Up Jumped a Swagman* did its star any good at all. And Frank, uncool as he might have become, still had much to offer. *VP*

But, as the sixties continued to splinter, what if the pop singer himself got behind the camera, and was let loose with a big-studio budget?

Can Heironymus Merkin Ever Forget Mercy Humppe and Find True Happiness?

UK | 1969 | colour | 107mins
Director Anthony Newley
Script Herman Raucher, Anthony Newley
Producer Anthony Newley
Production Company Universal Pictures
Cast Anthony Newley, Joan Collins, Milton Berle, Connie Kreski, Bruce Forsyth

It was the late 1960s. The sharp-suited executives at the Hollywood studios had a bit of a problem: they couldn't figure out what kind of films the younger generation wanted to see any more. Heck, they couldn't even figure out who was a boy, and who was a girl anymore, and over in London that guy in the Beatles was sitting on the floor playing a sitar. It was scary. They didn't much like it, but they were learning lessons from films like *Easy Rider* (1969), a grimy little movie about long-haired bums riding motorcycles. That didn't seem to have much of a plot, and they didn't understand it, but it was an unexpected hit, and they understood that it brought the money in. Confused, bewildered studio execs rushed to light up the joss sticks, grow their sideburns a little longer, and get with it, splashing out company money on a rum selection of weird, unusual film projects that would surely have seemed like commercial suicide in the good old days. Gambling uneasily on often untried talent, they crossed their fingers tightly as they awaited the end results and hoped that 'the kids' would dig it.

It seemed like a plan. For a while, until the figures came in and the accountants re-imposed order in tinseltown, a vividly-hued array of studio-backed cinematic oddities emerged in this uncertain era. Trying to cover all the generational bases, some of them even had all-star casts, awkwardly shoe-horning in members of the Hollywood old guard – e.g. ancient Groucho Marx in Otto Preminger's drug-addled *Skidoo* (1968) – alongside the psychedelic set. Odd film titles became de rigeur, tight narratives less so. Self-indulgence was almost compulsory. Suddenly, out popped song and dance man Anthony Newley's incredible *Can Heironymus Merkin Ever Forget Mercy Humppe and Find True Happiness?*, perhaps the most self-destructively self-indulgent film of all time, by turns eye-poppingly awful, eerily creepy, and dizzily wonderful. Unguardedly semi-autobiographical to an acutely painful degree, it was an incredible warts-n-all monument to Newley himself, simultaneously self aggrandising, self-loathing, and bewilderingly pseudo-psychedelic.

But let us pause for a moment to consider Anthony Newley himself – the man at the centre of this ornate folly Heironymus as he's not as familiar as once he was. You'd know him if you saw him, or heard his voice. Prominent of jaw, beetle browed, wire haired, knavishly good looking, he was a prolific singer, songwriter and actor. Yet even in his 1950s-1960s heyday Hackney-born Newley divided opinion. Prodigiously gifted, he was no shrinking violet; and too self-aware of his undoubted talents to ever really be loved by the public. Besides which, forever in search of new challenges, he veered on and off the mainstream like a man possessed. For every popular success that filled the coffers like the Bond theme *Goldfinger* (co-written with his friend and musical collaborator Leslie Bricusse) there would be an unwieldy experiment like *The Strange World of Gurney Slade* (1960) (a fascinating but understandably unpopular show-within-a-show about a performer trapped within a sitcom on trial for not being funny).

Understandably unpopular: cerebral comedy with Anthony Newley in *The Strange World of Gurney Slade* (1960). ›

His career upped and downed over the decades, from the dizzy 1960s heights of both writing and starring in the Broadway hit show *Stop the World…I Want To Get Off* (written with Bricusse), to 1980s lows like a minor part as a used car salesman in *EastEnders*. His acting was carefully studied, sometimes even underplayed; his singing quite the opposite. Many listeners of a melodramatic bent feel an affinity towards its overblown theatricality, and the 'tears of a clown' inner turmoil it surely hid. His singing style, an often impersonated highly distinctive nasal trill, with just a twinge of Norman Wisdom, transmuted over the years, and divides opinion. You'll love it or hate it. He graduated from early rock n roll, through pre-Beatles 'poor me' pop, to novelty numbers, into stagey show tunes, many self-penned. Always giving it his all, he acted out each song in a strange, mannered, overblown-cockney-in-Las Vegas style that was uniquely his. Big to begin with, it got bigger still, mutating slowly over the years into a strange grotesque parody of itself.

One of his biggest numbers was his own *What Kind of Fool Am I?* This became something of a theme song for Tony. 'What kind of fool am I, who never fell in love?'

He begins. 'It seems that I'm the only one I have been thinking of.' It turns into the ultimate tears-of-a-clown I'm a bad-boy, but I just want true love kind of number.

Take a look on YouTube, and you'll see how it looked. If you don't have YouTube handy, imagine it. Visualise it sung big, really big, with Newley living it – breathing it – gesticulating portentously – almost melting into his velveteen dinner jacket. Then multiply by ten. That's how Tony sang it.

And Tony's lonely clown torment was for real, albeit self-imposed. Tony truly had troubles with women. His main trouble was that one woman was never enough. Take a look at Garth Bardsley's splendid biography of the great man for details. For example: even after his marriage to actress Ann Lynn in 1954, Newley was compulsively playing the field; dashing between Ann, a designer called Gina, and a weather girl called Beverley. Just an average day for Tony. Anneke Wills, who appeared with Tony in *Gurney Slade*, eventually ousted Ann, but even gorgeous Anneke soon had to share him with actress Linda Christian, and, subsequently, a new-on-the-scene Joan Collins. And so it went on. His appetite was voracious, but seemingly one that could never be sated. One gets the sense that Newley's love-life was a conveyor belt of sexual encounter, in which Tony just couldn't – or wouldn't – as his song went, 'fall in love like any other man'. Certainly he seemed rather detached about it all. As Bardsley's biog revealingly notes, when Wills was finally thrown out to be replaced with Collins, there were no tearful farewells; as he bundled her into a taxi there was just a clipped 'No raging, Wills. No shouting.'

All of this must have been somewhat exhausting. By the time of his slow 1970s decline in the casinos of Sin City, Joan was gone, as were the glory days, but Tony was still up to his old tricks, sporting ever-more stiffly-synthetic ruffled shirts and alarming bow ties, as he performed the old numbers, pulling awful gargoyle faces, striking puppet-like poses, twitching his gangly actor's wrists portentously as he sang.

But back in '69, the time of *Merkin*, Tony was on the crest of a wave. Nobody in America had ever heard of *Gurney Slade*, luckily, and after the stage success, it looked like he was on track to crack Hollywood. He had a big part in the expensive musical extravaganza *Doctor Dolittle* (1967), alongside Rex Harrison, and starred in the melancholy comedy romance *Sweet November* (1968) (both were to be flops). Newley looked respectable enough. Sharply dressed, business savvy, safely into his mid-thirties, he smacked of an earlier generation of smart-suited entertainers. He was friends with Sammy Davis Jr. and Burt Bacharach: he must have looked like someone you could trust to bring in a good return on your initial investment. Jay Kantor of Universal thought so, at least: he handed over a cheque for $1,000,000,000, with carte blanche to make any film Tony wanted to make. The result: *Heironymus Merkin*. Oh dear.

'Everything appeared to be as good as it gets,' Bricusse wrote later of this high-earning period of Newley's life, 'but it wasn't.' Newley was well-off, a respected artiste, a father of two kids, married to the beautiful Joan Collins. On the outside, everything seemed hunky-dory; but it wasn't. Newley was haunted by memories of his troubled relationship with Ann Lynn, and despite his current dream-marriage, continued to exercise his overreaching libido with an ever-lengthening string of bright young things. And, what's more, he felt guilty about it. But instead of therapy, he decided to use his new film project to exorcise his demons on screen. In his musical *Stop the World*, Newley had already drawn upon himself for the central

Pulling the strings: Milton Berle sports an X-rated pair of bermuda shorts in *Can Heironymus Merkin Ever Forget Mercy Humppe and Find True Happiness?* (1969).

character, Littlechap the clown – who dallies with various women before finally realising his wife was the one all along. Why not go even further in *Merkin*? Bricusse thought it was a bad idea, and told him so. 'I would have enjoyed writing the songs, but I didn't like the implication of what the film was going to do.' So Newley hired Herman Raucher instead, the writer of *Sweet November*.

Raucher, glad of the gig, soon became aware of the frantic pace and confusion of Newley's life. 'Tony was totally fragmented,' he recalled later; 'like an exploding rocket he would go off in a million different directions.' Arriving in the LA office ahead of his collaborator, he discovered that he was required to turn aside from the typewriter to handle tricky phone calls from Newley's various women; Barbra Streisand, for example, with whom Tony was involved at the time. Incidentally Streisand, who was then married to Elliott Gould, referred to herself as 'Mrs Gould' when she phoned to set up dates with Tony. Newley finally finished off the script in the Park Lane Playboy building, occupying a suite of rooms that doubled both as office space and bedroom, while a procession of eager young actresses passed in and out, all keen to inspire the director. Without Bricusse's careful guiding hand, Tony went ahead and shot everything he wrote. And not much ended up on the cutting room floor.

Take a look at the film if you can find it. Its sprawling allegorical narrative centres around the mid-life crisis of the great Merkin, a multi-talented singer, songwriter and actor (remind you of anybody?), who, on the occasion of his 40th birthday, assembles the evidence of his life's work on a beach prior to sending it away to a special research institute where it will be preserved forever.

While his mother and his two children look on, Merkin/Newley – aware that time is growing short – tells the story of his life so far. He does this through a luridly-coloured multitude of dreamlike reminiscences, digressions and bizarre fantasies, some of which happen around him, and some of which he shows from 35mm on a screen he's had set up on the beach. It's one of those film-within-a-film films, and so it appears that the film we are watching is being shot, edited, rewritten – and critically panned – before our very eyes. Tony, various studio executives, writers, producers and film critics comment from within the narrative on the very film we're watching, disconcertingly enough, as Newley explores a weird amalgam of fantasy and strange autobiography, all punctuated with strange and often wonderful songs. And, unnervingly, it's all there, barely concealed – Newley's youth, marriages, affairs, hopes, fears, desires, everything. Stuff you'd expect him to keep hidden.

We meet various strange characters who comment upon or participate in the stream-of-consciousness action, which is frequently interrupted by

Merkin, stopping and starting the projector. Everything, like showman Newley, is gaudy, colourful, vivid, stagey, but beautifully designed. Early on we meet Merkin's Uncle Limelight (the splendid Bruce Forsyth), who seems to have a theatre stage set up on the beach. He's an old-school vaudevillian who sings a cynical song of showbiz, *On The Boards*, while youngster Merkin – in whiteface, on puppet strings, like a gawky marionette, watches the bold trouper agog. As Merkin matures, we see him grow increasingly confident, his libido is unleashed, and it is not long before his frenzied female fans are screaming and shouting for him. As it was for Newley. Indeed, in a potent and pertinent bit of imagery, a queue of young girls (and boys) is seen stretching across the beach, waiting to have their way with the young star, while he indulges himself, like Hugh Hefner's understudy, upon a big brass bed. As the kaleidoscope continues to turn, we witness flings, flirtations, and dalliances; a failed marriage to a girl who gets pregnant (echoing Newley's marriage to Ann Lynn), and Merkin's meeting with a beautiful young actress, Polyester Poontang. Mirroring Newley's life, this is all rather close to the bone. What gives it an added dimension of creepy melancholy, is that Polyester is played by his real-life wife, Joan Collins; Merkin's children are played by Newley's children. With his family as cast, Newley's acting out of his extra-marital urges – a dominant theme of the film – and his screen family's reactions to them – is disturbing to say the least. And he makes no bones about it. 'Some of you may have noticed a tendency on Daddy's part not to give a fig for other people's feelings,' Merkin bluntly admits to his children at one point. 'This is to get worse as Daddy gets older.' His children wriggle uncomfortably; so do we. But we keep watching.

Lest we forget that this is one of those pan-generational psychedelic studio pictures, Merkin is watched over by a strange duo of over-the-hill co-stars: devilish Goodtime Eddie Filth (comedian Milton Berle, in a horrific pair of plaid Bermuda shorts) and The Presence (aged cigar-smoking patter man George Jessel). These chaps may have been included for humorous reasons, but we cannot be certain. Flatly coughing out enigmatic sound bites like supper-club Mr Naturals, they themselves seem somewhat unsure as to their roles within the piece. We just hope they had better material when they played the Catskills. Filth leads Merkin always into temptation – encouraging him towards sensual excess – while The Presence, a god-like

Awkward frolics: Merkin (Anthony Newley) ravishes Humppe (Playboy model Connie Kreski) in this eyebrow-raising scene from *Can Heironymus Merkin Ever Forget Mercy Humppe and Find True Happiness?* (1969).

figure in a crumpled white suit – dispenses guru-like wisdom hidden within unfunny wisecracks. At intervals, there are the obligatory drug references: Merkin swallows small tablets that make smoke come out of his ears while sitar music plays.

But there is a darkness at the heart of if all: the tale of titular Mercy Humppe, the young girl with whom Merkin, despite his marriage to Poly, is obsessed, a tale that producers and studio executives – seen intermittently providing advice to Merkin/Newley – urge him not to tell. 'We've found a great way to avoid going into that Mercy Humppe stuff at all,' says one producer. 'They'll crucify you,' warns another. But Merkin ends up revealing a liking for 'young girls' nonetheless. Cue a self-destructively

270 The Bodies Beneath

sinister scene which sees Merkin in rain-mac and dark glasses guiltily emerging from woods to ogle doe-eyed Alice-like nymphet Mercy as she sits on a psychedelic merry-go-round, while Newley's eerie fairground song *Sweet Love Child* plays hauntingly in the background. Merkin sings and awkwardly frolics with the young beauty before he ravishes her in the damp grass. Incidentally, she wasn't actually as young as all that: Humppe was played by 19-year-old *Playboy* model Connie Kreski, and none of the actual reviewers who watched *Merkin* seem to have raised an eyebrow at the time – no crucifixions, it would seem, in swinging 1969 – but the Lolita-like undertones of this scene are somewhat uncomfortable to say the least.

Amidst the awkwardness of editorial control gone AWOL, though, are strewn wonderful songs and glittering set-pieces of splendour. Just one: a bizarre and superbly choreographed sequence set on a giant zodiac chart sees groovy dancers take on the personas of the signs, while Merkin splits in two: the 'real' Merkin, and a wind-up version of himself, dressed identically, but with an eerily blank cloth face. This is the shallow, cruel side of Merkin/Newley. Temporarily growing a vaguely disturbing animated mouth, cloth Merkin chats up Poly, while the actual Merkin hovers behind, cynically commenting on his real agenda. False Merkin attempts to hold her interest with his witty repartee; real Merkin sadly notes 'You realise we have absolutely nothing in common.' Poor Joan, for her part, playing out her marital difficulties in this very public arena, seems to be going along gamely with it all: she sings the song *Chalk and Cheese* about their fatally mismatched romance. And she gives a fine performance. But it's all rather close to the bone; especially as, by the end of the film, Poly/Joan walks out on the negligent *Merkin*/Newley. Merkin seems both to comment on Newley's past, and almost on a preordained future: shortly after the film was unleashed on an unsuspecting public, Joan's departure would, alas, be replayed for real.

'See it!' begged the publicity, 'To hell with the title!' But few did. Bricusse later suggested that *Merkin* marked the point that Newley's career took a wrong turn. 'Gradually, from the early 1970s, I started to worry as I saw Tony following a path that was wrong for him – the money trail – instead of the path that his manifold talents were meant to travel...when his Vegas bubble burst a few years later, he had nowhere to go...Broadway had forgotten about him, as had Hollywood and the film world.' Perhaps the problem was that they hadn't forgotten *Merkin*.

Can Heironymus Merkin Ever Forget Mercy Humppe and Find True Happiness? has, like the assembled bric-a-brac of Merkin's life on the beach, and outside the narrative like Newley himself and his extensive canon, ended up buried beneath the shifting sands of pop culture. However, in a 2006 poll, the *Chicago Tribune*, featuring it in *The Pop Machine* section, which promised *Entertainment With All the Fizz* (whatever that is), decided the film had *The Worst Movie Title Ever*, 'topping a poll of more than 500 *Tribune* readers'. Hard to imagine 500 *Tribune* readers having heard of it: I smell a rat. 'Newley died in 1999,' wrote Mark Caro, the journalist behind the 'poll', 'so we tracked down his co-writer, Raucher, 77, at his Connecticut home to accept this award.' Despite the banality of the premise behind the 'award', Raucher's response, half apologetic, half awed at memories of Tony, was interesting: 'It was Tony's title. I thought he was a little mad. But he was a little mad. Tony was one of the most talented people I'd ever worked with.' Caro's article scooted over any further detail about the film – could it be possible that he'd never seen it? – nor was there any further mention of forgotten Newley, except for Caro's incredulous comment: 'in those days when the studios actually let the creative folk run wild, Universal didn't insist on changing the title.'

I'd hazard a guess that when Newley turned in his finished movie, the long title was the least of Universal's worries. He'd pre-empted all criticism with the all-encompassing sprawl of the very artefact itself. All of the changes they would or wouldn't have suggested were already bundled up somewhere inside his colourful, oft-inspired but desperately unwise libido-crisis mess that nobody went to see in '69. But one thing's for sure: brave Newley's creativity never ran wilder, or more fearlessly, than in *Merkin. VP*

Other pop stars were more disciplined in their artistic efforts behind and before the camera, as the self-reflexive seventies progressed…

Ordinary man: Ray Davies wears his jim-jams high in the late-night experimental drama *Star Maker* (1974).

Star Maker

UK TV | 1974 | colour | 37mins
Director Peter Plummer
Script Ray Davies
Producer Dennis Woolf
Production Company Granada Television
Cast Ray Davies, June Ritchie, The Kinks

Ray Davies, lead singer and songwriter of The Kinks, had done some of his finest work in his 1960s heyday exploring the life of the 'ordinary man'. After his band's first flush of fame in the early 1960s – once he'd got all those noisy rock n' roll tracks out of his system – Ray settled down to write beautiful, brittle, fragile songs about everyday people in everyday situations. Amongst a plethora of fine compositions there was the one everybody's heard of, *Waterloo Sunset*, which you don't need me to tell you famously captured Londoners Terry and Julie milling about after work by the river, though the voyeuristic, reclusive narrator of the song confesses 'I stay at home at night'. But there were a plethora of other no less splendid but more obscure mid-sixties examples: the bewitching *Two Sisters*, as heard on *Something Else by The Kinks* in which Davies adopted the persona of a suburban housewife weighing up 'the drudgery of being wed' against her single sister's carefree antics, ultimately deciding domesticity was more worthwhile than the wild life; there was the ornate *The Kinks are the Village Green Preservation Society* LP, featuring *Village Green*, in which the one-time resident of a small parish 'far from all the soot and noise of the city' returns home years later – having missed village life – to see that the grocer's boy now owns the grocery. In 1969, drawing upon memories of his family life in post-war Muswell Hill as he often did, Ray had written a fine long player called *Arthur*, documenting the everyday life of an average chap from youth – *Young and Innocent Days* – via army service in wartime – *Yes Sir, No Sir* – to the uncertain semi-achievement of the suburban semi-detached – *Shangri La*.

The minutiae of everyday existence lay at the heart of what Ray was doing, and was what he did best. But as he explored it, and became renowned for doing so, it must presumably have become harder to do. It wasn't long before Ray was no longer an 'ordinary man' himself. He had become an internationally famous rock star and a highly regarded songwriter, with a string of hits to his name. But by the early 1970s all was not well with the Kinks' frontman. Great things were still expected from the fount of Raymond, but the hits had dried up somewhat. Nonetheless, influenced by 1970s rock's cynicism and self-referential mood, workaholic Ray had thrown himself into musical-theatre projects, *Preservation Act I* and *Preservation Act II*, grandly staged productions (which later became albums) further developing his Village Green concept, in which the Kinks themselves were often little more than session men for the musical dramas played out by Ray centre stage. Though they covered the territory of everyday life Ray was familiar with, they did not have the succinct appeal of his earlier work, and were not met with unbridled praise. Davies' personal life was suffering too. Shortly after the final break-up of his marriage in 1973, according to Johnny Rogan's fine biog of the Kinks, Ray, balancing a can of beer precariously on his head, is alleged to have told a stunned White City Stadium audience mid-show that he was 'fucking sick of the whole thing' and was packing it all in. Apparently, when the hospital rang up brother and co-Kink Dave Davies later that night, he was upset to discover that unhappy Ray had swallowed an overdose of tranquilizers before taking the stage that fateful night. Shortly after the show Ray had found himself in hospital, having his stomach pumped.

Slowly, Ray recovered, with the support of his brother. Times were not good for Mr Davies; yet still he remained astonishingly prolific. Further, according to Johnny Rogan's entertaining account, Ray was not very rock 'n' roll at all: he got up at 7am every morning, ate a breakfast of raw eggs, then got straight to work on the songwriting. Tired of his rock-star life, Ray yearned to be an ordinary man once more – spending free time wandering around London art galleries, and, ignoring his celebrity, using public transport whenever he could; but things could never be quite the same again. This dichotomy would soon find expression in *Star Maker*. Ray remained eager to create, despite his personal problems, and eager to work with the Kinks. 'Anyone who thinks they are only my back-up band is very mistaken. There are still things to extract from the Kinks on an artistic level – whether or not it turns out to be commercial remains to be seen.' Ray busied himself arranging a U.S. tour of his *Preservation* show;

before he went he was approached by Granada Television, asking if he would write a musical play – the brief for which asked for 'an experimental dream' – to be included in a new ITV series entitled *Late Night Drama*. Here his dream of the 'ordinary man', and his own sense of isolation, would find its most unusual expression; a distorted vision of domesticity, both longed-for and feared, fractured through the hazy lens of Davies' troubled psyche.

An ITV programme rather unlike anything you'd find in their schedules today, *Late Night Drama* went out on Thursdays in Summer 1974, the latter part of an evening that also featured such delights as *Don't Ask Me* featuring waggle-armed Magnus Pyke providing 'astonishing facts about everyday life' and the long-forgotten Arthur English sitcom *How's Your Father* ('Old Ted Cropper promises to give up drinking', noted *TV Times*, 'on condition that son Eddie gives up smoking…'). *Late Night Drama* was described – with perhaps just a hint of nervousness – as 'a late-night experimental drama series'. And it really was: other editions included *I Know What I Meant*, a reconstruction of events in the presidential office in the wake of Watergate, based on the genuine tapes, *A Brisk Dip Sagaciously Considered*, a study of a desperate man who attempts to drown his crippled mother, and *M + M*, a drama of a futuristic game show, written by *Doctor Who* K9 creators Bob Baker and Dave Martin. To top it off, the series ended with a new drama by John Osborne. There were no mystery or medical dramas in sight. Perhaps these challenging pieces went down well, perhaps they didn't. There were no letters about any of them in the *TV Times* and there was no second series.

According to Rogan, Ray's contribution to the series remained uncertain until he fell ill on tour in Chicago. Laid out in bed, Ray absorbed a steady diet of glossy afternoon soap operas on television, and was amused by the plastic perfection of their leading men. Suddenly inspired to create an experimental drama of ordinary life, Ray enthusiastically completed a script in bed, and returned to England ready to shoot.

His half-hour scenario centred on the silver-suited Star Maker: a charismatic super-being who would seek out the dullest man he could find, take over his mundane life, and turn him into a superstar. Eight new songs were quickly written to form the main body of the piece linked with dialogue also written by Ray.

The result, broadcast in September 1974, is remarkable. Ambitiously shot live, with no edits, apart from a gap for commercials in the middle, *Star Maker* must have been something of a challenging piece for the unsuspecting viewer. It begins as bewigged groovers – choreographed with genuine charm by Douggie Squires – beckon the viewers into the narrative. Wig-haired and sporting thick framed specs, they look much older than and singularly unlike any dancer you'd see on television today, and remind us of the days when dancers on television could be over 30 years old. The camera moves jerkily into a crowded, gaudily lit, but splendidly designed set, built across various levels; with a vaguely bewildered, hirsute, lank-haired audience gathered 'in the round'. At the centre, rather remarkably, is Davies, resplendent in shiny silver suit, as 'The Star', perched proudly but unsteadily atop a television camera in platform shoes and flares. The rest of the Kinks (shoved somewhere off at the back) noisily get cracking behind him, for a ramshackle but lively version of the theme song.

There are lots of songs to get through and it all rattles along at a relentless pace. Setting the tone for this breathless piece, Ray is soon hopping off his perch – as the camera operators scud about to keep Davies in shot – to sit in front of a television set, where he sees his co-star, June Ritchie, whom he speaks to on a phone, while an in-shot camera hovers behind him lending a claustrophobic air to this drama within a drama. 'Are you watching me on your colour TV?' Davies whines in a saccharin-coated voice. She is. It is her husband – Norman, an accountant – who is to provide the inspiration for The Star's new concept album, and he informs her that he intends to take her husband's place in her life for a few days. As the drama progresses, the Star moves in with Norman's wife – another part of the studio space has been designed to represent a 1970s house, with all mod cons – deciding that he intends to use Norman as inspiration for a new LP. 'I feel a few chords coming on already...I feel a whole concept album coming on,' he claims. In order to ensure authenticity, The Star does just what Norman does: wears his clothes, drinks his nightly hot chocolate, eats his evening shepherd's pie, gets up and goes to the office – and even sleeps with his wife. All of this is crammed into the action.

As one demanding theatrical follows another, Ray sings of *Ordinary People* while he gets ready for bed; and as a mic dangles above his head, he is dressed in his pyjamas by dancers wearing gold hot pants. But he never

It'll all come out in the wash: it may have been in the 'Best Buy' series, yet many copies of this pressing of the *Soap Opera* tie-in LP by the Kinks ended up in the remainder bins.

misses a beat. A blackout signals night time; this is followed by *Rush Hour Blues* which sees another costume change as Ray sings his song of the daily grind as he slips into a rather fetching all-in-one zip-up stretchy grey flared pinstripe suit, before he joins a procession of similarly suited workers as they groove symbolically towards a remarkably strange set – shaped like a giant horizontal clock face – that dominates the centre of the studio. Here, whilst singing *Nine To Five*, the 'hand' of this giant clock – on which Davies and his co-performers perch – unexpectedly begins to swing around slowly.

Audience members – unprepared from this assault by the scenery – are disbelievingly forced to duck as the set comes at them. Nobody has warned them; Ray makes no sign. This is live telly. If they don't get out of the way, they've had it. This kind of moment lends real nervous energy to the piece: one hundred things could go wrong at any moment, but they don't. Miraculously, nobody is clobbered by the set. Before you know it, Ray is waving a tankard about as he celebrates the after-work beer with *When Work is Over* and *Have Another Drink*, during which the audience is afforded a rare glimpse of Dave and the rest of the Kinks, playing brilliantly, but only occasionally spotted in this bizarre drama. *You Make it all Worthwhile* sees Norman return home, as one of a row of identical grey-suited office workers in deep focus being identically welcomed home by their wives. By now, the boundary between Norman and The Star has grown blurred; his wife begins to call The Star Norman, and claims 'since 1965 you've had this fantasy of being a rock star.' Eventually, after an emotional struggle, Ray/Norman decides it is time to take his place as *A Face in the Crowd* (one of Ray's most beautiful songs) and sits down amidst the audience with his 'wife'. Eating crisps with Andrea, he watches wistfully as brother Dave is briefly allowed to become the centre of attention. He suddenly emerges from the shadows, with the rest of the band, to play a cracking version of *You Can't Stop the Music*. Ray may have taken his place in the crowd; Dave certainly has not; and it's quite a jolt. Celebrating all the bands of yesterday (like the Kinks?) and all those that 'never made the grade', this rocker – like all the other songs included – sounds a lot more alive than it would on the subsequent RCA LP *Soap Opera*, to be released the following year. It did however include two songs not featured in the *Star Maker* television play, but that did feature in the subsequent stage show: *Holiday Romance*, an oft-overlooked latter day Davies classic about a brief flirtation abroad; and a song of suburban semi-detached rage *Ducks on the Wall*. Rather less essential than *Holiday Romance*, this latter number does feature some splendid duck-call noises.

As Ray sits and eats crisps – a somewhat strange end to his bizarre suburban odyssey – the audience take to their feet and cut loose alongside the Douggie Squires dancers, frugging stiffly, pasty faces glistening, and here, at last, are the real 'ordinary people' Ray wants to link with, but cannot: and, ironically, it would seem that they just want some good straightforward music to dance to – finally delivered by the boys in the band when Ray and his introspection take a back seat. The end credits roll and it's all over. What should we make of it all?

Ray's rock-star view of domesticity in *Star Maker* veers from well-observed, to naive caricature, to bewilderingly strange, and most stops in between. The drama loses its way at points. Is The Star Norman? Is Ray Norman? What's he getting at? Does he know? And the delicacy of Ray's greatest songs is not reflected in his clunky scriptwriting.

It would be easy to tear it all to pieces. But there is more to celebrate than to criticise – not least that Ray has produced a work that is incredibly honest, brave, and so ambitious that it cannot but fail. And he knows it – let's not forget, incidentally, he once wrote a number entitled *You Just Can't Win*. Yet it is vibrant, alive, bravely personal. It is fascinating – and occasionally uncomfortable – to see Ray exposing himself so acutely, yet so awkwardly.

It has been de rigeur to scoff at Ray's 'theatrical period' for years. To a large degree, it is still scoffed at. But, before scoffing, imagine a contemporary pop group attempting anything this ambitious today, and imagine a television company agreeing to commission it, or show it. Indeed, imagine a late night play slot on ITV. You can't, can you?

Ray's play was toured as a stage show, reworked with extra songs, released as an LP, then followed by another bizarre concept album vaguely drawing upon Ray's schooldays, entitled 'Schoolboys in Disgrace'. Alas, though the sleeve featured the band 'in character' in school uniforms, as well as a still more disquieting cartoon of a caned schoolboy with his shorts pulled down on the front (what on earth were RCA thinking?), there was no tie-in television drama. After this, Ray's nostalgia for the past, and his obsession with the 'ordinary man', was put to one side – as he reinvented the Kinks as a stadium rock band, and headed off to America. He would never concoct anything as strangely, sadly delightful – or oddly personal – as *Star Maker* again. Ray, though, never content to rest on his laurels, would doubtless say different. *VP*

The people behind the cameras in 1960s cinema for the most part evaded attention. They slipped, like invisible men, and sometimes women, between scenes and happenings, and some even suggested, via their rhetoric and movie titles, that what they were filming was objective reality, completely effacing their presence...

The Fire in the Water

UK Film | 1977 | colour and black and white | 90mins
Director Peter Whitehead
Producer Marc Sursock
Production Company Fontglow
Cast Nathalie Delon, Edouard Niermans

But whatever, in truth they had a power to create fame and influence things significantly, like David Hemmings' photographer in Antonioni's sinister Swinging London holiday jaunt film *Blow-Up* (1966), and almost everything went under the camera lens. Truth twenty-four frames a second – sort of. It was these people, hiding in the wings, like spies, travelling the world, changing identities, and sleeping-around with impunity, that made the sixties what it was, all refracted through a mysterious prism that made it all seem so spectacular. Even when it was depressive or downbeat, it was glamourous, and definitely seductive.

In this respect, Peter Whitehead was both a powerful and curious director. His name and way of being preceded him, and despite his personal intensity – and probably ultimately largely private if not antisocial ways – he was very well connected, being acquainted with the Rolling Stones, Pink Floyd and numerous other London pop musicians and counter-cultural figures.

His record of the important Royal Albert Hall Beat Poetry event, *Wholly Communion* (1965), all shot on black and white 16mm, with very few resources, and his psychedelic ode to the Swinging capital, *Tonite Let's All Make Love in London* (1967), played international film festivals, and were well received. His films were individualistic and creatively rendered, with highly-frenetic camera work and editing riffing off each other. But perhaps because of their documentary framing, they were largely received as reportage, or as direct expressions of the underground scene – kind of as cool, English film versions of Hunter S. Thompson's 'Gonzo' journalism being written-up in magazines in the States.

Which in many respects they were; they were direct expressions of him: his busy brain and libidinal nerves firing. People responded to his

Truth seeker on a visionary quest: Nathalie Delon reaches out in *The Fire in the Water* (1977).

camera as they probably did to him, opening themselves up, even submitting themselves to him. His voice is occasionally heard, as in *Tonite* when he quizzes, in slightly blunt fashion, Julie Christie, but curiously his image and presence is otherwise clouded. Yet his routes of access, commissions – such as following the Rolling Stones on a tour of Ireland in *Charlie is My Darling* (1965) – and people's preparedness to share thoughts and ideas implicitly foregrounded his personal reputation and charisma. The films frequently pull back and cut into the material in hard, collage fashion, throwing jarring juxtapositions and bleeding psychedelic lights at the viewer – but they're also intimate. Or present an intimacy fed through and partially facilitated by his camera, Whitehead's third eye and probe into the world. Whitehead is invisible but pervades every frame, his ever-growing yet partially mysterious reputation further encouraging this kind of reading years later.

His 1969 New York portrait, *The Fall*, included performance art pieces and interviews with noted counter-cultural figures. Whitehead altered his approach and now worked at a deeper, more overt level of reflection, and self-reflection. He became obsessed with questioning his position as a documentary filmmaker. He even filmed himself filming and death became a symbolic fascination. It was in many respects a parallel journey to that being made by the counter-culture as a whole towards the end of the 1960s. How could real change begin? What symbolic passing on or passing over needed to take place as the decade drew to a close? What did it mean to be fully conscious? The film stalked the need for a sacrificial victim and an answer to the apocalyptic mood, as students broken into revolt and the police smashed into them inside Columbia University, where Whitehead was installed, filming the carnage.

Whitchcad's sixties had been woven full of possibilities and yet had also brought personal crisis and a desire to move on. He made two films with collaborators in the early part of the 1970s but otherwise became preoccupied with bird of prey lore and began breeding falcons. (Artist Ian Breakwell remembered seeing a giant eagle in Whitehead's flat above the Pizza Express near London's Soho Square.) It must have been strange when, in around 1975, a Mr Marc Sursock approached him about making a film about the sixties, that strange decade that he was gradually leaving behind, perhaps even glad to be rid of. And yet his public persona was so inextricably tied to that time. It haunted him – in the same way he haunted the films, one being a shadow of the other.

Someone giving him money to make a movie was also unusual. Previously he'd borrowed money from the National Film Finance Corporation or raised it himself through pop promo production. He made, amongst many others, the classic Rolling Stones film for *We Love You*, where Marianne Faithfull played Bosie to Jagger's Oscar Wilde in a politically charged reenactment of the Wilde trial. Maybe the new film would provide a chance to process and detach himself from that unusual, feverish time.

Requiem For the Sixties, the initial title for *The Fire in the Water*, was a phrase that could mean many things. Cutting into the association, Whitehead flipped it around, and rather than making a compilation film of all his footage – as was expected and something eminently possible and indeed to an extent in vogue – see the strange Beatles tribute film *All This and World War II* (1976) – he built an interlinking, complex, personal narrative, combining a broad range of material and, unusually, a fictional scenario.

The Fire in the Water became an extended cine-poem built around images of nature, flowing lava and intense, psycho-sexual personal experience, as well as footage from Whitehead's archive of the 1960s. From extraordinary footage of Icelandic volcanoes, to firemen dousing a blaze, and a dramatic painting by Alder Taylor Mann, the film progresses in an associative, bricolage fashion. You can sense and feel the film's individual components and yet at every stage they also come together and create new chunks of meaning. During the sequence just described, the creative and destructive energies of heat and fire are brought together with great intensity. It could be both the beginning and the end of the world.

The story begins with a couple, driving a camper van and arriving in the Scottish Highlands where they unpack a large collection of film cans. The man – clearly a stand-in for Whitehead (he even looks a little like him) – begins to watch and re-watch sequences of rock performances and sixties happenings on a Steenbeck film viewing machine. Slowly and strangely, the footage seems to take on a life of its own, the screen of the Steenbeck mirroring the water that his female partner is looking into and through, out in the wilderness, as she wanders freely through the local untamed landscape. A flame is seen superimposed, flickering in front of the screen. Both the film material and the material of the landscape seem to live and breathe, controlling and influencing the couple like some kind of alchemical process.

The Fall had begun with the intertitle 'In the Beginning Was the Image' – deviating from the Biblical obsession with 'the Word' – and spoken dialogue features only very briefly in *The Fire in the Water* (though it does feature more prominently in the archival footage). The woman, Nathalie Delon, Whitehead's then lover (and ex-wife of actor Alain Delon), leaves the house and sets out on one of three exploratory journeys into nature. Asserting her independence, and refusing to fall in-line with a larger narrative, when asked where she is going, she repeats 'I don't know!'

The film's distinct lack of talk lends its images a presence and energy that was surprising given its background. First developed out of a project

Dark matter and alternative vistas: *The Fire in the Water* (1977).

originally intended for Bianca Jagger; several edits were attempted as numerous ideas and sources of input vied for dominance. Funder, Sursock, sought to make it more commercial, and at one point even introduced narration. But no matter, Whitehead's highly individual vision ultimately shines through. Maybe it benefitted from a little disruption along the way?

At one point bright, saturated footage of an astronaut floating in space (to the sound of the Beatles' *A Day in the Life*) cuts to Allen Ginsberg reading at the Royal Albert Hall (originally used in Whitehead's *Wholly Communion*). 'Come sweet lonely spirit back to your body. Come great God back to your only image,' he intones as the film is suddenly – but gently – sucked back into the present moment and different contexts, meanings and, indeed, the far distances of space, are traversed and once again grounded.

Crowd insanity and millennial fever threaten to truly overwhelm as the concept of progressive violence is introduced into the glutinous, cerebral flow. Footage of Columbia University students being beaten cuts into a Rolling Stones stage invasion, to the sound of their '68 protest anthem *Street Fighting Man*. Whitehead frustrates expectations by having the Steenbeck turn itself off and on, escaping the control of the filmmaker in supernatural fashion. As Laura Rascaroli has noted, inclusion of the Who saying they are 'talking about my generation' doubles up as a comment on Whitehead's activities, talking about his 'generation'.

Whitehead's inner explorations and interest in myth tunnel all the way through *The Fire in the Water*. He never filmed The Doors but the Oedipal references in their song *The End* ('Father, I want to kill you'), as heard here on the soundtrack, are significant, and as much about self-confrontation, as the usurpation of authority. Whitehead's alter ego's descent into the underworld in *The Fire in the Water* becomes a parallel event; he goes through the slippery images of the 1960s dream and into his mind. Does he in effect kill himself and then, to paraphrase Ginsberg, return 'to the body'? The Odyssey is now complete.

Or is it? What of the union with the female? To refer again to the Odyssey, the hero of the story must return and find his place in the world, reuniting with his wife. She has, however, had her own experiences and journeyed out in the wilderness on three separate occasions – three journeys of Lacanian self-discovery. Finally, walking amidst the bright light of the day, she peers down at and into a flowing river. A snake coils in its depths and a crow watches her. The proximity of woman with beasts of the sky above and the sea below, threatening violence, feels dangerous and sexual, and the landscape and her mood begin to merge with alarming intensity – and shortly after the man has become lost in his own reverie of images. Her encounter is like that of Eve in the Garden of Eden, her sexuality becoming overt and manifesting in strange, visionary terms, before she then dies, or at least transmutes into another form of matter. She goes through water, transcends the self-absorption of Narcissus and enters the underworld, like Orpheus.

The woman has passed on and unlike the man, chosen not to return to the earthly sphere. The choice of death and sacrifice has been hers to make and not her partner's, and he stands there, finally having quit his machine and looking at the land, uncertain of what has happened or quite where she has gone. But the magical broth that is *The Fire in the Water* is about post-modern or pagan time and it's perhaps significant that the film ends with the cottage in the snow. The heat of spring has passed to winter. Spring will come again. (Whitehead's cyclical myth-making is consistent: *Wholly Communion* begins with early morning sun, and ends with the darkness of night.)

The Fire in the Water is a powerful film. Documentary footage is used but it is in no way part of the so-called 'realist' tradition. Which is ironic given Whitehead's innovations as a direct cinema filmmaker, shooting sound-synch on location, documenting events. He was schooled in the technique, obtaining footage for Greek and Italian TV with his 16mm camera in the early 1960s. His style, however, began to change over the decade as he collided sections and small edits together. *Wholly Communion, Tonite Let's All Make Love in London, The Fall*; they are all collage films, *Tonite* perhaps most overtly. A close-up of a woman's face cuts drastically to bleeding lights at Piccadilly Circus, and then to an ace face at a club; freak out music also further churning-up the mesh and pushing the viewer's consciousness in different directions.

For all its shift to the countryside and isolation – and drastic moves between different contexts and locations courtesy of Whitehead's archive – *Fire* tried to work through and out of the millennial fever of the 1960s. It looked back, trying to process the post-war, H-bomb anxiety of the decade, whilst also stepping back and reflecting on the male and female split, and engaging with a kind of nature horror.

To what extent Nathalie Delon collaborated on the formation of this unusual vision is unclear. Whilst she receives no formal credit (beyond starring), she was Whitehead's partner, and the director worked increasingly closely with his lovers and close friends in this period. Whitehead explored male/female dynamics through creative dialogues with Penny Slinger and Niki de Saint Phalle in respective films *Lilford Hall* (1969) and *Daddy* (1973). Films became dialogues and psychosexual products of each relationship.

The Fire in the Water was, however, for all its dynamic construction, partially depressive and more reflective and inward looking than these other collaborative works. The male character is not in control and has to use a machine to reflect on the past, a machine that eventually disobeys him. It was perhaps a sign that Whitehead needed female companionship and collaboration to avoid the narcissistic tendency to which he and the male character in the film were partial. Otherwise, man and machine lock in compulsive, intense, masturbatory shut-down, his imprint in the film virtually taking over. Alternatively, if viewed in alchemical terms, the woman might represent Whitehead's more active and energized feminine side: the anima.

For a long time, *The Fire in the Water* might have been the last film that Whitehead would ever make, a line in the sand only revoked in 2009 with *Terrorism Considered as One of the Fine Arts*. Previously Whitehead would refer to *The Fall* as his last film, as if his seventies works were a coda, or simply didn't exist at all. He became a falconer, breeding and training the birds in Kuwait until the first Iraq War. The role of filmmaker ceased and with it that character, as he transmuted like the woman in *The Fire in the Water*.

Keeping up with the facts in Whitehead's story feels almost impossible. He's lived multiple lives and they all seem to overlap, different versions of his story gaining more or less of an upper hand depending on where and to whom he is speaking. The story is never fixed, like images rather than words, logic and concrete meaning remain elusive. Plotting all the things he did in the sixties is hard enough. He made films, ran a publishing company, travelled the world, shot events that still haven't seen the light of day, shot pop promos, and contributed to the founding of The Other Cinema, an alternative exhibition site and distribution body, all in the matter of a few years. But that says a lot about the 1960s counter-culture in general. Time worked in an unfathomable way and all manner of things were stuffed into each day. The archive can never recover all the facts and the feelings, and who would want it to? Like Whitehead's story and character, it's fluid and out of view, the romanticism of it all probably preferable to the reality anyway. Whitehead was emblematic of the decade. They key thing is the edit; how the sequences relate, the montage, the clashes, the collisions. Is the edit good? The past, and the self, can be anything you want, it just depends on the edit. *WF*

FANTASTIC FICTIONS

When it comes to other worlds, that's something the British do well. And we've done it in our own idiosyncratic style, from robot car-driver film *The Automatic Motorist* (1911) onwards. The big money for USA science fiction unexpectedly changed the cinematic landscape in the years following *Star Wars* (1977) but certainly British writers, while they may not have the big budgets, have no shortage of ideas.

Brits are good at eccentricity, which is what this section centres on: science-fiction, fantasy and big ideas done in a small way. We love the new technology and scientific advancement. But we also fear the homogenous uniformity that lurks somewhere within; and perhaps look to the peculiar individuality of the British eccentric to throw the potential for a more conformist future into relief. Here we celebrate unsung heroes and unusual British product, flagging up some of the individuals and outsiders who forged their own way, providing a low-tech spin on a high-tech future.

After World War Two, rebuilding the nation was a tough gig – and rebuilding the sense of security and stability that the post-war populace no doubt desired must have been a tougher one still. It was an age of wonders, of new atomic technology, but what had happened in Hiroshima

‹ **Leather, twigs, moss and a pair of gloves:** an 'alien' appears to grow and mutate amidst the hallowed arches of Westminster Abbey in *The Quatermass Experiment* (1953).

showed that this new world was not necessarily one of peace, harmony and prosperity. Despite developments in the domestic, for the post-war baby boomers, the threat of the bomb still loomed large. And the flood of low-budget atomic monster flicks mirrored a world concerned by the new technology that could no longer be ignored. In the US, Corman was concocting exciting exploitation along the lines of *The Monster From the Ocean Floor* (1954); in Japan, the threat was reflected in *Godzilla* (1954), and over here we had our own novel knock-off, *Gorgo* (1961).

Yes, in brave Blighty after the war comic readers could pick up a copy of *The Eagle* and read about the intergalactic exploits of lantern-jawed immortal Dan Dare, tune into *Journey into Space* (1953-58) on the radio, or watch Nigel Kneale's splendidly monochromatic space-menace drama *The Quatermass Experiment* (1953) on that thoroughly modern household wonder, television; assuming the thoroughly modern valves warmed up correctly. Anxiety and exhilaration seemed to run hand in hand in this brave new world of danger and possibility, where scientific research was forging a new intellectual reality.

Numerous and notable though were those who did not understand the new, or could not fit in – funny little men like Charlie Drake's work-shy *The Worker*, or Norman Wisdom's out-of-date milkman, as seen in *The Early Bird* (1966), still wheeling around his horse and cart under the employ of a tiny independent dairy run by Mr Grimsdale, in the face of mass-produced dairy produce, delivered by a faceless corporate army of electric-floated baddies.

But along with all those who could not conform, there were also those who chose not to, the eccentrics of whom we have spoken. The protagonist of *The Stranger Left No Card* (1952), for example; the secret agent who refuses to be a number, *The Prisoner* (1967-68), or the flamboyant Doctor of *Doctor Who* – confounding his alien adversaries by combining scientific genius with frilly shirts, weird haircuts, disrespect for authority and order, and corny wisecracks. For as well as being adept at darkness, the British are adept at humour, and it can be bewilderingly black: a complex fusion of darkness and comedy that can sometimes frustrate and confound those who do not understand its intricacies.

Oft flawed, perhaps thoroughly foolhardy, but oft fantastic, in one way or another, in concept if not always conception, the films and programmes in this section are prime examples of British filmmakers attempting to come to terms with social advance and societal anxiety, fearing conformity and homogenization, amidst the strangeness of an uncertain future. In their own weird ways, they juxtapose the outlandish, the unexpectedly individual, or the exciting and eccentric, against the bland backdrop of the everyday. Often they feature characters forced by the strangeness of their new circumstances to forge forward; and compelled to attempt to look like they have a plan – even if, in fact, they have not the slightest idea what they are doing. This is perhaps another tellingly British characteristic.

To demonstrate: oddness and innovation combined in a peculiar post-war anti-morality tale…

The Stranger Left No Card

UK Film | 1952 | black and white | 23mins
Director Wendy Toye
Script Sidney Carroll
Producer George K. Arthur
Production Company Meteor Films
Cast Alan Badel, Cameron Hall

Like directors Ken Russell and Barry Salt, Wendy Toye had a background in ballet. What did that mean? Her first film, the enigmatically titled *The Stranger Left No Card* was certainly different in tone and style to the highly celebrated Free Cinema films and documentaries also shot on the UK's city streets in the years immediately after the War. *O Dreamland* (1953) by Lindsay Anderson, the director most associated with the social realist movement, was impressively bleak in its portrayal of working class holidaymakers who glumly visit the Margate Waxworks Museum and witness scenes of torture and exploitation. Other Free Cinema films were less loaded, presenting midnight play at Piccadilly Circus in *Nice Time* (1957) and 1950s teenagers in *We Are the Lambeth Boys* (1959). The observation documentaries sought to present life as it was lived, unconstrained by the need for a happy ending, or by stylistic convention.

Wendy Toye had no such concerns. 'I am particularly interested in fantasy, which the English are not,' she said.

The confident, talented Toye had been appearing on-stage since the age of three and a half and was known as 'the pocket wonder'. She choreographed *The Japanese Legend of the Rainbow*, at the London Palladium, aged nine, and was later invited to perform with Serge Diaghilev's Ballet Russe, where she met the surrealist Jean Cocteau. She later choreographed routines for the legendary musical hall comedy outfit, The Crazy Gang, and eventually began to appear in films as an actress and dancer. In 1951, she directed *Stranger*. The short combined location shooting with considerable theatrical gesturing and a pronounced spoken and visual lyricism. A strange man, played by Alan Badel, wearing a floppy top hat, tails, a frilly bow tie, a pocket watch and shoes with a buckle arrives in town, accruing something of an entourage. Entering a local hotel, he dips the end of his umbrella in an ink pot and signs in, with a scratchy flourish: 'Napoleon'. His frivolous clothes give him license to mock a troop of soldiers with bearskin hats and he walks behind them, swinging his arm and pressing an umbrella to his shoulders. It's only seven years after the World War Two and the people look and laugh, not caring that he is mocking an esteemed national institution. Enthralled, the town folk wave and laugh at him whenever they see him over the next few days.

On the tenth day, he visits a Mr Latham, a local businessman in the process of checking his books before going home. Napoleon insists on showing Latham a card trick and the irritable businessman reluctantly goes along with it. Next Napoleon handcuffs his hands together, and then after raising his arms, frees himself with a flick of the wrists! Latham is impressed and is convinced to try it himself. But it doesn't work. The cuffs don't break. Latham is caught and bound, a captive audience to a strange man who begins to remove a false beard and eyebrows. Latham knows this man. He is the man who went to prison for a crime that he committed. In the stranger's words: 'I'm not really as tall as this, you know. In fact, I'm not tall at all,' removing the heels from his shoes and reversing his coat. And then he picks up his trusty umbrella and, taking off a cap to reveal a small blade, pushes it into Mr Latham's heart, killing him.

The piece is constructed like some hypnotic, hypnagogic dream, so caught-up in its own innocent world that it's hard to conceive of anything

Pocket wonder: Wendy Toye made a name for herself as a dancer and choreographer from an early age.

Halt! Who goes there?: Alan Badel sticks out from the crowd in *The Stranger Left No Card* (1952).

going quite so drastically wrong. The stranger sweeps everyone along, narrating his mission in the manner of a children's story, and subsequently as a perfect crime.

The man then leaves Latham's office. 'No one paid any attention to him. Why should they? There was nothing peculiar about him' he says to both himself and the viewer. He has changed from a verbose dandy to a sad, embittered, vicious killer, and the mood and the look of the film changes with him. Alan Badel's performance is measured and exacting; he crumples and peers ahead, packing up his things very slowly, somehow sadder now, even though his plan appears to have concluded successfully. He makes his way back to the train station where he first arrived and sits glumly, waiting for the train to leave.

Badel, who'd previously performed with the Royal Shakespeare Company and at the Old Vic, plays directly to the camera, using his body and facial expressions very carefully. He was one of several specific personnel suggested by Toye when approached with the project by George K. Arthur, a producer for whom she had choreographed the Wartime American Eight Army Air Force show, *Skirts*. Arthur pitched a number of ideas to writers and directors through his company Meteor Films, including the intriguing sounding *The Gentleman in Room 6* (1952), a short work about Hitler living out his last years in a state of poverty in a shabby room in the USA.

Her suggestions were varied and specific, demonstrating Toye's knowledge of who was working and what skills would benefit the piece, whilst also anticipating future stars. Doreen Carwithen, who oversaw orchestration, later wrote over thirty-five film scores for Rank; Alix Stone looked after costumes and had worked with several major theatre set designers, including artist John Piper; and music director Muir Mathieson had extensive experience and would conduct and oversee Bernard Herrmann's score for Hitchcock's *Vertigo* (1958). Perhaps most notable was Jonah Jones who had been a member of the GPO (General Post Office) Film Unit and shot classic 1930s and 40s documentaries *Night Mail* (1936), *Rainbow Dance* (1936) and *London Can Take It* (1940), and was taken on by Toye as cinematographer and cameraman.

It was all shot on location, in Windsor; the special cameraman keeping the dandy tight centre frame whilst still taking in selected details; faces, buildings and other particularities. Nimbly following the coattails of Badel as he strode down old-timey cobbled streets, Jones channelled the musical, semi-hallucinogenic qualities of *Rainbow Dance*, evoking place whilst still creating something fantastical.

It was perhaps the conception of working as a gang, establishing a kind of personal repertory company, that led to her very clear thoughts about the film's shape and look. It was made 'very much as independent films are now', Toye said when discussing it in 1986, i.e. small and on-the-fly. She used a metronome to ensure that Badel walked consistently in time, and later cut it to the music; the swaying, steady rhythms driving the film – and all the shots and action in it – forward; not unlike the rhythm of the train matching the syncopation of a W. H. Auden poem in the aforementioned *Night Mail*, and acknowledging Toye's background in dance.

The documentary look was taken in a very different direction to that affected by the Free Cinema crowd, and Toye was inventive as she went about it. 'The first TV play I did was terribly technical and had all sorts of overlay and complicated cueing', Toye recalled, illustrating her creative ambition. 'When I asked the BBC if I could go on a crash course for director, they refused. They said it would have killed my spontaneity.' Would Toye and her original ideas have got to this point without her ballet, in terms of opportunities and the gaining of a certain level of professional respect? It's unlikely. There were very few women film directors working at this time. Muriel Box, virtually her only contemporary, had been head of Rank's scenario department before and then given opportunities to direct through her husband's company London Independent Producers. She focused on the female experience in *Street Corner* (1953), *The Beachcomber* (1954) and *The Truth About Women* (1957), and, frustrated by gender prejudice in the film industry, founded the publishing house Femina, in 1965, as a way of further exploring feminist themes.

In the USA, there was experimental filmmaker Maya Deren. Like Toye, Deren had a background in dance and choreography and she made short psychodramas that confused and manipulated the reading of space. Her influence on both underground and overground filmmaking, by way of *Meshes of the Afternoon* (1943), has been significant. Deren spoke about establishing a 'chamber cinema' for small personal films (i.e. a form of cinema that was intimate but also exclusive) whereas Toye was more of a populist; but both filmmakers were influenced by Jean Cocteau and engendered a balletic and fantastical sensibility. With its mirroring and internal journeys, *Meshes of the Afternoon* would have been strongly influenced by Cocteau's *The Blood of a Poet* (1930), and Cocteau said *The Stranger Left No Card* was a 'little masterpiece'. More strikingly, Deren and Toye were born only two days apart. The former, 29th April 1917; the latter, 1st May. The more magically inclined might like to note that they were both Taureans. Weirdly, Deren's first husband, Alexander Hammid, would make *The Gentleman in Room 6*, the aforementioned fantasy film about Hitler in the USA, overseen by the producer of *Stranger*. If she and Toye never met, they clearly should have.

There may have been few female directors working when Toye's film won best short at Cannes but the press focussed on other matters. *The News Chronicle* said it cost £3,500 and that it was 'easily dubbed in foreign languages and planned every inch of the way. [It] open[s] up a field previously rejected as impractical and profitable.' *The Manchester Guardian* called it a 'short feature' but its 23-minute running time meant that it failed to qualify as a quota and thus, on release, would not receive a share of the cinema tax obtained from non-British features at the box office (see also *Screamtime*).

The story was a mutable creation and it was promptly reworked in the American comic *Black Cat Mystery*, which established a bewilderingly different mood. In *Here Today* from issue 50, June 1954, by Sid Check and Frank Frazetta, the town's new arrival wears a grotesque mask and leaps around distributing gifts and sweets with nihilistic abandon. 'Enjoy yourselves! Everyone must enjoy themselves! I can't stand long faces! Laugh!' he says. The town responds in kind, entering into a collective hysteria. The stranger then shoots two of three intended victims before revealing himself as a dashing, distinctly chiselled villain, wearing a dark suit and coiffed hair, on a mission to fulfil gang reprisals. (Reprinted in *Four Color Fear* in 2010, the notes for *Here Today* acknowledge the influence of *The Stranger Left No Card*, but credit the film to George K. Arthur.)

The story was later remade again as an episode of *Tales of the Unexpected* (1979-88), with Toye once again directing. Derek Jacobi played the stranger (as 'Sir Columbus' rather than 'Napoleon') and eagle eyes will also spot a young Jennifer Connelly (later star of *Labyrinth* (1986)) in one scene. The framing opens up early on to reveal real life punks, sporting mohicans and 'The Exploited' pin-badges, seated grumpily on the streets of Norwich, where it was shot by Anglia Television, giving it a certain verisimilitude. The original's musicality is far from view, however. *Stranger in Town* (transmitted 23/05/1982) incorporated no surface niceness. Latham (Clive Swift) is a shrewd, hard-nosed property developer and the crime, never specified in the original, is now murder. The tone, and alterations in detail and context, say a lot about what had changed, in society and dramatic expectation, between the 1950s and the 1980s. (The fact that it was in a series called *Tales of the Unexpected* also undermined the final twist.)

The original film appeared to have no sympathy for a country struggling to pull itself together after the War. Rather, it highlighted corruption, capitalism and division, quietly mocking small town trust and good old quaint England. It's not just the stranger who is underhand; the murder victim, the businessmen is also revealed to be a crook. The story is creepy, harsh and brutal, a reflection of the post-war malaise and ongoing rationing, still in place when Toye and Badel made the movie.

Here Today: an unlikely, high-octane, 1954 American comic-strip adaptation of *The Stranger Left No Card* (1952).

Are these qualities part of the English whimsical tradition, the mix and meeting of light and dark? Mole and Rat must go to the dark wood to meet their fears and eventually speak with the wise Badger in Kenneth Grahame's *The Wind in the Willows*. It becomes a personal challenge. Refreshingly, the darkness remains in *The Stranger Left No Card*. There is no return. And it uses the crisp pleasures of the first half to crushingly drop all and sundry in the second. It's more modest and direct than the films of other English romantics like Powell and Pressburger, piercing the veneer of class and composure.

Toye and Badel were later reunited for *Three Cases of Murder* (1955). Conceived as portmanteau film of three separate stories, made with different crews, it indicated the extent to which producer Alexander Korda was impressed with his new charges who he signed-up after seeing *Stranger* by accident one evening. He was endorsing short filmmaking craft whilst trying to increase its press, profile and profit margins. It was a bold experiment, and one that would be repeated many times over in the 1970s by British horror company Amicus amongst others.

Following Korda's death in 1956, Toye's contract moved to British Lion who had earlier bought *The Stranger Left No Card*, releasing it with *Moulin Rouge* (1952). To her regret, Toye was now given comedies to direct; such as *We Joined the Navy* (1962) which told the story of a Lieutenant Commander transferred to a new naval academy when he falls out with his dim-witted superiors. Her last cinema work was a short, *The King's Breakfast* (1963). British Lion appeared to understand only part of what made *The Stranger Left No Card* work and Toye moved into television.

Free Cinema did a lot for the profile of the short documentary in the post-war period but the world of short fiction pieces has received little equivalent boost of profile. Their relative invisibility, in a historical sense, shows how much feature films have dominated. The short film is now largely seen as a calling card, not something of interest in its own right, but when the Eady fund existed, a tax that gave money back to supporting British cinema films, some companies and directors actually made their living that way.

Ironically Toye's film was too short to qualify for the Eady fund but as efforts go *The Stranger Left No Card* is a fine and highly memorable piece of work, and it is a shame that it has lain forgotten. Short films don't command the respect and interest they sometimes deserve. In the case of Toye, and her post-war anti-morality tale, that glued fantasy and a crushing realism together via her balletic and very original sensibility, we'd say it was her best work. And she thought so too. *WF*

Unexpected sci-fi strangeness in early seventies TV comedy now, my darlings, with a somewhat forgotten giant of the small-screen schedules…

The Worker: The Saucerer's Apprentice

UK TV | 1970 | colour | 30mins
Director Shaun O'Riordan
Script Lew Schwartz, Charles Drake
Producer Shaun O'Riordan
Production Company ATV
Cast Charlie Drake, Henry McGee, Kay Frazer

Spare a moment, pals, to hail forgotten funny-little-man Charlie Drake. 'Hello, my darlings!' as he used to say. 'Hello, Charlie!' we might answer. 'Haven't seen much of you on the television nostalgia shows lately.' Or ever. *The Saucerer's Apprentice*, a particularly bizarre episode from *The Worker*, the diminutive, curly-haired, baby-faced comedian's most popular television series, was screened as part of a Flipside cinema show in 2011, and we took the opportunity to canvass opinion on Mr Drake after the event. Some of our guinea-pig viewers found the programme interesting; a few particularly enjoyed the performance of supporting player Henry McGee. Intriguingly, perhaps tellingly, we were hard pressed to find anybody who would confess even to liking Charlie Drake, let alone finding him amusing.

Yet Drake, a close friend of the rather more legendary Tony Hancock, took his craft seriously, devoted himself wholeheartedly to the business of being funny, and was, in his heyday, critically acclaimed and heaped with awards and honours for his work. If his numerous comedy series and frequent appearances in (and on the cover of) the *TV Times* of the late 1960s and early 1970s are anything to go by, he must certainly have had a large and devoted following, once upon a time. However, while other 'vintage' humour has lasted – *Dad's Army*, for example, is still repeated every Saturday night, half a century down the line – Drake's star has dimmed – disappeared, even – in the intervening years between then and now. Repeats there are none. What happened?

Drake had spent a large part of his formative years as one half of a double act on children's television, appearing on the BBC's *Jigsaw* (1954-55) with Jack Edwardes in the mid 1950s. Drake and Edwardes were old RAF buddies: Edwardes was a bomber pilot; Drake was a rear-gunner. They'd

Hallo, my darlings: yes, it's chirpy Charlie Drake, seen here on the cover of *Radio Fun* comic, 'the all-star picture weekly', 1959.

developed their act one summer season after the War while they'd worked together as holiday camp entertainers, and continued to bill themselves as *Mick and Montmorency*, a straightforward slapstick double act in the silent comedy tradition. Their skits proved popular with youthful viewers and they were tempted over to the other side when they were snapped up for an ITV series. The formula usually remained the same: Mick (Drake) would suffer at the clumsy hands of Montmorency (Edwardes) as the pair struggled to hold down a different job every week. A hefty ninety-one episodes later, Drake was wearying of the programme, or perhaps he was wearying of Edwardes; one way or another, their partnership was terminated. It was 'an act that couldn't transfer to an adult audience,' Drake later noted; and he re-launched himself as a solo act in the show that broke him with mature viewers, entitled *Drake's Progress* (1957-58). Success saw him busy on television, starring in feature films, and married with a family in a large house in Weybridge: 'my big house by the river…two boats, cars, the full lot, all the things I wanted…and three children,' he recalled later.

The Worker (first seen in 1965) was a reworking of Drake's old character from the *Mick and Montmorency* days. By now, though, Drake's comedy – aimed squarely at the adult viewer – had become considerably more complex. Increasingly billing himself as 'Charles Drake', his holiday-camp humour had mutated into a strange mixture of the old-style slapstick, Chaplinesque pathos, and strange, stylised sequences that pierced the illusion of verisimilitude: the complex set-up was becoming more important than either the pay-off gag, or maintaining plausibility. An episode from the 1965 series of *The Worker*, *A Punting We Will Go*, for example, featured an elaborately staged routine in a crowded betting shop. Drake's pugnacious 'little man' – maintaining an interior monologue throughout – repeatedly struggles to push his way through a crowd of punters, then repeatedly tries and fails to put on a bet, as a miserable bookmaker slams down the window on the counter. Each time Charlie fails to put on a bet, the horse he would have backed wins. The joke (eventually) finds its resolution some races later when, by way of contrast, the mass of other punters step aside as if by magic, and, despite Charlie's deliberate slowness, he cannot seem to miss the chance to make his bet; which of course he loses. The joke is in the inevitability of Charlie's failure (whatever he does, the opposite will happen: he can't win). It's all very clever, and impressively staged, but, you might argue, not very funny. You could imagine it featuring in similarly unfunny latter day ITV *Hancock* episode. *The Worker*, though, was a successful show in 1965, and was repeatedly revived; but looking back, it's difficult to appreciate exactly what it was about this 'little man' that proved so popular.

Putting Drake's shows together was an elaborate process. Co-writing the programme with collaborator Lew Schwartz, Drake would painstakingly rough out his comedy sketches on a drawing board before shooting began and spend much of his limited budgets on unusual props and location shooting. Director Shaun O'Riordan – who worked on many shows with Drake throughout his career – knew this well. 'Charlie is a great "prop" man and perfectionist, and isn't happy until we find the craziest product of his comedy imagination,' he noted in a *TV Times* interview.

The products of Drake's imagination did indeed get crazier, if *The Saucerer's Apprentice*, an episode from the 1970s era of *The Worker*, is anything to go by. The programme begins as it always does with Charlie at the Labour Exchange, looking for work as usual, but this time there's an added twist: he's accompanied by an alien being, who feeds on plastic. At least, he says it's an alien – when it creeps into the Labour Exchange it looks like a lithe young lady inside a large pillowcase (the alien is played by Kay Frazer, more often seen – wearing considerably less cloth – in early 1970s editions of *The Benny Hill Show* (1955-91). Odd-looking indeed, the creature stretches the encasing sheet to makes a snout shape with the beak-like pointed hand within, while electronic bleeps, zaps and warbles reverberate around he/she/it. Though it is obviously somebody in a pillowcase, there is nonetheless a disconcerting air about the creature: Frazer, jerking and twitching, really throws herself into her otherworldly performance.

Mr Pugh, Charlie's regular adversary behind the counter at the Labour Exchange, splendidly hammed up by comedy stalwart Henry McGee (another veteran of *The Benny Hill Show*, and the long-suffering 'keeper' of Honey Monster in the Sugar Puffs adverts), initially refuses to believe the being is an alien ('that's a girl in a pillow case!', he declares indignantly), though Charlie resolutely tells him it is. Rushing towards the creature, Pugh is repelled by a 'force field'. To see McGee, his square jaw jutting, pretending to be blocked by an invisible extra-terrestrial barrier, like a kind of gawky Marcel Marceau, is splendid indeed, and worth the price of admission on its own account. After singeing Pugh's toes with a 'thought bolt', the creature

All in a day's work: *The Worker* confronts a walking pillow case on ITV, this Thursday.

eats every plastic appliance on the desk (a pen and a telephone disappear in what now looks like a charmingly slow-moving 1970s video effect, but which was doubtless a tricky set up back then). Pugh is ultimately reduced to a quivering wreck: the scene ends with him cowering in the corner, regressing to childhood, screaming 'I want my mummy!' It is compelling – and just a little uncomfortable – to watch.

The middle part of the programme is a little more routine, and a strangely sad air descends on proceedings, as Drake is seen alone in a darkened room teaching his alien 'pet' tricks – such as flipping buttons from its 'beak' and swallowing them. Next, he uses it in a money-making scheme – passing the hat around in the street while the alien jerks about. Intriguingly, he passes it off as a war-veteran under a witch-doctor's spell doing a sand-dance; you'd think that it would have been easier simply to capitalise on the creature's extra-terrestrial origin.

The scene climaxes with the hungry alien eating every scrap of plastic available within swallowing distance – cue a statuesque blonde's plastic mac vanishing, inevitably, to reveal her in her underwear. The woman, credited in very 1970s fashion as 'snooty girl', was played by Celestine Burden, who, according to a short piece of *TV Talk* in the *TV Times* found working with Charlie Drake 'hilarious'. Just two weeks earlier, also in an episode of *The Worker*, she'd had another important part to play when her pants were snatched from her by a giant vacuum cleaner. Was she in danger of being typecast? The piece was accompanied by a picture of Celestine in – surprise, surprise – her pants. Away from the screen, though, she was 'head girl in a troupe of eight dancers who appear at a West End hotel'.

Her bawdy business is topped in this episode – still more hilariously? – when a policeman's trousers fall down. The alien ate the plastic braces holding them up, apparently (have you ever heard of plastic braces?). The scene ends in reassuringly old-school fashion with everybody chasing Drake off the screen, shouting and waving their fists in the air. It's all very British and such corny by-the-numbers old humbug that it makes the more outlandish aspects of the show – thrown into sharp relief – seem weirder still.

Next is the haunting, bittersweet sequence that finishes the programme. The alien, hiding in an alley with Charlie, spies a pillowcase on a washing line, and, with much bleeping and cloth-fondling, falls in love with it.

Charlie is initially baffled when, suddenly, the alien becomes similarly inanimate, by teleporting itself to hang next to its mate, becoming just another pillowcase out to dry on the line. Eventually realising what has happened, Charlie ties the two pillowcases together to symbolise their love, and, in a bizarre, melancholy moment of pathos, stares solemnly into the distance.

It's a serious moment, and Charlie plays it like he means it. Interestingly, it is this intentionally laughter-free coda that works the best. And, overall, despite it's being a comedy show, and swamped in canned laughter, it must sadly be confirmed that *The Saucerer's Apprentice* is not very funny. Neither, though, was the comedian's life at the time. Drake often drew upon his own life for his scriptwriting (he was a compulsive gambler and *A Punting We Will Go* must have reflected many of the comic's own experiences down at the bookie's shop). Perhaps Drake's own sadness was somehow permeating the programme. A sufferer from depression, Drake had reached a difficult and lonely moment in his life. His first marriage broke up around this time, and by early 1971, he had, according to a strangely melancholic interview in the *TV Times*, left the luxury of his 'big house by the river' for the painful solitude of a small bachelor flat – complete with a painting of a sad clown above the fireplace – high above Leicester Square. Also in Drake's flat, according to the article, were 'some items of luxury furniture – a couple of leather armchairs, a grand piano, some pictures on the walls – a couple of grey-fleshed nudes, and one of Charlie Drake himself in equally sombre hues, his head and shoulders framed by a television screen…' At that time, work was all that mattered. Work-shy as his character was, the real Drake was unfailingly industrious. He told the magazine: 'I'm not a genius. I get no flashes of inspiration. I have to discipline myself. There are times when I wake up, but I don't want to get up. I don't want to start the day because the day has no end. But I force myself to get up, to bath and shave and put on a suit and tie even when I am not going out. I need to do that to make me work. Because I know I am no good if I do not work.'

Perhaps the sentiment of Drake's brief, bittersweet friendship with the otherworldly creature, and the odd poignancy of the final scene with the pillowcases, was a creative reflection of an inner sadness within the performer. With all that turmoil going on in his life, no wonder some of his humour fell flat, or to be more precise, was made strange.

But this can't entirely account for the evaporation of the humorous content of *The Worker* in the decades since it was created. McGee is still good for a laugh, and the timeless low-brow corn of the sight of a policeman with his trousers down will always appeal to some less-discerning viewers. But the passing of time has somehow made Drake's cheeky, wilfully work-shy persona seem as alien as that pillowcase creature. Somewhere in the passing of the years Drake's little man has lost its appeal; and what's more, it's tricky to understand how it might have appealed even then. Perhaps it is simply that tastes change; perhaps it's because jobs have become careers, and the world of work is all taken so desperately seriously now; but I can't help thinking that part of the problem lies with Drake himself. Are we supposed to identify with his irritating 'little man'? Mugging and winking at the camera throughout, he seems rather pleased with himself; unsettlingly seeming to drift between the character of 'The Worker' and what seems to be the real and rather pleased-with-himself Charles Drake. He just doesn't invite the kind of sympathy you'd think he would want for his comedy-everyman character.

Yet, at the same time, something valuable has endured. There is something unique and special about Drake's risk-taking, in his highly personal comedic tunnel-vision, in his defiantly off-kilter world-view, remarkably played out over the course of many years, in the very public forum of the early-evening ITV schedules. Somehow, perhaps against the odds, he captured the imagination of the masses. Is it any wonder he seems a little proud of himself? Shouldn't we be celebrating him? Either way, one gets the sense that Drake was pursuing his own artistic vision wherever it led him – whether we liked him, or his programme, or not.

But humour does not always age well. By the 1980s, as his star faded, and with the onset of the new 'alternative comedy' that swept away many of his generation of 'light entertainers', Charlie was wise enough to know that times were changing. Interviewed in 2001, for *Drake's Progress*, a melancholy *Arena* documentary about the comedian, Charlie's agent, Laurie Mansfield, spoke of an arrangement he'd made with Drake. 'People's tastes change. I don't think people now necessarily laugh at the same things that they laughed at twenty or thirty years ago. It was a conscious decision between the two of us that perhaps the time had come to make a change… we couldn't live forever on comedy and slapstick.' Charles eventually turned to a career in serious theatre, and played in Pinter, scooping plaudits for his part in *The Caretaker*, and never looked back. Perhaps we should, though, if only for twenty-five minutes, to revisit the melancholy space oddity that is *The Saucerer's Apprentice*. VP

When it comes fantasy and sci-fi, the combination of eccentric individuals with left-field work can make for baffling viewing. But then even masters of the form sometimes swerve in unexpected directions in order to bring new product to the screen...

Kinvig

UK TV | 1981 | colour | 7 x 25mins
Director Les Chatfield, Brian Simmons
Script Nigel Kneale
Producer Les Chatfield
Production Company LWT
Cast Tony Haygarth, Patsy Rowlands, Prunella Gee, Colin Jeavons

Considering his list of fans, his influence and the style of his work, it still seems wonderfully strange – indeed, brilliant and peculiar – that in 1981 sci-fi horror writer Nigel Kneale created *Kinvig*, a comedy. Kneale, who died in 2006, had a massive impact on British television, and on general sci-fi and horror writing internationally. His *Quatermass and the Pit* (transmitted 22/12/1958 - 26/01/1959) caught people's imaginations in an almost entirely unprecedented way when it was first broadcast by the BBC back in 1958 and 1959. Sinister and exciting, it combined reflections on post-War British culture, racism, an alien invasion and the occult; at least one seat of local government attempted to adjourn its meeting so that members could catch the final episode, according to *The Times*. (*The Daily Express* – not to be left out – meanwhile shrieked 'Woman Killed By *Quatermass and the Pit*', detailing how a lady had died whilst watching it and doing the ironing.)

Kneale adapted the serial for Hammer in 1967 and like his big screen versions of *The Quatermass Experiment* (18/07 - 22/08/1953) and *Quatermass*

II (1955) – *The Quatermass Xperiment* (1955) and *Quatermass 2* (1957) – with all three featuring the rocket scientist character Professor Bernard Quatermass, it again did very well. Kneale continued to work in TV through the 60s, 70s and beyond and established himself as something of a horror and sci-fi master. Many drew from his rich pot of ideas over the years and in 1982 he wrote *Halloween III: The Season of the Witch*. In the early 90s, Chris Carter asked him to write for *The X-Files* (1995-2002 & 2016-), then in development. Kneale declined.

Humour had featured in his work before *Kinvig* but only ever occasionally, and when it did it was typically dark and ironic in tone. A wife of one of the intrepid astronauts in *The Quatermass Experiment*, for example, asks her husband to 'bring me something back' before he blasts off into space. And he does. A creature invades his body and he mutates into a giant alien organism on returning to Earth. (Kneale was at one point going to call the whole story 'Bring Me Something Back'.) Darker and more challenging still was an entry in *Tomato Cain and Other Stories*, a book of short stories written by Nigel Kneale before he joined the BBC in 1951. *Oh, Mirror, Mirror* retells the story of *The Ugly Duckling* except here the ugly duckling is a curvy white girl in a world where everyone else is black. And unlike the duckling, she remains as she is: ostracized and rejected. In which dark, strange universe did Kneale write a sitcom? Ours, it turns out.

TV Times announced the new show with a photo and a simple description: 'Down-to-earth Des Kinvig (Tony Haygarth) is suddenly transported to another world when he meets the glamorous Miss Griffin (Prunella Gee).' The married Kinvig runs a run-down electrical repair shop and meets the said beautiful alien Miss while out walking his dog late one night. Will he help her and her decidedly less attractive male counterparts to fight the evil Xux? Of course he will. They'll meet again in her UFO, she says, but also in his shop that she'll visit in the form of an angry and irritable woman. She'll never admit her 'true' identity, however, just berate him and make demands. Is it real or is it a dream, a fantasy about a domineering woman with whom he can never have an actual relationship? We never find out but Jim, his UFO-obsessed friend, definitely believes the story – and so does Des.

That's the scenario for all seven episodes of *Kinvig* broadcast by London Weekend Television between 4th September and 16th October 1981.

Loving the alien: Prunella Gee and Tony Haygarth promote Nigel Kneale's *Kinvig* (1981).

It's a curious collision of the banal and the fantastic, mixing as it does the humdrum activity of bored middle-aged men with the intergalactic salvation of a doomed race. Not that there ever appears to be much urgency about saving the aliens.

Sci-fi/comedy hybrids *Metal Mickey* (1980-81) and *Hitchhiker's Guide to the Galaxy* (01/05 - 02/09/1981) were also broadcast at the beginning of the eighties (as noted by Andy Murray in his *Kinvig* DVD booklet essay). Perhaps humour felt like the only realistic option for new sci-fi at that time – to go for laughs and silliness and avoid hard sci-fi and the inevitable cheap special effects. After all, how could television companies compete with the mega-budget, space-romp *Star Wars* (and its sequels), very much still on everyone's minds? Are these other programmes really *Kinvig*'s closest bedfellows, however? Watching it, it feels more like a cross-between *Terry and June* (1979-87) and *Steptoe and Son* (1962-74) (of which Kneale was a big fan): the focus being everyday mundane relationships and their occasional transcendence. Des and Jim's friendship comes alive with the discussion of the alien while Des and Netta – his wife – carry on as before: him bored and her quietly distracted and in denial.

The mood of the show is like the repair shop inherited from Kinvig's father-in-law; dusty and depressive with sudden moments of garish energy, like when the angry Miss Griffin comes to visit. Is it any wonder that Des and Jim try to seize on something, anything that might bring a little adventure to their lives? Jim is convinced that Des has a doppelganger in *Double, Double* (18/09/1981): he's not, he's just another man stuck in his life, wearing a light brown raincoat. Was Nigel Kneale trying to tell us something – about himself?

Kneale had a history of creating vulnerable, sensitive characters and then using them to support and build the unfolding drama. The elderly woman who recounts an old ghost story in *Quatermass and the Pit*, for example, has an eerie, eccentric charm. She reads tea leaves too and attends to her sick husband; her everyday actions and story serving to ground the viewer in domestic normality while simultaneously preparing them for the horrors to come. The scene with the tramp in *Quatermass II* – played by Wilfrid Brambell – has a similar power. Discovered amongst the ruins of a desolate village, he represents a sort of tragic forgotten past, a culture apparently swept away by 'progress' but, deep down, still very much alive.

These moments turned the TV into a mirror when they were broadcast live back in the 1950s. Domestic scenes at home reflected domestic scenes on screen and the TV that enabled that reflection also symbolized the threat of coming change.

All three of the *Quatermass* stories grappled with the changing and uncertain times in which they were made. Suez, the end of colonialism and the Cold War all featured directly or indirectly but, despite the drama, *Quatermass and the Pit* could well have been perversely reassuring after World War Two. Superstitions and the Devil are presented and reinterpreted here but significantly the principle of their power still remains. For all the story's chilling bravery at facing the dark recesses of the human mind, Kneale was telling us that the world had changed – but not that much.

Kinvig and its characters are more mixed – to say the least. Des is the most likeable and curiously a bit like Bernard Quatermass. He's another little man outsider, someone who stumbles into his adventures and puts up with bureaucrats: Quatermass resists incursions into his rocket group from the army while Kinvig objects to increases in the rates – and takes it up with the Bingleton Borough Council (BBC) in *Creature of the Xux*. (Note that Nigel Kneale fell out with the British Broadcasting Corporation (BBC) after they failed to commission a fourth Quatermass story just two years earlier.) Kinvig has a grounded, weary quality and it's invariably through him that the other characters express their obsessions and frustrations. Netta has her dog, Jim his sci-fi magazines and Miss Griffin her anger. Somehow, Kinvig has to make it funny.

It's a struggle and the canned laughter doesn't help. Take the very beginning of the first episode: Des dreams of little green men – creatures that look quite a lot like the aliens in *Quatermass and the Pit* – and waves his arms in the air as if to push them from his mind (they're superimposed and we can see them too). Cue laughter after about three seconds – before we even know what it's going on, before the gag can even raise a laugh. It's like someone telling you something's funny before it happens; it slightly deflates the moment. Is it even a gag?

Kneale developed *Kinvig* after going to a science-fiction convention in Brighton and meeting fans close-up. 'They were the craziest lot of people I'd ever encountered. They were dreadful. The whole thing consisted of just dancing about in masks, giggling and having too much to drink. I was just

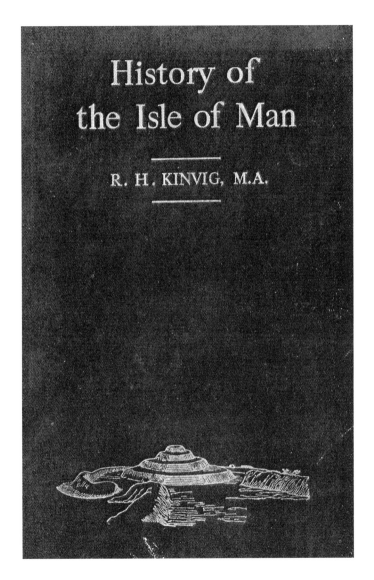

Manx to the core: the history of Nigel Kneale's family home, as told by R. H. Kinvig, M. A. The surname Kinvig is a common one on the self-governing – but UK-affiliated – Isle of Man.

disgusted.' From there, he thought two science fiction obsessed men would be good for laughs – to laugh at, that is – and created Des and Jim. If they believed everything they read about UFOs then it would be easy for them to enter into a fantasy about a beautiful alien female. It's not really a great start for a comedy show. If the writer doesn't like his characters, why should we? We need to be able to laugh with the people we see on screen and not just at them. It works when Des is by himself – Haygarth projects a quiet charismatic sadness – but put him with the character Jim, for example, and it all goes flat.

What was going on? Kneale was very particular about his writing and how a story should be constructed. He complained about people's use of the 'Macguffin' when writing *Halloween III* and insisted that everything should contribute to the drive of the unfolding narrative, not distract the viewer from the matter at hand. 'Each episode is planned, each quite distinct in style and content' he said about writing TV in 1983.

Television was a live medium back when Nigel Kneale first started in the 1950s, closer to theatre in many ways than it was cinema. Different studio-sets could be cut-between (and in that way TV developed or exceeded traditional theatre) but everything had to happen in real time: costume and make-up changes, new camera set-ups, the actors getting from set-to-set, etc. Film inserts increased over the years but were still only ever used sparingly. Scripts required careful, intricate planning then and this naturally established the scriptwriter as the key voice in developing the mood and pace of the story in question. Early TV dramas weren't called 'plays' for nothing and when it came to development and structure, Kneale was the master. His stories are like giant pass-the-parcels. They unravel layer by layer; each stage in the narrative leading slowly and shockingly to the next. At their best, they're absolutely compelling.

And that's what's so strange about *Kinvig*. Sitcoms can be brilliant but they're an anathema to what Nigel Kneale was good at. They're about familiarity and repetition – the inherent drama within a single situation – not change and development.

The representations of TV in Kneale's *The Year of the Sex Olympics* (29/07/1968) and *Quatermass* (24/10 - 14/11/1979) are pretty telling here. In both cases, TV has turned into a kind of decadent comedy porn. In 'The Tit-uppy-Bum-Titty Show' in *Quatermass* people in bright costumes go through absurd sexual acts with a giant banana. 'It's the only show that anyone watches anymore – don't they realize?' shouts the director at one point. There's a sense of despair about *Kinvig*. This is all that TV's good for, all that people want to see, perhaps thought Kneale. Kneale looks forward to the final end point of popular mass entertainment

Looking through his work, Nigel Kneale seems to see two highly distinct – and conflicting – sides to the human spirit: an innate goodness, as witnessed in *The Quatermass Experiment* when an appeal to the humanity of the astronauts absorbed by the alien allows them to defeat it; and a propensity for absolute evil, as seen most clearly in *Quatermass and the Pit* – and there most damningly. 'We…have knowledge of ourselves and the ancient destructive urges in us that grow more-deadly as our populations increase…Every war crisis, witch-hunt, race riot, purge is a reminder and a warning: we are the Martian and if we cannot control our inheritance, this will be their second dead planet' states Bernard Quatermass. Human potential hangs continually in the balance in Kneale's scripts and by the time of *Halloween III*, it seemed to be TV that was triggering the badness. It's a childish yet sinister television advert that causes all those wearing a Halloween mask made by the mysterious Silver Shamrock company to die.

Nigel Kneale's status as a pioneer in British television and his subsequent frustration and disillusionment have parallels with the career trajectory of Peter Watkins. Watkins directed *Culloden* (15/12/1964) and *The War Game* (1965); two extraordinary and highly challenging fake documentaries (see The War Room). When the latter was controversially prevented from being broadcast by the BBC, he left the corporation and went independent. He has in more recent years developed a critical thesis about the limited and manipulative qualities that still dominate mainstream moving image practice. Kneale never went that far. *The Year of the Sex Olympics* may have asked 'is television a substitute for living? Does the spectacle of pain at a distance atrophy sympathy? Can this coffin with knobs on furnish all that we need to ask?' – as noted by *The Sun* in 1969 – but Kneale still stuck with the mortuary. He continued to write television plays and adaptations and in 1996 wrote his last, an episode of the courtroom drama *Kavanagh QC* (1995-2001) starring John Thaw: *Ancient History* (17/03/1997).

'All in all, *Kinvig* is still a disappointment and given Kneale's proven creative brilliance and an originality second to none, I can only assume that his ideas and scripts were watered down and compromised during the long pre-production period' said magazine *Starburst* in 1981. Kinvig has a better reputation online. Internet forum writers have said how they liked the way it was never clear whether Miss Griffin was actually an alien or not and others say it was a shame that the second series was never commissioned. We might go back to *Starburst* and another quote: 'It's a bit like hiring James Joyce to write *Charlie's Angels.*' It's snobbish, but how could you not want to watch a show like that? *Kinvig* is a mixed bag, disappointing and quite odd, but it's also the fall-out and direct expression of someone losing faith in the potential of television as an art form. *WF*

By way of contrast, new technological forms could be a profound source of inspiration for some, even if the results were sometimes bleak and sadly prophetic in terms of how we use to internet today...

Electric Dreams

UK | 1984 | colour | 112mins
Director Steve Barron
Screenplay Rusty Lemorande
Producer Rusty Lemorande, Larry De Waay
Production Company Virgin Pictures Ltd
Cast Lenny Von Dohlen, Virginia Madsen, Bud Cort

Rarely has a fantasy film been so quickly financed, and in such unusual circumstances. Backing was secured for *Electric Dreams* in four days, and in four weeks it had been sold in South East Asia, and North America. Shooting began two months later.

At one level Virgin Films, and their backers, were taking a risk but first-time feature director Steve Barron already had a major career as a pop video maker, most famously shooting the video for Michael Jackson's *Billie Jean* (1982), an early MTV hit. Also, *Electric Dreams* wove a number of contemporary pop songs directly into its story, and many of the musicians involved – Boy George, Heaven 17, Giorgio Moroder, Jeff Lynne – were signed to Virgin. Barron shot pop videos as he went along, incorporating

Screen burn: an accident with a champagne bottle leads to *Electric Dreams* (1984) for nerdy architect Miles Harding (Lenny Von Dohlen).

sequences from the feature film and shooting new material on Twickenham Studios' special sound stage, and the film could be sold at many levels, reducing risk, whilst appealing to a whole new visual culture.

The meeting of music industry finance with the international film market no doubt felt pregnant with possibilities and Virgin Films were not alone in attempting to pull the two worlds together. Pop videos were big business, popular but also a frame for the new and experimental. Pete Townshend announced plans for a video album and nightclubs installed screens above the dance floor. The labels behind Paul McCartney, Mick Jagger, The Style Council and the Pet Shop Boys all got involved too, their charges actually appearing in full-length feature films, acting and singing. The pop musical was reborn into a strange new glitzy, glamorous, cynical world – and it felt distinctly exciting to those used to only four channels on TV and whatever was playing at the provincial cinema.

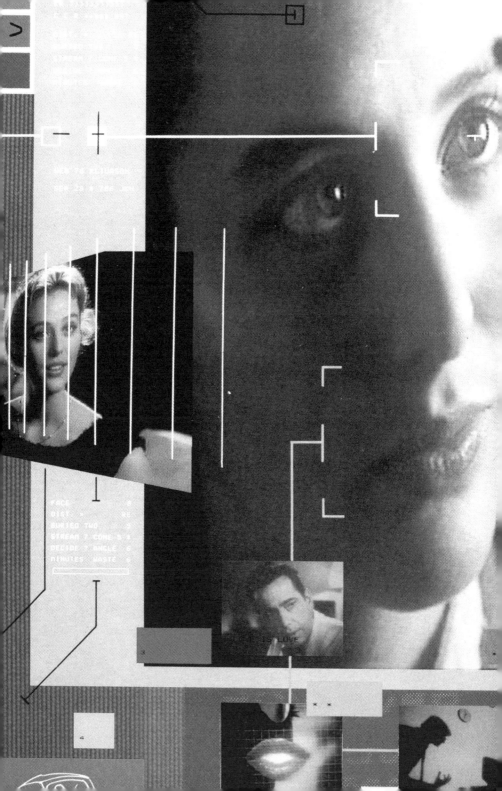

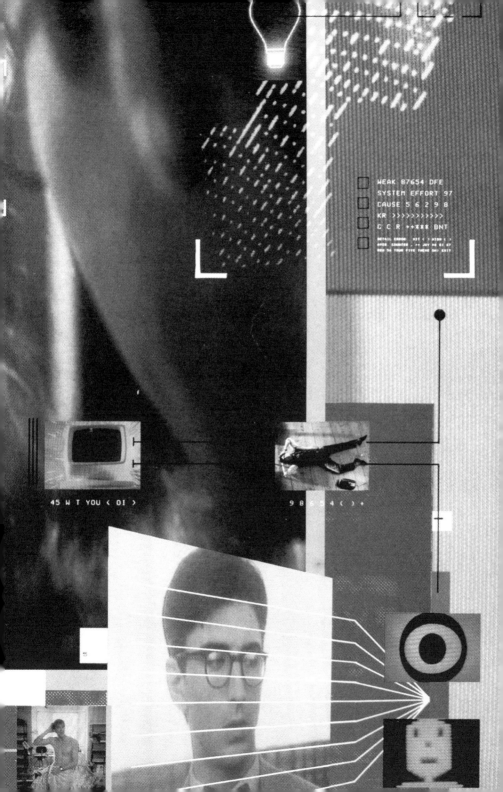

WEAK 87654 DFE
SYSTEM EFFORT 97
CAUSE 5 6 2 9 8
KR >>>>>>>>>>
C C R ++*** BNT

45 W T YOU ⟨ OI ⟩

9 8 6 5 4 ( ) +

« **Computer love:** a network of gazes, incorporating an intimate moment between Virginia Madsen and Lenny Von Dohlen; the *Electric Dreams* (1984) soundtrack LP inner sleeve.

Mick Jagger's *Running Out of Luck* (1987) was a particularly unusual effort. Kicking-off with a staged pop video shoot, it saw Jagger play opposite real-life wife Jerry Hall whilst lip-synching to a song from his new solo album, *She's the Boss*. Kidnapped after the shoot, he wakes-up in a Brazilian banana plantation. He makes his way to a shop and talks to the two assistants, but they don't speak English, or recognize him, even when he points at a Stones record and starts singing *Jumpin' Jack Flash*. They'd have heard of the Rolling Stones, but who's this guy in tight white trousers and a tailored eighties jacket? Who indeed, right? He's either a different person, or lost – in every sense – without his band. Director Julien Temple may be a genius.

'Meet Edgar. He'll make you sing, make you dance, make you laugh, make you cry, make you jealous, make you nuts,' read the *Electric Dreams* poster. The main character, Miles, is a bow-tie, glasses-wearing nerdy architect – visually pre-dating, or perhaps inventing, millennial hipster-gay fashion and was somewhat different to the still vaguely hip Rolling Stones singer. Out in San Francisco, he is a man out of step, and trying to invent the earthquake-immune brick. Madeline, his neighbour and love interest, by way of contrast, is more overtly sexy, but still bookish. She plays the cello and hangs out at home. The film is mundane and domestic, a family picture, perhaps aimed at pre-teens and early teens, not older kids already going-out and buying music.

Fed-up after arriving late to an important meeting Miles decides to get organized and buys a computer, the Pinecone. Setting it up that evening, it starts to overheat and in a flap, he pours champagne on the keyboard. The lights flash, toasters pop and like Frankenstein's monster, the beast comes to life; Miles' computer assumes a consciousness: Edgar, the third character in a rather strange love triangle.

Trying to pretend everything is normal – it isn't – Miles heads off to work and leaves his computer stewing at home. Enter Madeline, who gets underway with her daily cello practice. Miles and Madeline would never get it together without Edgar. Hearing her play, electronic entity Edgar sends electronic purrs and bleeps back through the air-ducts. Intrigued, thinking it's Miles, Madeline returns to the tune with renewed sweaty vigour. A high-octane duet ensues (in real life realized and recorded by Giorgio Moroder), and then it's over. Madeline sits back breathless, post-orgasmic even?

There's something Cyrano de Bergerac-like about the story. Or to take a different approach, is Edgar (voiced by Bud Cort, Harold in black funereal comedy *Harold and Maude* (1971)) a Mister Hyde to Miles' Doctor Jekyll? Is he the part of Miles that wants to be brash, childish and seductive? The mismatched Miles and Madeline begin to date; Edgar helps out by composing music on his owner's behalf. Later, he gets angry, resentful even. He blocks Miles' credit card and creates chaos with the lights and locks. His owner goes into one of his charming, over-the-top neurotic spins, reaching out to the boy nerds watching in the cinema, the gay audience, and any women with maternal tendencies. It gets virtually slapstick at times. What's at the heart of this romance – two lonely people drifting in a technology obsessed San Francisco (future home of the computer industry) or some unusual seduction techniques and a lot of front?

Of course, novel romantic comedies are rarely the stuff from which cult films are made and there's no radical attempt to get the process underway here. Even the director expressed mixed feelings about the film, saying that it 'was a little bit like an extended music video. I didn't help that cause in a lot of ways.' The cause being pop video directors making 'legitimate' films. But this may be self-protection, an attempt to offset criticism. The film is light in tone, certainly, but there is much pleasure to be had in its neurosis and dark details.

Consider the very beginning of the film, when, waiting nervously in an airport lounge, amidst remote-control cars and bleeping toys and digital watches, Miles sees a woman apparently talking to him. 'Hello, how are you? Where do you live? Where do you work? Where is the post office? Do you have any bananas?' And more enigmatically: 'I like the blue dress.' She's not speaking to him, however; she's repeating phrases from a 'teach yourself English' cassette tape playing in one of the new-fangled Walkman machines, this one being clamped to her ears and hidden in her big eighties hair. He responds, and then slumps when realizing that she's otherwise engaged. There is no communication, just self-absorption and alienation – despite the taped language lesson.

Reviewers criticized *Electric Dreams*. 'The machine-protagonist possesses more acting ability than its human counterparts', said the *Journal of Popular Film and Television*. But this seems to be either stating the obvious or missing the point. It's essentially a medium budget, commercial film (with weird, unacknowledged dark undertones) aimed at a general audience. The characters are archetypes, and the pleasure and sadness comes from seeing them fumble and stumble in the metaphorical dark as they try to reach out to each other. With Edgar in tow, they're either too advanced to fit neatly into this brave new world, or somehow still lagging behind. Like when Miles takes a pager to one of Madeline's concerts and Edgar starts obsessively paging him (or messaging him, to use modern parlance). Beeps fill the air to the disquiet of the stiff oldies also in attendance, and Miles goes into one of his panics, running around the building and eventually flushing the damn thing down the toilet.

Electric Dreams wasn't the first movie to feature a computer out of control. The monotonous Hal lost it in *2001: A Space Odyssey* (1968) and Julie Christie's computer tried to do truly awful things in *Demon Seed* (1977). In those days computers seemed to represent an external threat to humanity. But later, as electronic technology became more domestic, the 'threat' changed. Edgar is like Kitt in *Knight Rider* (1982–86) or Johnny Five in *Short Circuit* (1986). He's fun, larger-than-life, but he also symbolizes sadness and disconnection; man and machine beginning to blur under the veil of laughter. The alienation is there too, if in considerably more violent terms, in *Terminator* (1984) and *Robocop* (1987), and not just in the stories of the individual robots, but in the very fabric of the worlds that they inhabit; answering machines and other devices helping people whilst keeping them apart too.

It's present in *Electric Dreams* but arguably just to pass Miles off as a figure of fun, someone to laugh at – and may be with – as he fails to get to grips with eighties modernity. It also exaggerates the unlikeliness of his union with the chilled out, sexy Madeline.

But the dominance of technology in the film goes beyond Miles and his numerous pratfalls. When Miles and Madeline go on a tourist trip to Alcatraz, Edgar is left to write a love song. He peruses the TV and telephone lines as a way of learning about modern love – now he'd use the internet – and he creates a strange cut-up love song. The music reflects and even exaggerates the fun time they're having whilst commenting on the proceedings too, technology trapping them as they smile and laugh. The high-energy collage forms a musical backdrop as Miles and Madeline wander the legendary prison, and at one point, tellingly, sit in a prison cell.

The film's theme song, *Together in Electric Dreams*, by synth-pioneer Giorgio Moroder and Phil Oakey of the Human League, becomes a song that Edgar writes and sends around the world. It too works at various levels. It plays on the radio – everywhere – and Miles and Madeline listen to it as they drive off from San Francisco at the end. We're all together, stuck, stuck in '*Electric Dreams*'. (But at least the computer helps Miles to invent and realise his earthquake-immune brick.)

Steve Barron had used the self-reflexive approach before, notably with his video for *Don't You Want Me* (1981) by the Human League. The number one hit, which incorporated self-referential lyrics, partially evoking how, supposedly, singers Phil Oakey and Joanne Catherall had first met, was presented as a British film noir/romantic thriller, and it documented the process of its own making. We see images of the band shooting the video in which they appear (wearing long, sharp macs), and then reviewing it in a preview theatre, everyone looking very tense and projecting ill feeling, reflecting the emotions of the song. Again, life, technology and the process of being in an artificial, constructed world all weave into and inform on each other. The emotions are confusing, but still real.

The new technologies and new approaches in *Electric Dreams* went down badly with the critics, and the fact it was made by an upstart video director was a problem too. They were suspicious. Many felt that Barron and others like him had had it easy, slipping effortlessly from 'throwaway' pop promos to full-blown features. The main criticism seemed to be that pop video directors paid scant regard to plot. 'While promos are a medium in which the imagination can continually break conventional bounds, unlike an advert, it has no built-in concept of narrative – the crucial weakness of *Electric Dreams*' said *Films and Filming* in October 1984. Looking back from the perspective of the internet age these anti-narrative, non-realist tendencies feel prophetic. 'Personal computers taking over our lives could well be where it's at' said Steve Barron in his autobiography, looking back to 1984. Yes, it could.

Whatever you say about Barron, he put his time in. He worked for Samuelson's film equipment and was later a clapper loader/camera operator on *A Bridge Too Far* (1977), *The Duellists* (1977) and *Superman* (1978). If anything, he was actually something of a tech-head and had learnt about feature filmmaking at the coalface. Later he directed episodes of *The Storyteller* (15/05/87 - 10/07/1988), plus features *Teenage Mutant Ninja Turtles* (1990) and *Mike Bassett: England Manager* (2001), with fantasy themes often playing a part.

Unloved and only very recently available on DVD, *Electric Dreams* was, in its own way, part of a vanguard movement in the British film industry. Production and profit had been in decline but, like the other 'pop musicals', it built on new trends and new technological developments. With MTV being in the ascent, the approach was savvy.

It and its cousins were certainly different to the 'Heritage Cinema' of Merchant Ivory and their films *A Room With a View* (1985) and *Howard's End* (1992). This is the British cinema of the establishment, of a world frozen in aspic, reassuring to some but just as cynically crafted to sell like holiday brochure propaganda to the American market. *Electric Dreams* may be unreal but it has at least in some way proved to be prophetic – the film looks forward, not back.

For all its future visions, cynical or otherwise, the film did still, however, make romantic references to classical culture. Madeline plays her instrument in the day, has a classic musician boyfriend (at first), and she performs concerts in the evening. The sexy cellist is something of a recurring eighties character. The sophisticated, feminine archetype crops up in *Ghostbusters* (1984) and then again in *The Living Daylights* (1987). And in each case, the tousled-hair siren needs rescuing from a stiff, European – read 'queer' – boyfriend. He's up against it, but thankfully nerdy Miles has Edgar to help him in *Electric Dreams*.

The cellist archetype didn't entirely go away, rather it transmuted. Alan Rickman took up a twist on the role in *Truly, Madly, Deeply* (1990), the British, sedate, middle class equivalent of Hollywood's *Ghost* (1990). He's passed on and his partner bears the confusion and pain of being a widow. He stays with her, chatting with the other dead people in her house, also occasionally knocking-off tunes on his instrument. But he gets bored. He has to do something in this strange new time, the end of the eighties, the end of life. What does he do? He looks back, he rewinds, he fast-forwards, he watches movies – on good old VHS. The old, the new, the fantastical;

they all interrelate and overlap in strange post-modern fashion in these movies. We're all stuck, stuck in 'electric dreams'. And in the case of *Electric Dreams*, the storyline may seem a little sappy to some – others would say it was charming, and funny – but at least it also had Steve Barron to introduce tight, multi-layered edits, and a strange, existential darkness. *WF*

TALES OF TERROR

When independent British film production company Hammer remade *Dracula* in colour in 1958, and scored international success, it appeared to reclaim the classic British gothic tale back from the USA and Bela Lugosi's iconic 1931 Universal Studios portrayal. Careful design, art direction and bright punchy colours reinvigorated the cinematic imaginary surrounding Bram Stoker's brilliant book and placed it more clearly amidst the period textures and environments of the Victorian era in which it was set. And of course, Peter Cushing and Christopher Lee brought a profound, studied seriousness to their roles as Van Helsing and the Count respectively, vigorously lunging at each other with charismatic intensity during moments of battle. Lee brought simmering sexuality to his Dracula, too, outranking everyone in the height department, compelling in his command of his female victims and followers – who understandably seem imminently glad to do this bidding, as he flourishes his long, red-lined cloak around his grand, imposing, steely frame. An actor of some experience already, finally hitting the big time with this portrayal, he'd never escape *Dracula* – the role that would make his reputation – and would reluctantly be drawn back to the character through the 1960s and 1970s. Even his much-vaunted turn in the *Lord of the Rings* (2001-03) trilogy failed to sever the link to the fictional

‹ **Some of us are looking at the stairs:** Linda Hayden and Isla Blair stalk a wet, cold Highgate Cemetery, hoping to *Taste the Blood of Dracula* (1970).

vampire that had mastered him – and obituary photos of the actor after his death depicted him once again as the bloodshot-eyed, commanding, undead master of darkness.

Naturally, one would expect more outrage and more extreme horrors after 1969, when the salacious sounding 'X certificate', which had already been oft-exploited and highlighted by filmmakers (as with *The Quatermass Xperiment* (1955), or *X The Unknown* (1956)) was raised to only allow admission to those of eighteen years and above, rather than sixteen. And in certain respects, outrage and extremity were delivered, as the form changed and began to mirror the grimy, grotty decade that was the 1970s. Kubrick's *A Clockwork Orange* (1971), if you want to call it a horror film, with its unsavoury assortment of ultra-violence to the accompaniment of classical music, would never have been released before the relaxing of censorial restriction that came with that 'permissive' decade.

And away from the big studios, by the 1970s the great independent filmmaker Pete Walker was also notably strident in his glorious efforts to update the form, describing his films as 'terror pictures' rather than horror films. Walker, with the aid of ace scriptwriter David McGillivray, wanted to, and succeeded in, rattling the cage of the establishment. Thus the judges, priests and mothers in his film narratives were often deranged; abusers and even destroyers of life, truly out of control and yet somehow maintaining that stiff-upper lipped-look of respectability whenever anyone appeared likely to challenge their credentials. Walker's product, for all the controversy it caused with the moral guardians, was top quality stuff; and he was, like other entrepreneurial filmmakers over at companies Tigon, Amicus and other even smaller operations, able to crank out modestly-budgeted films and for the most part make a profit, simply by being able to offer something that television and the mainstream could not – or rather would not – dare to deliver.

But for the likes of Hammer, in this slightly later time, their strange, almost experimental updates of their previous successes still seemed in thrall to earlier years, their growing reputation as the elder-statesmen of Brit horror creating boundaries of sorts to a true update. A vampire might appear in contemporary times in *Dracula A.D. 1972* (1972) and *The Satanic Rites of Dracula* (1973) but notably it was still Christopher Lee, Dracula hairpiece carefully positioned, shoved into frame to stare hypnotically, perhaps partially in a trance, perhaps partially bored, at an ever-more hollow-cheeked Peter Cushing as Van Helsing, clearly a similarly eternal foe, despite all the happening young vampires surrounding them in groovy black polo-necks and aviator shades. Hammer's more novel ventures at this time – like the excellent *Dr Jekyll and Sister Hyde* (1971) and *Hands of the Ripper* (1971) – took some enjoyably odd risks with the brand – but they just never went quite as far as you thought they might.

Charismatic, personality driven horror is written into British film DNA, it would seem. As far back as the 1930s, the underrated barnstorming board-treader Tod Slaughter delighted audiences 'in the provinces' with his sinister, scheming mustachios-twirling villains, as portrayed in his proto-horror Gothic-styled old school melodramas, including *Sweeney Todd, The Demon Barber of Fleet Street* (1936) and *Crimes at the Dark House* (1940). Bela Lugosi, the great Universal Studios Dracula himself, was lured to the British Isles in the 1950s to undertake a theatre tour version of Stoker's story – and then, when his own ill health curtailed the tour, just prior to a West End run – helped to pay for his passage home by appearing in the marvellously misguided music hall mash-up *Mother Riley Meets the Vampire* (1952). Once he got back, of course, he'd join forces with that awful auteur Ed Wood, appear in a superlative string of Eddie's micro-budget masterworks, and end his career posthumously popping up in Wood's unforgettable *Plan 9 From Outer Space* (1959). But that's another story.

Gothic tropes have always pervaded British popular culture – and let's give a nod to early-independent pop producer Joe Meek's recording artiste-extraordinaire, theatrical, Kensington-gore spattered, entrails-at-the-audience-chucking rock and roller Screaming Lord Sutch. The gaudy full-colour Cinebox music-jukebox promo film for the Lord's shock rock serial-killer song *Jack the Ripper* (1963) saw Mr Sutch indulging in some thoroughly distasteful theatrics, very much in the early-Hammer mould.

By the seventies, of course, you could buy a Dracula lolly, and a pair of plastic fangs. There was space for horror everywhere it seemed; but none of the old ghosts and ghoulies stuff seemed that frightening anymore, in a post *Texas Chainsaw Massacre* (1974) world. Bram Stoker's nephew, journalist Daniel Farson, wrote and presented the documentary *The Dracula Business* (transmitted 06/08/1974), which reflected how vampires were now the stuff of package tours abroad; in 1979, the classic BBC drama series *Play*

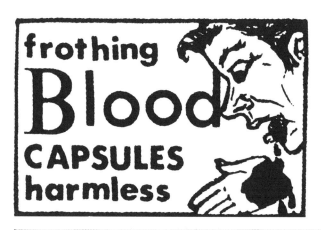

Please rush me a Dracula T shirt: bloody brilliant vampire merchandise for your nearest and dearest.

For Today even made a genre related piece, *Vampires,* which demonstrated very clearly how Dracula had become strictly kids' stuff, compared to the world-weary realities of family life.

Though they may have seemed increasingly old-school and hackneyed, the classic Gothic horror themes refused to stay entirely buried, their archetypical components giving oxygen to more contemporary forms of alienation and transgression. The aforementioned Pete Walker – perhaps mellowing as years went by? – remained seduced by the art form's early years, the modern terror master opening the 1980s with the *House of the Long Shadows* (1983), bringing together classic horror stalwarts Vincent Price, Christopher Lee (not playing a vampire), Peter Cushing and John Carradine in a semi-post-modern reworking of the classic old dark house story of yore. Walker couldn't escape the traditions of the genre; and in this late work he embraced them.

In the 1970s and 1980s, dreams of the old Hollywood, the Hollywood Babylon of dream imagery and magic, captivated and lingered in some quarters as filmmakers groped toward old aesthetics whilst simultaneously updating them for the modern era. Andy Milligan, assuredly of this school, travelled from his native America to the UK to find new opportunities for film production – reversing the journey of filmic forebears like James Whale, who had founded an ex-pat film colony Stateside known as 'Hollywood, England' back in the early 1930s – and employed curious camera techniques and styles that mimicked, in distinctly low-budget, weird fashion, both the work of Whale, and the German Expressionists before him. Milligan's films were shot on location, however, distinguishing them from the more studio bound work of early cinema.

Despite those Dracula lollies, in the naughty 1970s, horror assumed many unlikely guises, and even innocuous screen narratives were embedded with distasteful ideas, and associations with the unpleasant and the corrupt – at least in the eyes of the National Viewers' and Listeners' Association. hoping to turn back the clock and realign the nation's moral compass. BBC television show *Casanova '73: The Adventures of a 20th-Century Libertine* (13/09 - 29/10/1973) was a curious case in point. Starring Leslie Phillips as a philandering businessman who leads a double life of covert sexual exploits, this controversial TV comedy series, scripted by *Hancock's Half Hour* writers Ray Galton and Alan Simpson, challenged the current mainstream of social protocol – at least to Whitehouse's outraged eyes. After much fuss-making, she succeeded in having the show moved to a later slot in the evening. In doing so, she allied it with a whole range of films and programmes that were deemed – by her and her legion of supporters, at least – to be horrific and unsuitable.

Yet the call of horror has remained a compelling one, for studios and audiences alike. Despite the back and forth of that endless game with the censor, the genre has developed and dragged itself towards ever more grotesque and gory arenas. Body snatchers, undead men coming back to life, madmen, molesters, serial killers; all have hit – if not actually splattered onto – the country's cinema screens over the years. But maybe the most enduringly pertinent point of all this is that filmmakers still somehow seem to be able to expose and shock our nerve endings. They still find ways to express and articulate our traumas and shameful sexuality, to dig at our very deepest fears and dreads, and to exhilarate us by exhuming – or at the very least reconnecting us with – that same age-old frisson of fear. Though sometimes assuredly silly, horror rightly remains a serious business. And in today's terrifying society, we need it to be.

Speaking of which, no actor ever took horror more seriously than Bela Lugosi. So how did he end up making a British comedy film with a man dragged up as an Irish washerwoman? Read on…

Mother Riley Meets the Vampire
aka *Old Mother Riley Meets the Vampire*
aka *My Son the Vampire* aka *Vampire over London*

UK Film | 1952 | colour | 74mins
Director John Gilling
Script Val Valentine
Producer John Gilling
Cast Arthur Lucan, Bela Lugosi

It was the oddest of meetings between two eccentric film stars, past their prime, in financial trouble, in the twilight of their careers. Back in the

1930s good old days, one of them, Bela Lugosi, had played Dracula in Hollywood, a role for which he was still remembered. Yet he had struggled to emerge from the shadow of the bat, and two decades later, according to some passed-down-over-the-years accounts of his life story, he found himself penniless and marooned in England with only his trademark cape and a customised velvet-lined coffin to his name. The other aging star was Arthur Lucan, a provincially popular music hall comic who dragged up to become his elderly Irish washerwoman alter-ego Old Mother Riley. He/she could also reflect on 1930s glory days, having performed at royal command way back then; but like Lugosi, Lucan's popularity and prospects had narrowed over the years. Accidentally allied, in an act of ingenious if desperate entrepreneurship, they would unexpectedly throw their hats (or bonnet, in the case of Lucan) into the filmmaking ring one more time to appear in one of the strangest collisions of Anglo-American exploitation ever committed to celluloid: the impossibly ludicrous team-up picture *Mother Riley Meets the Vampire*. How did it happen?

Despite becoming the iconic screen vampire, things hadn't worked out right for Bela Lugosi ever since he turned down the role of Frankenstein's monster, the part made famous by Boris Karloff. A rivalry – real or imagined – would forever be perceived between the two actors; career-wise, Karloff had won hands down. Lugosi was doomed to be cruelly neglected by casting directors at Universal, the studio responsible for *Dracula*, for reasons still uncertain. Some claim that Lugosi rubbed people up the wrong way, while others effusively proclaimed his friendliness on set. What can't be denied is that he was denied his rightful cloak in the Dracula sequels, suffering the indignity of seeing unsuitable types like lumbering Lon Chaney Jr stiffly taking his role in *Son of Dracula* (1943). The indignity! The choice of Chaney Jr. as Dracula is mystifying, while the original and best Bela was forced into countless thankless parts, for ever-smaller studios, sometimes involving a ridiculous surfeit of glued-on facial hair. Lugosi, alas, was an old man by the time he finally got to play Dracula on screen once more, in the successful fusion of comedy and chills, *Abbott and Costello Meet Frankenstein* (1948), and perhaps he expected the phone to start ringing again; but it did not herald a new era of plentiful work. In latter days, Lugosi was often forced on to the road, making money through undignified personal appearances at cinemas. Following the screening of one of his films, Lugosi would perform a ramshackle sketch with 'a giant gorilla and a manacled girl' to audiences of noisy, disinterested children. One imagines Bela didn't like it much, but it was a living.

1951 saw Lugosi, in search of the better things he deserved, lured to England to play a provincial stage tour of *Dracula*. Lugosi was encouraged because the gig was set up by Richard Gordon, a devoted fan of the actor. Gordon had befriended Bela in the States, when he and his brother, asking for an interview for an amateur fan magazine, had been amazed to be invited to dinner with the actor. Lugosi, swept up with Gordon's enthusiasm subsequent to their meeting, was filled with renewed hope when he heard of the offer, and so agreed to the tour. Ever the showman, he even suggested he should be carried off the boat in a coffin (alas, the customs officials were not so keen).

Arriving in England in March 1951, Lugosi was contracted to appear in the first full-length production of *Dracula* he'd played in for some years. Produced by John Mather, and directed by Richard Eastham, the show ran for more than 200 performances at venues across the UK. Opinions were initially mixed as to the show's quality; with British actress Megs Jenkins (later so memorable in *The Innocents* (1961)) commenting of the dress rehearsal 'This is pretty poor'; and apparently director Eastham agreed. But after some teething troubles, and despite problems with an unwieldy smoke machine and a rubbery prop-bat on wires which sometimes crash-landed unexpectedly, the show garnered some good reviews; with Lugosi attracting especially favourable notices for his proud and time-honed portrayal of the Count.

Despite some new padding, to elongate the show, Lugosi's cues and speeches remained unchanged, and thus his performances were, in the main, impeccable. However, old trouper Bela was not the strapping young fellow he used to be. He couldn't appear in the coffin for the final scene and was replaced by a dummy. The reason? 'We might not have got him erect for the curtain calls,' Eastham recalled to Frank Dello Stritto, Lugosi biographer supreme, and author of the seminal *Vampire Over London*, some decades later.

Producer Mather, who was negotiating a deal to book the show into West End theatres following its provincial run, was also well aware of his star's frailty. 'Bela looked as if he were going to die,' he remembered later; 'he

MY SON THE VAMPIRE
B/W Running Time 68 Minutes
STARRING: ARTHUR LUCAN as OLD MOTHER RILEY
Old Mother Riley receives a crate intended for the crazed (Bela Lugosi) known as The Vampire. She "inherits" a robot which turns his life upside down. Whilst the police are hot on the trail of the Vampire, the Vampire is hot on the trail of the robot. An enjoyable partnership of comedy and terror. Including Hattie Jacques, Dora Bryan, Richard Wattis and many others.

An enjoyable partnership of comedy and terror: the first early 1980s pre-cert UK VHS of *Mother Riley Meets the Vampire* (1952), released in its US cut as *My Son the Vampire*.

always looked that way.'The only times Lugosi came to life, it would seem, were whilst leafing through his scrapbook of Hungarian newspaper reviews of past glories, or rejuvenated onstage as Lord of the Undead. Mather recalled that, then, 'the transformation was complete: he looked 40 again, erect and towering. When he was Dracula, he had this twinkle in his eye.'

Apparently, drugs helped with that twinkle. Bela was an addict; and his wife Lillian would be waiting in the wings to administer his injections. But eventually, despite the artificial stimulants, exhaustion got the better of Lugosi. The tour had to be curtailed, on the very brink of Mather negotiating to get the show a West End opening at The Garrick Theatre. Years later, still Mather recalled Bela's anguished words, gasped out backstage at a theatre in Derby: "'John, I can't go on," he said, "It's taking too much out of me. Please finish it quickly." I put up the closing notices that week.'

With the tour unexpectedly ended, Bela still remained a long way from home with no work prospects and – thanks to the demands of his drug addiction – it might well be that, though – contrary to some accounts if this period – he was certainly paid for the tour, he soon had no money to pay his return fare to America.

Things had not turned out as planned; but Richard Gordon was still keen to help. He approached George Minter, head of the independent company Renown, looking for a potential film for Lugosi. Renown handled the *Old Mother Riley* series, starring the aforementioned Arthur Lucan. The series was petering out, but another comedy was on the cards. *Abbott and Costello Meet Frankenstein* had recently done better than expected at the box office, in the UK and the US. Bela Lugosi was at hand; why not fuse British comedy with American horror? And so, *Mother Riley Meets the Vampire* was conceived.

Lucan was easily as eager as Lugosi for money. In trouble with the tax man, he desperately needed work. The good old days were a long, long way back. Born Arthur Towle in Lincolnshire in 1885, he'd been treading the boards since he ran away from home aged fourteen to take to the stage. Appearing in Ireland in 1913 – there choosing Lucan as a more Irish sounding stage name – he'd married young Kitty McShane, with whom he developed the double act that made him famous. Growing out of a sketch entitled *Brigette's Night Out*, in which he donned a dress and played a fast-talking Irish washerwoman, he'd created the Old Mother Riley character, starring in a successful series of cheaply made comedy films, and playing a Royal Command Performance in 1934. His reputedly volatile wife Kitty played his daughter. The act was billed as *Old Mother Riley and her daughter, Kitty*. But latter days brought a downturn in the star's fortunes. The Lucan / McShane relationship, so cheery and chucklesome on screen, was tempestuous and tortuous in real life. Comedian Max Wall – who glimpsed what went on off stage – later attested that Lucan had suffered greatly, as a battered husband. Endless rows, marital discord and bouts of violence meant that in later films, the two stars could no longer bear to share the same sound stage. Ultimately, their scenes were shot independently, to be edited together later; they parted to perform in separate stage shows.

Resourceful Kitty did not allow her dislike of her spouse to prevent her from touring with her own rival *Old Mother Riley* show – with one of Arthur's understudies, Roy Rolland, taking the leading role. Lucan, too, carried on, replacing Kitty with a stand-in. But still the horror continued, it would seem, culminating in Kitty – according to Slim Ingram, Lucan's show manager – attempting to burn down a theatre at which Arthur was appearing. Lucan – free of Kitty, but still afraid of her influence – was soon really on his uppers; possibly even harder up than Lugosi, and teetering on the verge of bankruptcy. He did not hesitate to sign up for Minter's film.

Gordon had reservations; he worried that Old Mother Riley might not cut the mustard with US audiences. But Minter was determined. Though Lucan and Lugosi were culturally miles apart, there were some professional similarities. Both were star names that still had some marquee value – albeit very different marquees. Both performers badly needed work; both were synonymous with one particular strange, pervasive fictional characterisation that had eerily displaced – or perhaps even to a degree replaced – their own identities. Lugosi, forever the undead count, travelled everywhere with his own cape and coffin; even hard times did not see him parted from them. Lucan had his own little ways, and seemed too to have melted into his stage persona. He would arrive at film studios in full Old Mother Riley costume, wig and make-up; at night he returned home the same way. Nobody – except Kitty, perhaps, assuming the wig sometimes came off – ever saw the real Arthur Lucan. And he preferred it that way. Lugosi was addicted to drugs; Lucan drank heavily. Lucan hoped to appease his tormentors at the tax office; Lugosi was paying for a boat ticket home.

A baffling conception to Lugosi: Arthur Lucan as Old Mother Riley, as seen on a 1940s cigarette card.

Time was of the essence. Lugosi was hired for a month, and John Gilling – later to go on to better things at Hammer – was enlisted to direct. In a shameless bit of screenplay piracy, the script was a hasty rehash of the Abbott and Costello film that had been such a success. Shooting took place at Walton's tiny Nettlefold Studios. How did Lugosi and Lucan get on? According to Richard Gordon, Lugosi was a bit puzzled at first as to whether Lucan – arriving, as usual, in feminine garb – was a man or a woman. More worryingly for Bela, Lucan was prone to the odd ad-lib, which disturbed the hard-of-hearing horror star – such things would put him off his cues – but generally speaking he was simply glad to have a job. Lugosi's main worry was that Old Mother Riley would make him appear more ludicrous than he would wish. Old Mother Riley was a baffling conception to Lugosi, entirely unfamiliar with cornball British music hall comedy, and with no prior knowledge of humorous Irish washerwomen. Yet, surprisingly, their scenes together, in the finished product that quickly emerged, are some of the best in the film. Bizarre but true.

Watch it if you dare. The plot is a bit of a jumble, but let that not concern us too deeply. Lugosi plays a fanatical scientist, Von Housen, who seems both to be abducting women and plotting to take over the world with an army of robots. Von Housen is known as 'The Vampire'; except that actually he's not one. Great pains are taken to demonstrate that he is not a vampire who is also an atomic scientist, but an atomic scientist who merely thinks he's a vampire. And sleeps in a coffin, in a vampire cape. And thirsts for blood. Clear? Gordon and Minter were worried that if Lugosi actually played a vampire, the film would get an 'A' certificate – preventing unaccompanied children – Old Mother Riley's core fan base – from seeing it. So Bela does not play a vampire here, even though the title says he is. This is rather a disappointment, so you may choose to decide that he is a vampire nonetheless. As for Von Housen's robots, he's only built one so far, and it's en route to the obligatory spooky house in a packing case. Meanwhile, Old Mother Riley, who works in a shop in this one, has just heard that she has inherited Uncle Jerimiah's fortune, comprised of a crate full of brassy bric-a-brac. Guess what: labels fall off, etcetera, and the crates get swapped. You guessed it. The robot is delivered to Old Mother Riley.

Controlling it by radio, Von Housen commands his robot to kidnap Riley. It's one of those great old cheapo-movie robots, and the scene of the robot going to get Mother Riley is actually pretty good. Why does Bela want her, though? He thinks he's a vampire, remember, so he decides that Riley is to be his next victim. Interesting choice. Having captured her, he offers her a job, while he does his best to fatten her up with steak and liver. Yeeuch! There are further complications: it would seem that aside from the vampiric exploits and his robot army, Von Housen is also after a uranium mine. I won't bother you with the ramshackle twists and turns, but there is an intriguing bit with the robot driving around with a drunk, some business involving revolving doors in the walls, a woman strapped to an operating table, secret passages, and punch-ups with gangsters.

Graham Moffatt, sidekick to Will Hay in a string of rather splendid British comedies, suddenly appears, up a ladder, for a cameo appearance. Oddly nobody bothers to attempt to write him any funny lines; as in most of his post-Hay appearances, he seems to be there purely so viewers can reflect upon how much he has aged since he played the cheeky fat boy in Hay's entourage. Other more familiar faces lurk about in the background: Hattie Jacques, Dandy Nichols, Richard Wattis. None would ever reminisce about this one. At the end, it's back projection ahoy as there is a frenzied car chase, before a boat-based finale. Old Mother Riley ends up in the water, after some riding about on a motorbike. Of course she does. Disappointingly, Bela does not get much to do in the end, as he is rather feebly subdued by some coppers. Surely he should have been surprised at dawn, and then had a stake bashed into him? Alas no. For he is not a vampire. He just thinks he is. Bah.

But before this damp-squib end, Lugosi is impressive. He delivers some so-so lines with splendid timing and restraint – he actually almost makes them funny. And – in their scenes together – he tempers his performance carefully to compensate for Lucan's shrill mugging. Lucan's stock-in-trade is to wave his arms and writhe about; Lugosi, by contrast, is calm and collected and – it must be said – very good indeed. This is the viewer's last chance to see Lugosi looking healthy and robust – whatever his medical issues, whatever his addictions, here, though he is obviously older, for the last time, he looks pretty much as we would like him to look: like the King of the Vampires. Despite the ludicrosity of it all, this is not such an ignoble end for Bela, is it? Who knows what he might have done with a better thought out script? Though it's a feeble film, Lucan and Lugosi – an impossible combination – work well together. Who'd a thought it? Certainly not British cinema audiences, who steered well clear.

Lucan's fee was presumably quickly spent: he continued to tour the country, until he dropped dead in the wings of the Kingston-upon-Hull Tivoli while awaiting his cue. Apparently his understudy went on in his place and – until afterwards – nobody was any the wiser. Bela got his fare home, and also managed to do a bit of advertising work, too, presumably earning a few more quid: he was photographed, in his beloved cape, proudly stepping out of a Humber Pullman car, as seen in the film. Clever old Bela.

It is a measure of Gordon's dedication to the film business that though he had previously failed to sell Old Mother Riley to American audiences, he was prepared to give it another go. He'd attempted to flog *Old Mother Riley's New Venture* (1949) to the Irish population of New York, later telling horror buff Tom Weaver 'it was a total disaster'. So, too, it must be remembered, was this. One significant stumbling block to overseas sales was the presence of Old Mother Riley. So an ingenious plan emerged to disguise the fact that Lucan starred in the film altogether, by removing him from the title. Gordon's suggestion was *Vampire Over London*. It was a fine title, but one can only surmise at the reaction of New York cinemagoers, having handed over their hard-earned, to be unexpectedly confronted by Old Mother Riley's lacklustre British provincial schtick.

So, ever ingenious, they considered removing Lucan from the film altogether, planning to rewrite the film as *King Robot*, and shoot more Lugosi footage. This failed owing to a deterioration in poor Bela's health – the new footage would not have matched the old. So it was back to the drawing board. Years later, attempts were still being made to wring some money – any money – from this seemingly unsellable product. As the 1950s became the 1960s, Minter even wanted to change the title to *Carry On Vampire* to cash in on the British comedy series. This would have been quite a stunt, had he gotten away with it. But he didn't; he was sued. The last throw of the dice saw it become *My Son, The Vampire*, a title which referred to a now-forgotten series of LPs of light-hearted Jewish reworkings of folk songs by Allan Sherman. Sherman even knocked up a song for the title sequence, which was clumsily glued on to re-release prints, but audiences were not fooled, and still steered well clear. But perhaps the day is finally coming when we can appreciate *Mother Riley Meets the Vampire* for the valuable filmic artefact it is; without worrying about whether it is 'good' or 'bad'. Apparently, it went down a storm when it was screened some years back at the Manchester Festival of Fantastic Films. 'They applauded it wildly!' according to Gordon, in attendance, and still trying to sell it, by the sounds of things.

Don't worry, we're not going to even begin to attempt to convince you that this is a good film. However, it sure is a fascinating one. This is the last chance to see Lugosi in full Dracula mode; with coffin and cape, seemingly energetic, definitely enthusiastic to the last. It is not a fine film, but he gives a fine performance. And for Lucan, it provides the key to a hallowed immortality rarely bestowed upon British music hall comedians. Many of his contemporaries – arguably far more talented ones – are already slipping into obscurity. How many of today's kids know of or care about Will Hay or George Formby? But Lucan's portrayal of Riley *will* endure. It'll have to – as long as Lugosi's depiction of Dracula remains iconic – which looks like it might be for long, long time yet. Even if everything else Lucan ever did is forgotten, and it may well be, he/she will remain eternally embalmed in a celluloid casket deep within Lugosi's filmography. Thanks to their accidental alliance, Old Mother Riley may truly live forever. Like a vampire. Or, at least, like a mad scientist who thinks he's one. *VP*

The old horrors might suffer disrespectful parodies but many filmmakers were keen to draw on their blood and life force as a way of infusing their own new efforts with something special – however weird the results. Two decades later, another American abroad in London dabbled in his own delightful kind of deranged English gothic…

The Body Beneath aka *Vampire's Thirst*

UK Film | 1970 | colour | 82mins
Director Andy Milligan
Script Andy Milligan
Producer Leslie Elliot
Production Company Cinemedia Films
Cast Gavin Reed, Jacqueline Skarvellis, Berwick Kaler

An unusual American exploitation filmmaker obsessed with the past, Andy Milligan frequently set his films in all manner of different times and locations: Victorian London, the old American South, and the European Middle Ages, to name just a few. Budgets were small, even for independent horror, and his films became highly theatrical, with lengthy chunks of dialogue, and idiosyncratic costumes, made by his own fair hand, dominating. In unfinished epic *The House of the Seven Belles* (1979), strange garish collars jutted out at unusual angles and stiff, bright fabrics flowed straight to the floor. Milligan took a supporting role, and talked – a lot.

His stories very often centred on dysfunctional families, whilst still finding space for transgressive gore as a way of attracting audiences in the grindhouse cinemas of New York where they typically played. *The Ghastly Ones* aka *Blood Rites* (1968) saw gloopy, syrupy music poured over the tale of a late eighteenth century family gathering while out on the lonely marshes skin was gouged out of arms and legs by an unseen assailant. In the UK, it became one of the oldest of thirty-nine films released on home video in the early 1980s that were seized and banned by the State. In theory, before 1984, anyone of any age could have purchased this very strange film, and taken it home to experience, what? Confusion? Pleasure? Laughter? The gore was surprising realistic, everything else being plastic and over-wrought. But whatever anyone felt about, Milligan's commitment was undoubtable. Something very personal, and special, wove its way around the strange, mannered, melodramatic dialogue.

Milligan had been at the beck and call of producer William Mishkin who essential underfunded and misused his talent whilst helping to get his – any kind of – films made. In 1968, in an attempt to escape Mishkin – and to perhaps create something yet still more personal – Milligan moved to the UK. His first effort was a vampire film, shot, as all its attendant publicity stated, 'in the Graveyards of England.'

> *You all know how close we've come to being discovered by the police for what we are. You all know how difficult it is to move about London after 11.30pm! London is a police state after midnight. Anyone can be stopped and asked where they are going at any-time of the morning!'*
> – Reverend Ford, *The Body Beneath.*

One of seven cemeteries built to address the overflow of London's dead: Highgate Cemetery in the Victorian era.

Relocating from the USA to London, the mysterious Reverend Ford invites a distant relative, Anna Ford, to his new small manor house near a cemetery. The Reverend, it emerges, is a vampire, and he locks-up Anna's husband and later humiliates and tortures his own manservant, the strangely named Spool. Susan Ford, another family member, is lured to the house, so that they might breed incestuous vampire babies. But things start to untangle. Spool helps the Reverend's prisoners to escape, and the increasingly tetchy clergyman calls his long-established USA vampire brethren to a grand party, where he weighs up the pros and cons of his new British homeland, and then departs. The whole thing resolves in atmospheric theatrics, Susan left apparently dead, but then flicking her eyes open, now also a vampire.

The plot was fantastical but appeared to trace a line through Milligan's various preoccupations and even paralleled the finer elements of his own biography, a detail easier to pick-up on in retrospect, notably in light of more recent speculations that he had a very difficult family background, and may have been abused by his mother. Plus of course it referenced his move across the Atlantic, and it was set in the present day.

The Body Beneath retained the director's unique vibe and aesthetic – partly grindhouse, partly something else – and, whilst the film felt more American than British, it still chimed with UK horror's new, increasingly contemporary and/or (Swinging) London focus. Milligan's characters dressed-up in chunky knitwear, de rigeur mini-skirts and heavy eye make-up; and the film's use of Highgate Cemetery connected it to both other movies, and the underground, occult and gay subcultures of the period.

Built in the Victorian era as one of seven commercial cemeteries located on the city's fringes, Highgate Cemetery was designed to attract the wealthy and appealed very much to the macabre, ornate tendencies of the age. By the 1960s, however, it had fallen into disrepair, but was still open to the public. The graveyard featured in several movies from the 1960s onward, most notably in *Taste the Blood of Dracula* (1970), the fifth instalment in the Hammer *Dracula* cycle. Here its thick undergrowth hinders the passage of a group of aging Victorian gentlemen in their progressive hedonistic descent through the different layers of the capital, traveling from the suburbs to the centre, to a club, to a backroom with dancing prostitutes, and then finally Highgate Cemetery, all the time lured on with promise of an untold salaciousness by a modish Ralph Bates.

The run-down cemetery was like a jungle in the midst of the city, with ornate architecture modelled on fallen empires awkwardly poking out from the chaotic greenery. It appeared to call out to, even demand, strange activity. On 14th October 1970, Sean Manchester and Allan Farrant (aka David Farrant) appeared amidst its crumbling walls on BBC London news programme *24 Hours*. Both briefly stumbled on their words as if trying to remember dialogue written and actualized at that very moment – like a spell or a summoning. Or perhaps they were just nervous. Manchester: 'a spectre [later referred to as a vampire] was seen by that gate there, appearing to come from here, which leads to the catacombs.' Farrant wandered by the gravestones, vacantly clutching a wooden stake, and stared at the grass. 'I have seen it, yes. I saw it last February and I saw it on two occasions.'

Everything seemed wild in this strange place, and whilst Amicus film *Tales From the Crypt* (1972) would later open with an impressive, surveying crane shot of the sinister site, *The Body Beneath* took a different approach. Starting on the ground, Milligan slowly wandered amongst the gravestones with an Auricon newsreel camera, the same model favoured by Andy Warhol, following a mourning woman as she passed into and through the gothic, strange passageways cut into the hillside. Peering into the wet, misty air, a smoky dampness infiltrated his out-of-date 16mm stock, and hard colours smudged together, whilst the sound was recorded directly onto a magnetic strip that ran down the edge of the 16mm film as it wove its way around the camera, like a snake. The woman encounters three female vampires (all wearing long-flowing gowns, naturally) who intone with a collective shimmering, undulating voice 'hello-o-o-o-o'. Is this distortion on the mag track? No, it appears to be a special effect.

The Highgate Cemetery vampire story, as reported on the BBC's *Tonight*, unfolded after Andy Milligan had completed *The Body Beneath*. But did his movie somehow influence the reported sightings and subsequent grave desecrations that slowly began to obsess the local press? London was in a state of weird upheaval, the sixties comedown beginning to merge with a new permissiveness that was almost millennial, or fin de siècle, in tone. Occult thinking was on the rise and Milligan's rant about late night London, as delivered via the lips of Reverend Ford, suggested he was frustrated by his new home, whilst also drawing energy from its raw, nocturnal delights – not unlike the Victorian gentlemen in *Taste the Blood of Dracula*.

He became, by all accounts, obsessed with the story of the Hampstead Heath crucifixion. Joseph de Havilland had been found impaled through the palms of his hands to an 8ft cross on 25 July 1968. His accomplices said he thought the act would make the world 'a happier place'. ('There was also talk of the Pope being dethroned, but he denied saying he would have a following greater than the Beatles,' reported *The Times*.) Milligan's version: 'A guy nailed to a tree, bled to death all night. In leather, S&M. Bled to death! Ecstasy.' The hands of servant Spool were nailed to an external wall in *The Body Beneath*, and then a character was pinned to a tree in subsequent movie *Guru, the Mad Monk* (1970). These kind of gay sadomasochist acts strongly appealed to the low-budget auteur and in fact he often himself pushed for blatant violence on stage in his early days as an 'Off-Off-Broadway'

Cometh the man, cometh the hour: secret vampire vicar Reverend Ford, played by Gavin Reed, calls the shots in *The Body Beneath* (1970).

theatre director, perhaps invoking Antonin Artaud's ideas about a 'Theatre of Cruelty' as a way of engaging the audience, directly and viscerally.

It was an unusual time and both *The Body Beneath* and Milligan himself were set at the periphery; the periphery of the city, the periphery of legal sexual practices, and the periphery of the film industry. The cast and crew remained ensconced in North London, shooting in Highgate Cemetery and a small manor house located on the edge of Hampstead Heath, Sarum Chase, the same depicted on the back cover of the Rolling Stones album *Beggars Banquet*. Ornate but curiously sparsely decorated, and a bit rough around the edges, it was renamed 'Carfax Abbey', a la Dracula, and used as the base for the jeering Reverend Ford.

The trashy director himself, however, bedded-down in Soho, at flat 6, 58 Dean Street, and his office was on Wardour Street, putting him in touch with a whole other hedonistic, sexual and creative world. It 'wasn't such a

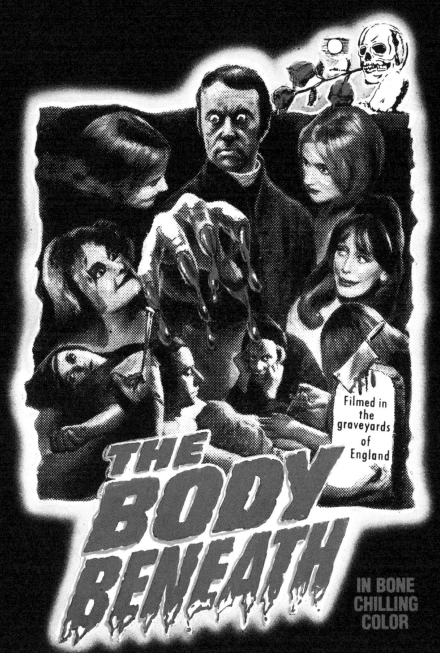

great place – a lot of topless dancing places, striptease places' remembered Milligan actor Hope Stansbury, who came over from the States in August 1969. Soho shop fronts and clubs became more explicit towards the end of the sixties, plus homosexuality had recently been de-criminalised, leading to an increase in 'gay friendly' pubs and clubs. Milligan was well situated to exploit both central London and Hampstead Heath, which for a long time had also been associated with impromptu gay encounters, as well as occult and witchcraft activity.

He had been an active, long-time, late-night cruiser in America. On arriving in London: 'first week there I did research. I went out and talked to the kids in Piccadilly.' By which he meant the rent boys. 'Hang out with the street people, that's how you find out about any country. You don't need to go to the libraries; you go to the street corners, the dives, with the bums and the street peddlers. That's where you see the story,' he told Jimmy McDonough, author of Milligan biography *The Ghastly One*.

The weird thing is, despite all these contextual details and unusual deeds, *The Body Beneath* pursued rather traditional, if not outright old-fashioned horror stylings. For one there was very little actual sex and gore, but also: the 'trio of mute, green-faced harpies swathed in neon-coloured dresses who creepy-crawl in and out of shots like creatures from a Murnau film accidentally shot in comic-book colour,' as observed by McDonough (also using a timely Charles Manson-ism, the 'creepy crawl'); plus the very Igor-like put-upon, bullied hunchback manservant, Spool; and finally, the true man of the hour, the bitchy, compelling Milligan-avatar, Reverend Alexander Algernon Ford, his name presumably deriving in part from weird, gothic fiction writer Algernon Blackwood – all these characters feel like strange, re-worked archetypes drawn from the horror lexicon book of yore.

Gavin Reed who played Reverend Ford is brilliant, commanding the film and everyone in it, propelling it forward with continual barbed pronouncements. He's a different type of vampire to Bela Lugosi's, loading-up on blood via transfusion for one thing, and yet when he aggressively snaps shut an old-style mirrored cigarette case (protecting his obscured visage), he channels the spirit of another time.

‹ **Filmed in the graveyards of England:** lurid video cover for *The Body Beneath* (1970), based on the original grindhouse release poster.

'I love horror films,' Milligan would say. 'All the early Frankenstein and Dracula pictures, the ones that came out in the thirties – all the James Whale. One of the best ones for German Impressionist sets is *Son of Frankenstein* (1939). Wonderful abstract sets, all the camera tilts. That's before he started becoming just a monster, still had the human soul.' Did Milligan want to find his human soul? He was remembered as a tyrant and saw off at least two of his small cast and crew during his London spell; John Borske, who had flown over from the States with Milligan in late '68, quit after just one day's shooting. And yet as Reverend Ford says 'it's strange. I have no soul, yet I feel compassion. It doesn't make sense, does it?'

The shooting of his movie, at times, recalled these earlier works, with Vaseline being smeared around the lens during the climatic vampire banquet scene to channel tensions and Milligan's love of the past. Bright, lurid colours and strange faces loom out of the haze and the assembled vampire clan looks terrific. It evoked Kenneth Anger's occult, underground party gathering film, *Inauguration of the Pleasure Dome* (1954), and yet it was all done in camera, with no unusual cross-cutting or special effects, as was the way in cinema's early days.

Milligan's 'whirl up camera' technique, his way of ending a scene, by twisting and quickly pointing the camera up into the air, also created unusual, DIY sensations; time somehow speeding-up, indicating confusion and high-drama. Was it Milligan's equivalent of the camera tilt, a way of evoking German expressionism, as in *The Cabinet of Dr. Caligari* (1920)?

Of course, *The Body Beneath* was clearly lower budget than other horror films made at this time by the likes of Hammer, Amicus or Tigon. But Milligan appeared to exploit this and pull out a different tone and energy, focusing on his camp street edginess, and on the interplay between the camera and the acting, giving it a certain directness, rarely pulling back to set the scene. It appeared to highlight Milligan's theatrical beginnings; it was in many respects a 'live' production, the director operating the camera and taking in sounds directly onto the filmstrip, the edit, in turn, becoming like a strange jump-cut jigsaw. Its refusal to establish context and a wider view of the landscape allied it with other horror films shot in the UK by foreign directors. Landmarks, class and authority are all heavily sign-posted in Jacques Tourneur's *Night of the Demon* (1957) and Jorge Grau's *The Living Dead at the Manchester Morgue* (1974) and Lucio Fulci's *The*

The fabric flows freely: Gavin Reed dresses to impress – all costumes being made by the director, Andy Milligan – at a final orgiastic vampire banquet in *The Body Beneath* (1970).

Black Cat (1981), yet they're all cut-up versions of the UK, informed by guidebooks and established in the mind's eye of each respective director.

Milligan was only in London from August 1968 to early 1970 but incredibly shot a total of five films there – *Nightbirds*, *The Body Beneath*, *Bloodthirsty Butchers* (1970), *Curse of the Full Moon* aka *The Rats Are Coming! The Werewolves Are Here!* (1972) and *The Man With Two Heads* (1972) – later finishing and unleashing them to audiences in New York.

Milligan's interface with the British film scene was brief, so brief in fact that Jackie Skarvellis (Susan Ford), interviewed in 2012, couldn't even remember appearing in *The Body Beneath*! Berwick Kaler, who played Spool, has had better recall. Watching it and other Milligan titles with writer Steve Thrower he became impressed with how 'proper' they seemed. *The Body Beneath* is certainly unique amongst British films, if we can call it British. A weird transatlantic collision of grindhouse aesthetics with broader influences; it mixed-up British gothic, German expressionism, and early Hollywood.

'What is America? What is it made of? Pimps, prostitutes, religious fanatics, thrown out of England a few small centuries ago. They're the scum of the earth,' says the Reverend Ford, actually quoting the man who pulled the plug on Milligan's British career, the father of Milligan's British producer, Leslie Elliot; Elliot senior misconstruing what he thought was an anti-Semitic comment and stopping the cash flow. And yet paradoxically America is exactly where *The Body Beneath* ended up, a brilliant piece of strange art-trash left rejected, unspooling, spilling images onto screens well-versed in, if not outright jaded by, blood, guts and gore on New York's 42nd Avenue. It was a weird, brilliant mix of ideas, tropes, aesthetics, and experiences. Let's hope it made a good impression. *WF*

Also in the early seventies – another American, who also happened to be a screen horror veteran, was suddenly traversing unexpected television terrain here in dear, unhealthy olde Englande…

Cooking Price-Wise

UK TV | 1971 | colour | 6 x 24mins
Script Vincent Price
Cast Vincent Price
Production Company I D Television

Strange as it may seem, it's not until halfway through the fourth episode of Vincent Price's *Cooking Price-Wise* that the latter-day King of Horror makes any reference at all to his career as a master of the macabre on screen.

He finally gets the chance as he concocts a crocodile-monster out of a cucumber, carefully balancing the cucumber creature on short cocktail stick legs and adorning it with green olive eyes and spines and scales fashioned from cheddar cheese. This whole sequence – entirely unlike the rest of the series, all cheaply cranked out on cheapo video tape – is shot in shadowy low-light, while Price slides suddenly into horror mode, and his voice takes on that special terrible twang. His cucumber-monster complete, Price concludes this little sequence by declaring 'it may not be to everybody's

Carving knife clowning: horror-meister Vincent Price scoops a huge lump of cheese from a simmering psychedelic saucepan amidst fine formica for the cover of the *Cooking Price-Wise* tie-in paperback.

taste, but I can assure you that the creation of monsters is certainly very lucrative.'

It surely was, but *Cooking Price-Wise*, a six-part series cheaply cranked out on unforgivingly garish videotape in the early seventies for British television, surely was not. This must have been a labour of love for Vincent, whose enthusiasm for all things culinary was well-known in Hollywood, if not to the British cinema going public at the time – or now, in fact. And though Price gamely clowned around with a carving knife for some promo photos that accompanied this outstandingly odd and bizarrely brilliant series, he almost entirely resisted the impulse he may have had to ham it up for the cameras (if you'll forgive the expression).

Instead of lunging at viewers with something sharp, Vincent instead wielded rice, bacon, cheese and potatoes – or, as Vincent insisted on pronouncing it, 'the poe-tato'. Let's assume he did that in tribute to the popular series of AIP horrors he made for Roger Corman. He revealed his love of British cuisine – unexpectedly enough – in a 1971 interview for the *TV Times*. 'My special delight is British cookery. I think it's very hard to do well. Take a steak and kidney pudding – it's so difficult to get it absolutely delicious. We don't eat suet in America, simply because it's the national pastime to worry about obesity.' Wise words, Mr P; though his subsequent claim that you'd never get indigestion from British foods may be going just a little beyond the pale.

Cooking Price-Wise was broadcast on Thames Television in London, as well as regionally, in 1971. It's hard to imagine earlier Kings of Horror doing a show like this – though it would have been fascinating indeed to see Lugosi in a striped apron, or Karloff buttering a baking tray – but the rationale becomes clearer when you remember that Price was a great gourmand, and a keen cook. He produced more than one cookery book with his wife Mary – including *The Treasury of Great Recipes*, a hefty, leather-bound tome filled with the couple's favourite dishes, interspersed with a selection of splendid wide-focus photos of the pair enjoying themselves supping cocktails, cooking and entertaining in their lavish home.

Cooking Price-Wise, though, does not look lavish. One suspects that Mr Price was over here to make a movie, and on a couple of days off, took rather less than his usual fee for making it. It appears to be a peculiarly personal labour of love, and whether you like cooking or not, it is well overdue for revival.

A bewildering theme-music tattoo of bongo drums – apropos of nothing in particular, but pretty damned funky – and a couple of quickly knocked up pop-art title cards usher us in to Vincent's kitchen, or rather an imaginary knocked-up-in-the-studio vision of that of the ordinary 1971 English housewife. This is certainly no kitchen that Vincent Price ever used, that's for sure. He probably had broom cupboards that were bigger. But it is stocked with the latest in Day-Glo psychedelic kitchen equipment, pans covered in loud, lurid floral patterns, and the wall behind boasts a poster about preserves so groovy that it looks more like a one-sheet for a Hendrix concert.

Vincent himself is no less splendid, greeting us each episode in his blue striped apron, flamboyantly clad in a rotation of ornately cuff-linked polyester western-wear shirts, and a selection of stylish neckerchiefs. These – perhaps significantly, style fans – are always worn above the apron.

Over the course of six superb episodes, each beginning with the cordial greeting 'hello, I'm Vincent Price', the great man invited British housewives to accompany him on a culinary trip around the world, using 'your cooker instead of a jet plane'. It wasn't about Vincent's beloved British cookery, though; all the dishes were rather more exotic than that. What, foreign muck? This was quite something back then. Things like yoghurts were only for hard-line health freaks; bottled water, and most fresh vegetables – certainly green ones, and not in a tin – had still to be invented.

Just look towards other celebrity chefs of the time and look for a moment towards Richard O'Sullivan's cookbook, produced to cash-in on the success of the fab television comedy *Man About the House*. This useful volume, *Man About the Kitchen*, featured little of an exotic bent, and certainly nothing his on screen cookery-student counterpart, Robin Tripp, would be at all pleased with. On the cover, O'Sullivan can be seen grinning grubbily out of a gloomy kitchen, beaming from behind a grimy-grey industrial size saucepan (the kind in which we used to boil up our socks) and, inside, recipes teach you how to live well on baked beans and Smash.

So, Vincent's show was something of a delightfully cosmopolitan departure. But because the programme was made in the 1970s, and it is well-known that no food was bad for you in those days, each and every exotic dish seems to be drowned in butter (or 'greaze', as Vincent puts

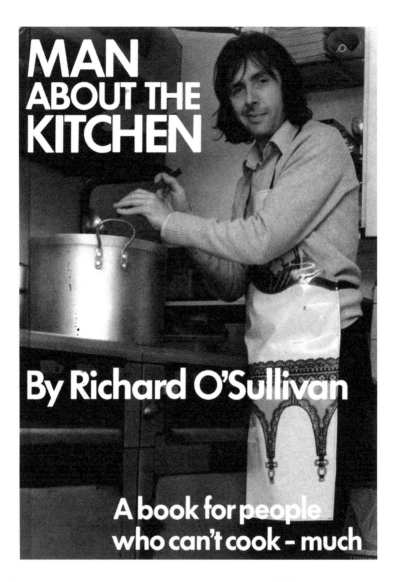

MAN ABOUT THE KITCHEN

By Richard O'Sullivan

A book for people who can't cook - much

Robin's nest: *Man About the House* (1973-1976) star Richard O'Sullivan – wearing the best apron in the world – is either cooking an industrial quantity of Smash or boiling up his socks and pants on the cover of his 1970s cash-in cookbook.

it so wonderfully), or cream, or swamped in oil, lard, or covered in sugar or bits of bacon. Or both at once, maybe – Vincent would surely have approved. As noted, each episode has a theme: cheese, bacon, lamb, potatoes, rice and cream. Nowadays, the recipes would come with a government health warning.

Each episode also seems to have been shot live, with Vincent shifting deftly from chopping board, to blender, to cooker and back again, periodically presenting us with previously prepared dishes 'thanks to the wonders of modern television'. As he cooks, he drops in anecdotes about the history of some of the ingredients he's using. The first episode, which focuses on the poe-tato, is filled with essential information about everybody's favourite root-vegetable, abetted by the insertion of cartoony illustrations of great moments from the potato's past. However, this educational stuff disappears entirely as the series progresses, perhaps to allow Mr Price a little more time to actually cook (the whole first episode seems like rather a rush).

How can it be that Vincent made this show for humble British TV? Whichever bizarre accident brought it about, it's great that it did. Vincent is an exceptionally genial, welcoming host. You may have absolutely no interest whatsoever in cookery; no matter. It remains a very real pleasure, to be a guest of the great man. Just don't expect tales of his horror film career. Instead, we are regaled with titbits about his trips abroad with the wife, and fragmentary glimpses of their lifestyle dynamics. 'I'm a messy cooker, but my wife never minds,' grins Vincent as he busily bungs ingredients about; 'she makes me clean up afterwards.'

It may be that the viewer does not quite believe that Vincent has travelled quite as far and wide around the globe to collect his recipes as he might attest – especially when he confesses how much he enjoys the version of one exotic dish as prepared at 'the restaurant at the airport in Los Angeles, California' – but his fierce enthusiasm and enjoyment of all things foody is undeniably obvious.

And to be honest, this is about as intimate as the public ever got with a king of screen horror. As the all-too-short-series progresses, we start to glimpse the Vincent Price nobody ever saw in the movies. Vincent has a little verbal tic, for example, a habit of going 'hmm?' at intermittent moments; which he attempts to hide at first, but, rather endearingly, can't entirely disguise, and he does it every episode. We hear much about his predilection for garlic – 'I happen to love garlic' – he says over and over, and don't forget, horror fans, he didn't ever play a vampire until *The Monster Club* in 1981. We learn too of his preference for white pepper over black pepper and, most fascinating of all, the reason for it. The makers of the programme, he says, have provided him with black pepper, but he doesn't like the sight of the black specks, 'which are unsightly, of course.' Certain standards *must* be maintained.

Incidentally, Vincent ad-libs in a delightfully ornate manner, often throwing himself into confusion in the process, and, pressed for time, tries to do too much at once. He has a jolly set of quirks. Often, about halfway through an episode, he'll gaspingly seem to run out of steam somewhat. At the outset of each episode, he offers to remind us later on of all the ingredients for his dishes, but he doesn't seem to like doing it very much. Pointing out all the bits and pieces with his wooden spoon, he gets rather confused with the details. What's more, he sometimes has a good hearty cough over whatever it is he's making (no problem if it's dinner for one, but surely not so good if he's rustling up supper for the wife).

What is clear though, is that Vincent really does want to expand the horizons of British cooks – to demonstrate that it really isn't that hard to make some more unusual dishes. All it is, he tells us with a smirk in an episode centred around cheese, is 'cutting, beating, measuring and cooking…and a lot of luck.' Such good sense is, though, also interspersed with crackpot stuff. In the same episode, Vincent makes a chess-set out of cheese, and describes the salad he's produced as 'so good you could almost wear it'. Deciding where the good advice stops and the madness begins is all part of the fun.

We also discover that Vincent, like so many great chefs, enjoys a drink. When he adds booze to a dish, he really adds it. What he describes as a teaspoonful is usually a glassful; and when he adds the brandy to his Irish coffee, he seems to have the measures reversed – it seems to be three-parts brandy to one-part coffee.

'Good eating', says Vincent, as he sits down at the end of the first episode to tuck into some vegetable soup he's made, slightly suspect in that he made it with chicken stock. Perhaps he was planning to say 'good eating' at the end of every edition; but by the next one, he seems to have forgotten in his rush to get through all the recipes in time.

Six episodes is all we got, and one wonders why. Probably, Vincent was back over to the States (stopping off at the restaurant in LA for an exotic dish of some sort) and there was never to be another series. But there was a tie-in cookbook, produced by Corgi and Thames Television. Harder to find than a restaurant serving Vincent's crocodile-monsters, copies of this tasty curio now cost a bundle.

There's no other cookery show to touch *Cooking Price-Wise*. The abundance of cream, sugar, salt and butter may disconcert you; the almost absolute absence of green vegetables may disturb you; and some of the dishes may provoke an attack of the horrors in those of a nervously health-conscious 21st century disposition; but even if you don't want to eat his dishes, it sure is great to be able to sit around in Vincent's kitchen and chew the fat with the great man for a while. *VP*

As we've mentioned already, and as Vincent would doubtless remind you over a generously-loaded Irish Coffee, by the end of the 1970s, the old Dracula bit was strictly Scooby Doo stuff and not to be taken too seriously. Or was it? Let's ask some school kids...

Vampires

UK TV | Transmitted 09/01/1979 | colour | 50mins
Director John Goldschmidt
Script Dixie Williams
Producer Tara Prem
Production Company BBC
Cast Peter Moran, Paul Moran, Tommy White, Linda Beckett

The Dracula Business

UK TV | Transmitted 06/08/1974 | colour | 49mins
Script Daniel Farson
Producer Anthony De Lotbinière
Production Company BBC
Cast Daniel Farson

Once upon a time, an untried writer could simply send in a script to the BBC and, if it was good enough, it would get made into a television drama. Dixie Williams' script for *Vampires*, which became a 1979 entry in the BBC's long-running *Play for Today* strand, was just such a phenomenon: an unsolicited submission from an unknown writer. 'These days, it would never get made. A script wouldn't be read unless it came to you through an agent,' Peter Ansorge, the script editor who commissioned the drama, told us.

And it was made at a time when a television drama could be made without a familiar face in the lead role. Shot on the streets of Liverpool, *Vampires* had two untrained children as its stars. Paul and Peter Moran had no ambitions to become actors; they were signed up by director John Goldschmidt when he spotted them in a Liverpool school. Their unconventional audition sounds like every schoolboy's dream. 'We had to do Frankenstein walks, Dracula noises and werewolf howls,' Peter told the *Radio Times* in January 1979, when the play was transmitted.

Peter and Paul play Liverpool schoolboy horror film fans Stu and Davey, seen watching the Hammer horror *Dracula: Prince of Darkness* (1966) on telly with their mate Dingo at the beginning of this bittersweet, autumn-hued play, while their widowed mum goes out to the pub with another new boyfriend. All three kids give terrific performances throughout – there's a real dynamic chemistry between them. As The Count is reconstituted before their very eyes in his coffin, on the flickery old telly, the intensely registered, lip-chewing reaction shots of the boys – the sight of their faces reflected in the screen as they watch transfixed – will strike a chord with all those who remember naughtily staying up too late to watch a film they shouldn't really be watching. We soon discover that Stu – who regularly bunks off school to prowl around the town in a fantasy world of cinematic horror, wearing a pair of plastic fangs, and top-buttoning his parka so it becomes a cape – is convinced that a vampire haunts the local cemetery. The boys attempt to track him down with the help of their school friends in what ultimately coalesces into a quietly melancholy and oddly affecting drama.

What makes it really special is the beautifully but economically drawn character studies of the boys and the people around them, all seemingly perceived through the eyes of the boys themselves. The kids are all brilliant, excitedly engaging with youthful fantasy, but already beginning to realise and accept the adult world of disappointment beyond. They learn about

Gothic daydreams: Stu and Davey (Peter and Paul Moran) face up to grave realities in *Vampires* (1979).

this from Peter's mum, as she struggles from one unsuitable new fella to the next, disconsolately serving up the Ready Brek on an endless succession of dismal grey mornings, doling out the dinner money and puffing on endless ciggies.

While the drama centres on the secret world of the boys' experience, they're surrounded by equally fascinating adult characters, perhaps slightly less rounded and more influenced by kitchen-sink stereotype, but all economically and entertainingly sketched in with some memorable – if sometimes enigmatic – scraps of downbeat dialogue. There's Mum's latest dodgy boyfriend – hopefully tripping up the stairs half-cut, asking that most romantic of questions, 'I bought you a bottle of Guinness – what more do you want?' There's the nicer-seeming ex-boyfriend, bequiffed 'Uncle' Georgie (a pre-*Hi-de-Hi* Paul Shane), who works down the local chippie, all tired wisecracks, sideburns, grease-spattered green cardi and string vest, who has to remind Stu 'I'm not your Uncle anymore, Stu. We're buddies now. I'm an ex-uncle,' before flipping him a 50p to spend in the joke shop.

And what a joke shop it is, miraculously hidden somewhere off a cobbled-corner of a dingy back street. The Wizards' Den is the kind of strange emporium childhood dreams were made of, crammed full of horrific rubber heads, fading Houdini posters, creepy masks, and skeletons dangling everywhere. It all looks grubby and lived-in enough to be real. As does its proprietor. Lurking amidst the clutter is a rubber-faced joke shop man – a practitioner of gurning no less, just like everybody's granddad used to do – who plays magic tricks with Stu's 50p before telling him the history of vampires.

It's all shot on location, and on film. So there's not a studio set, or a dodgy reality-check cut between too-bright video and 16mm, to be seen. Hence the joke shop looks like a real joke shop, and the viewer gets the full flavour of the cramped terraced houses, with the peeling paint, and really feels the freedom when Stu escapes onto the cobbled streets, or naughtily vaults the cemetery walls to dash between the gravestones in his own private dream world.

Of course, wherever fantasies are used to obscure hard-to-swallow realities, there is an underlying sense of sadness. Writer Dixie Williams seems to know all about dreams dashed and eroded by age. Nobody here –

except perhaps the enigmatic joke shop man, a fellow fantasist with whom Stu can perhaps relate – seems particularly fulfilled by their lives. Meanwhile, death strikes suddenly and randomly, as Stu's school teacher suffers a heart attack halfway through school assembly. Luckily, Stu can build her death into his Gothic daydreams: if she has been bitten by a vampire, as he decides she has, there is, at least, some kind of rationale behind her demise. A rationale that once, perhaps, was offered by religious belief.

The play was one of a scant handful of writing credits for Williams – a talented but troubled character, Goldschmidt told us – who died young. Gifted with a knack for dialogue, the barbed thrusts of Williams' sharp-as-a knife script emphasise the futility of it all, cauterising the wounds caused with soothing swabs of dry, cynical humour.

It's all written from Stu's point of view. We share his bewilderment at the strange behaviour of adults, and see that they are pursuing fantasies – love perhaps, religious belief, perhaps – no less absurd than his own; but made socially acceptable purely through the passing of the years. As we see a visiting priest sermonising to the kids at Stu's school – 'You all know, I'm sure, that there's a battle going on between God and the Devil,' he says attempting to sound portentous, clutching the lectern. A vaguely absurd figure, he gazes out ominously from beneath beetling brows – doing his best to instil the fear of god into the increasingly disinterested youths forced to listen to him. Is it any wonder that Stu hounds the 'vampire' of the local cemetery, ultimately confronting him with 'You're a vampire!' while all the other kids make crucifixes with their fingers? The religion they have been schooled in is surely no less theatrical and absurd, Williams seems to be suggesting, than that served up by the Hammer horrors.

By the time of *Vampires*, we have noted elsewhere, the heyday of the Hammer horrors was well and truly over. Dracula was old hat. Not seriously considered threatening any longer, it had become an escapist fantasy for unruly schoolboys. It would be a while yet before *Buffy*, and later *Twilight*, would seriously rekindle interest in things vampiric.

Dracula had, though, spawned a worldwide commercial operation, as was reflected in another BBC programme, *The Dracula Business*, made just a few years before *Vampires*, in 1975. This documentary, fronted by the aforementioned investigative journalist Dan Farson (the great nephew of Bram Stoker, no less), demonstrated that though perhaps Dracula had run

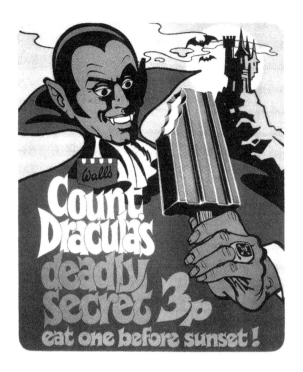

Eat one before sunset: a long nailed Dracula gets stuck into his lolly – only 3p!

out of cinematic steam, the universal importance of the vampire mythos remained. Kids knew all about it: one sequence in the programme shows youngsters enthusiastically enjoying an ice-lolly named Dracula's Secret, which the adverts proclaimed, was 'now deadlier than ever with blood red jelly'. But for adults too, vampires – though not necessarily scary – were still very important, as Farson discovers. We are treated to dinner with the Dracula Society – where gaunt faced intellectuals and eccentrics, some wearing strange amulets, wave their cigarettes at each other while swigging port and discussing vampires with gleam-eyed gusto.

In another sequence, one mild-looking woman, interviewed by Farson in a science fiction and fantasy bookshop, reveals her enthusiastic relish for the bloody violence of vampire fiction. 'My husband left me and I couldn't do anything about it,' she admits cheerfully, but with a strange

Tuesday tv

Dracula Tour

A ruined castle, a flutter of wings in the night. This is the (50p-a-time) world of the undead: 9.25

Fantasy violence: Dracula Tours, 50p-a-time, as seen on TV.

glint in her eye. 'As I couldn't do anything to him, I took up fantasy violence instead. I couldn't do anything to him – in the way of attacking him or hurting him in any way – because I'd end up in prison, obviously; so it's much safer to do it this way, by fantasy. My sympathy is with Dracula, not the victim.'

As Farson solemnly follows stern-faced tourists on their Dracula Package Tours, one wonders if the line between fiction and fantasy is blurred for them. At least the would-be violent vampire-supporting spurned-wife seems self-aware of her obsession. But interviews with churchmen lead the programme towards more serious territory. The priests seen here certainly profess a belief in vampirism, and still extol the values of exorcism, throwing the previously mentioned rhetoric of the priest of *Vampires* into intriguing relief. Perhaps, here then, really was a cinematically-inspired hook with which to catch an increasingly secular and disinterested public. Certainly, one senses, the public needed *something* to believe in.

As Farson concludes, 'there is this ache for something better and less artificial, a return to more spiritual values, a less soulless way of life, even if it means the occult.' With all this in mind, Perhaps Stu and his friends' unswerving belief in vampires wasn't as fantastic, or at least not so foolish, as his teachers seemed to think. *VP*

And lo, there was home video; and the punters said it was good. It brought new kinds of horror...for viewers, for the cinema managers, and for the government. And an English filmmaker we've met many times already in these pages nipped abroad to shoot some lurid links for his naughty – but ultimately still distinctly British – video nasty...

Screamtime

UK Film | 1985 | colour | 89mins
Director Al Beresford
Script Michael Armstrong
Producer Al Beresford
Production Company Manson International
Cast Robin Bailey, Ann Lynn, Jonathon Morris, David Van Day

The video rental shops are gone. Everybody streams now. But when home video first affordably arrived around 1980, by the cringe, it was incredibly exciting. The very idea that you could watch a film of your choice on your own TV whenever you wanted to was a revelation. But even affordable home video was an expensive business. Just buying a blank tape was something many households had to save up for. And as for actually owning pre-recorded tapes, that was virtually unheard of, unless you were of the upper classes. Hence you had to rent tapes from video rental shops, of which there were very many, precisely because the tapes were so darned expensive. And when you did rent out a film, in those early days, you had to leave a hefty deposit.

But for a brief period at the beginning of that decade – an era soon to become associated with the idea of the 'Video Nasty' – you could get away with showing anything you liked on a video. Sod the cinema. You'd rent your VHS player from Radio Rentals, borrow a couple of video tapes for the weekend, and away you went. No restrictions. Every entrepreneur raced to release any film they could – the gorier and sexier the better – to a hungry market of viewers, many eager to be shocked, excited and/or aroused by material as yet unsullied and uncertificated by the dictates of the government censors, still getting their legislative act in gear.

Screamtime was a video specifically released to capitalise on this demand. It was 'The newest thing in nightmares!', according to the tagline on the lurid cover, which depicted a cartoon skeleton threatening a large-chested woman with a knife, already dripping blood. As was absolutely de rigueur in those days, the back cover boasted a selection of photographs from the film, showing some of the most sordidly violent scenes from the movie. As was also de rigueur in those days, the cover was somewhat misleading: though designed to look like a sleazy American production (the American ones, we all knew, were always the scariest and the most horrid), the newest thing in nightmares was in fact anything but. It was actually a late entry in a long and distinguished line of British portmanteau horror films, harking back both to the glory days of creepy portmanteau specialists Amicus, and to *Dead of Night* (1945), the Ealing portmanteau that had helped start the whole subgenre back in the 1940s.

The newest thing about it, in fact, was that it was a video-only release, specifically crafted for home viewing. But its roots, not that you would have known it, lay in the British cinema, and it was the brainchild of two British exploitation veterans, who we have met before in these pages. It was co-directed with tongues firmly in cheek by Stanley Long, the man behind *Primitive London* (1965) and, later, the *Adventures* series; and Michael Armstrong, writer and director of *Mark of the Devil* (1970), grisliest and most gruesome of all the *Witchfinder General* (1968) rip-offs, whose involvement – and unflinching readiness to include gorier material – seems particularly apparent in the second and most sinister of the stories.

To create the illusion of a sleazy flick from across the water (all the average punter had to go by in those days was the packaging – once you got it home from the rental shop you had to watch it, regardless of whether it was any good or not, that was that), they adopted the American-sounding pseudonym of Al Beresford, covering the sleeve with blood, to conceal the relatively innocent old-school horror theatrics within. In his biography, Long described the name as 'a tribute to my mother's side of the family… it was a new name for a new start.' After years of trouble with the BBFC, it

SCREAMTIME

Ed is a horror video freak — he doesn't even notice his girlfriend enjoying his best-friend as he settles down to watch his latest:
A revengeful Mr Punch doll who comes alive with psychotic intensity.

Corpses with no intention of staying buried and lots of very nasty Gnomes.

But Ed's real terror begins when our little fiends refuse to be switched off at the end of the film!!!

The newest thing in nightmares!

Running time 91 mins. approx.

MEDUSA

MEDUSA

18 Suitable only for persons of 18 years and over

Not to be supplied to any person below that age

Don't believe the rumours about all the dead bodies...
they're the ▪ people who fainted watching!

SCREAMTIME
The newest thing in nightmares!

...ng JEAN ANDERSON, ROBIN BAILEY, DORA BRYAN, ANN LYNN
...YVONNE NICHOLSON, IAN SAYNOR AND DAVID VAN DAY.
...rectors of Photography: DON LORD, ALAN PUDNEY, MIKE SPERA
Screenplay by MICHAEL ARMSTRONG
Produced and Directed by AL BERESFORD

A. MANSON INTERNATIONAL PRESENTATION

« **The newest thing in nightmares:** Blood, naked ladies, nasty gnomes, and a 'revengeful Mr Punch doll' on the VHS sleeve for *Screamtime* (1985).

was no wonder that it was time for a change. Perhaps the pseudonym also reflected a lingering reluctance on Long's part to be associated with the horror genre: 'It was the goriest thing I've ever made, but I was bowing to commercial pressure, if you like.'

The bulk of the package comprised three short films, released a couple of years earlier to British cinemas to provide support to the main feature, another practice that has gone the way of the VHS tape. Stretched out just long enough to qualify for the Eady Levy – government film funding incentives eventually dismantled a few years later by the Thatcher administration – the three films originally played as second features to American horror films. To create *Screamtime*, they were trimmed down a bit and tenuously connected by a newly-shot linking story.

Ominous music leads us into the first part of this linking sequence. Speedily shot in the US of A by Stanley Long and his brother Peter over three days and designed to provide the package with some international appeal, it begins with a smoky vista of New York, where we see two shifty looking young men emerging from a subway to enter a video shop. It all seems authentically Transatlantic – until the young men steal some video tapes and dash out of the store. Suddenly there is the sense that this is a British production. These, their behaviour soon confirms, are juvenile delinquents as seen through British eyes. Cheerfully dumb rather than sinister, it all quickly becomes more reminiscent of *Grange Hill* (1978-2008) than *Last House on the Left* (1972). Shots of an attractive girl in a shower soon follow: this is territory that we know by now that Stanley Long is more comfortable with. After some cheerfully gratuitous nudity, the two young hooligans arrive at the girl's apartment to watch movies – on a top-loading VHS player, that's built like an audio-tape deck, just like the ones we had from Radio Rentals. Though they speak with a nasal US twang, these kids still somehow seem like they might live somewhere in suburban Slough.

Close up on the television screen for the first of the three main stories: *That's the Way to Do It*. Clearly inspired by the ventriloquist's dummy sequence in the aforementioned *Dead of Night*, this spin on an old classic is a chirpy portrait of a misunderstood Punch and Judy man driven to madness by his juvenile delinquent son. We are back in reassuringly British surroundings: a windswept Brighton seafront, where a Punch and Judy Show is in progress (do they even have Punch and Judy in America?) Having begun his career shooting documentary for the military, Long always delivered on reportage-style footage. This was no exception. Everything looks cold, grey and desolate; you can almost smell the cold chips rotting on the promenade.

We meet emasculated Punch and Judy man Jack Grimshaw. Clad in sensible tanktop and more interested in painting his puppets than in spending time with his attractive wife (an uncharacteristically shrewish Ann Lynn), he surely can't maintain his authority over her boy, his stepson, Damien (played by an intriguingly cast Jonathon Morris, later to appear in the sitcom *Bread* (1986-91)). He's so bad. Naughtily fashioning a smiley face from his bangers and mash, and refusing to eat any peas, Damien, having brought his girlfriend to tea, humiliates his old man. 'My real dad used to race motor cars instead of playing with dolls,' he smirks. It's all so British, right down to the HP and tomato sauce on offer, and the garden peas in a nice china dish. Later, things escalate, with Damien and his gang knocking over a dustbin – we're in *Grange Hill* territory again, though these kids say 'fuck' instead of 'flip' – but there is a moment of genuine poignancy when he burns his stepdad's Punch and Judy tent down, mostly thanks to a believable portrayal by Robin Bailey, playing the impotent puppeteer who seems to get it in the neck from everybody. Luckily, Damien gets it in the neck himself later on, when he's attacked on the beach while a dog barks at his assailant, in a nice bit of hand-held camera work by Long, before things escalate for an enjoyably grisly conclusion.

Which we don't see: just at the final moment, the action cuts away, back to the linking story – where we see Ed squirming away, in a very old-fashioned way, apparently revolted by the shockingly gory horror on screen. 'They're British movies…I can tell by the way they talk!' he tells his friends.

The next story is *Dream House*: a genuinely chilling tale of premonition with the grubby authenticity of a Pete Walker movie. It begins something like an episode of *Tales of the Unexpected* (1979-88), and a limited budget is apparent: this tale of a new couple arriving home to find horror after their honeymoon is entirely shot around an undecorated suburban house. But it works. As new wife Susan grows ever more frightened by strange visions of murder about the premises, the claustrophobia of the setting is unexpectedly effective, and it's all tied up tightly in a neat twist ending. Best of all is an uncredited, gangly, bald-headed actor whose matter-of-fact performance as the murderer of Susan's hallucinations is chillingly plausible. Indeed, the film was shot at a house owned by one of the production company's staff; apparently he would not allow his wife to see the finished film for fear that it would deter her from moving in. Influenced by Hitchcock's *Psycho* (1960) and Spielberg's *Jaws* (1975), Long was keen to make cinema audiences jump – and manages it here more than once. 'I saw it happen when I went to various theatres where the movie was playing,' he wrote in his autobiography, 'That gave me quite a buzz, I can tell you.'

There is an intriguing part for Veronica Doran, cast here as a psychic, who, apparently an enthusiastic believer in the occult, comes to exorcise the house, for a fee – yet, in a moment of very Pete Walker-esque cynicism, she reveals her true sceptic colours, quietly suggesting afterwards to the unhappy woman's husband that it might be advisable that she should be encouraged to see a psychiatrist.

We return to the linking story to find Ed has sent his buddy Bruce away for cigarettes; Bruce, meanwhile, is ensconced in bed with Marie. Ed, continuing his interior monologue on the effects of video horror, mutters 'I'm not scared…I know they're actors in stories.'

This is arguably not entirely the case in the most bizarre of the three tales, *Do You Believe in Fairies?* For leading man David Van Day was not an actor. But he was popular in the musical duo, Dollar, and plays Gav, working in a gentleman's outfitters, resplendent in v-neck Pringle jumper. He's in need of money for his motocross habit (there's another good bit of documentary footage, of a motocross meet, at the beginning of this one, too). The problem is bikes are expensive. 'That's gonna cost a packet!' his shifty friend proclaims. So Gav takes a gardening job at the house of two strange old ladies – veteran actresses Jean Anderson and Dora Bryan, both of whom play their dotty-old-bint parts with a twinkle. An eccentric array of garden gnomes frame their doorway. Later they come to life, to guard the old ladies when Gav and his friends attempt a robbery – or at least, perhaps for budgetary reasons, one of them does: a giant one, looking suspiciously like a little fellow in a pointy red hat. Later, as the action grows stranger still, a young girl in an old painting comes to life to attack the hapless Gav with knives – after snogging him first. A nice little in-joke sees Mary Whitehouse – long-time nemesis of Stanley Long – mentioned on a radio broadcast.

If this third tale is perhaps the weakest, there is a rip-roaring conclusion still to come, as a hand emerges from the television screen to strangle Ed; meanwhile, in the bedroom, Mr Punch appears with his wooden club to club the lovers. As the camera pulls out to reveal the New York skyline once again, we hear Mr Punch singing to himself. The ending provides an intriguing alternative to the prevailing view of the day, that films influenced youths to commit crime. Instead, here, the film commits the crime itself, in an extreme form of vigilante VHS justice.

Originally released on video only in the UK, the film did, apparently, get a regional cinema release in the USA, in February 1985. 'Picture was released regionally commencing February 1985, subsequently available in the home video market,' according to *Variety*, July 9 1986. *Variety* went on to bemoan the fact that it was shot 'on the cheap' and that 'some excellent thesps…are wasted in nothing roles'; but *Screamtime* is consistently better than it ought to be or needed to be, and despite any budgetary limitations, or the cut and paste way it was put together, is a dignified late addition to the British horror portmanteau sub-genre. All the ingredients are there: ludicrous stories in the horror comic vein; stars of yesteryear doing a hammy turn late in their careers; pop stars who can't act getting a brief chance at a starring role. It's all wrapped up in a suitably ludicrous linking story, which, in its efforts to be contemporary and American, seems most dated of all, and just serves to emphasise how very British and very traditional the main part of the content actually is, don't you know.

Long was never that comfortable with horror – he preferred to make his cheeky sex comedies – and that is occasionally apparent in *Screamtime*. 'Blood, entrails and screaming women were now the "in" thing, but they certainly weren't my cup of tea,' he wrote in his autobiography. But this was a distinguished excursion into unusual territory, managing to be by turns both chilling and ludicrous; and was a distinguished end also to Long's career as a filmmaker. And now, as we put down our shovels, and lay the Bodies Beneath to rest once more, we bid our old catalytic chum Stanley a fond farewell. *VP*

References

Books and articles

Bardsley, Garth. *Stop the World: The Biography of Anthony Newley*. Oberon Books, 2003.

Barnouw, Erik. *The Magician and the Cinema*. Oxford University Press, 1981.

Barron, Steve. *Egg n Chips & Billie Jean: A Trip through the Eighties*. CreateSpace Independent Publishing, 2014.

Blackman, Inge. *"Our Forefathers – The Pioneers of Black British Filmmaking"*, Black Filmmaker v5, n20 (Summer 2003).

Booth, Rupert. *Not a Number: Patrick McGoohan – A Life*. Supernova Books, 2011.

Brown, Richard, and Barry Anthony. *A Victorian Film Enterprise: The History of the British Mutoscope and Biograph Company 1897-1915*. Flicks Books, 1999.

Brownlow, Kevin. *How It Happened Here*. Doubleday, 1968.

Burroughs, William. *Nova Express*. Grove Press, 1964.

Burroughs, William. *Naked Lunch*. Olympia Press, 1959.

Carter, Steven. *"Avatars of the turtles"*, Journal of Popular Film and Television, v18 n3 (Autumn 1990).

Clébert, Jean-Paul. *The Blockhouse*. Secker and Warburg, 1957.

Dacre, Richard. *Trouble in Store: Norman Wisdom, A Career in Comedy*. T. C. Farries & Co., 1991.

Debord, Guy. *The Society of the Spectacle*. Black and Red, 1970.

Dello Stritto, Frank J. and Andi Brooks. *Vampire over London*. Cult Movies Press, 2000.

Dello Stritto, Frank J., and Andi Brooks. *"Dracula's Last Hurrah – Part 3"*, Cult Movies Magazine, n35 (Autumn 2001).

Duke, Jas H., *"Cutting With a Keen Edge"*, Cantrills Film Notes, Issue 23/24, 1976.

Fansler Behrman, Cynthia. *Victorian Myths of the Sea*. Ohio University Press, 1977.

Farson, Daniel. *Never a Normal Man: An Autobiography*. Harper Collins, 1997.

Field, Mary, and Percy Smith. *Secrets of Nature*. Scientific Book Club, 1939.

Fleming, John. *"Kinvig Preview"*, Starburst, n35 (July 1981).

Ford, Derek, and Alex Sanders. *Secret Rites.* Gadoline, 1972.

Frazer, James. *The Golden Bough.* Macmillan & Co., 1890.

Gardner, Gerald. *Witchcraft Today.* Rider & Co., 1954.

Genet, Jean. *The Miracle of the Rose.* Grove Press, 1966.

Gifford, Denis. *British Film Catalogue Vol. 2: Non-Fiction 1888 – 1994.* Fitzroy Dearborn Publishers, 2000.

Hamilton, John. *Beasts in the Cellar: The Exploitation Film Career of Tony Tenser.* FAB Press, 2005.

Hutton, Ronald. *Triumph of the Moon: A History of Modern Pagan Witchcraft.* Oxford University Press, 2001.

Johns, June. *King of the Witches: The World of Alex Sanders.* Pan Books, 1969.

Kenny, Robert V. *The Man who was Old Mother Riley.* Bear Manor Media, 2014.

Kneale, Nigel. *Tomato Cain and Other Stories.* Collins, 1949.

Lawrence, D. H. *Lady Chatterley's Lover.* Penguin Books, 1960.

Lewis, Roger. *The Life and Death of Peter Sellers.* Century, 1994.

Long, Stanley, with Simon Sheridan. *X-Rated: Adventures of an Exploitation Filmmaker.* Reynolds & Hearn, 2008.

Lynn, Frances. '*Steve Barron's Electric Dreams*", Starburst. n77 (January 1985).

Marcuse, Herbert. *One Dimensional Man.* Beacon Press, 1964.

McDonough, Jimmy. *The Ghastly One: The Sex-Gore Netherworld of Filmmaker Andy Milligan.* A Cappella Books, 2003.

McGillivray, David. *Doing Rude Things: The History of the British Sex Film 1957-81.* Sun Tavern Fields, 1992.

Morris, Marc, and Nigel Wingrove. *The Art of the Nasty.* Redemption, 1998.

Murray, Andy. "*Kinvig - Mercury Rising: A Series Overview*", *Kinvig* DVD booklet. Network, 2006.

Musser, Charles. *The Emergence of Cinema: The American Screen to 1907.* Charles Scribner's Sons, 1990.

Paskin, Sylvia. *"A Picasso For every season*", The Monthly Film Bulletin. British Film Institute, v53, n631 (August 1986).

Pixley, Andrew. "*Danger Man: The Battle of the Cameras – A Complete Production Guide*", *Danger Man: The Complete 1964-1968 Series* DVD book. Network, 2008.

Rayns, Tony. *"An Interview with Antony Balch*", Cinema Rising n1, April 1972.

Reekie, Duncan. *Subversion: The Definitive History of Underground Cinema.* Wallflower, 2007.

Rhodes, Gary Don. *Lugosi.* McFarland, 1997.

Rogan, Johnny. *Ray Davies: A Complicated Life.* Bodley Head, 2015.

Rogan, Johnny. *The Kinks.* Elm Tree Books, 1984.

Sadowski, Greg & John Benson, eds. *Four Color Fear: Forgotten Horror Comics of the 1950s.* Fantagraphics, 2010.

Savage, Jon. *1966: The Year the Decade Exploded.* Faber & Faber, 2015.

Sheridan, Simon. *Keeping the British End Up: Four Decades of Saucy Cinema.* Titan Books, 2001, revised 2011.

Starr, Michael. *Peter Sellers: A Film History.* McFarland, 1991.

Stoneman, Rod, and Hilary Thompson, eds. *British Film Institute Productions 1979-80.* British Film Institute, 1981.

Svehla, Gary J., and Susan Svehla, eds. *Bela Lugosi: Midnight Marquee Actors Series.* Midnight Marquee Press, 2008.

Szwed, John. *The Man who Recorded the World: A Biography of Alan Lomax.* Arrow, 2011.

Thompson, Harry. *Tintin: Hergé and his Creation.* Hodder and Stoughton, 1991.

Thompson, Kenneth. *"Secret Rites"*, The Monthly Film Bulletin. British Film Institute, v39, n458 (March 1972).

Tibballs, Geoff. *The Secret Life of Sooty.* Interpet Publishing, 1990.

Tulloch, John, and Manuel Alvorado. *Doctor Who: The Unfolding Text.* St Martin's Press, 1984.

Vick, Rebecca. "Savage Voyages: Eric Marquis", In *Shadows of Progress: Documentary Film in Post-War Britain,* edited by Patrick Russell and James Taylor. British Film Institute, 2010.

Wakelin, Michael. *The Man Behind the Gong: J. Arthur Rank.* Lion Publishing, 1996.

Walker, John A. *Left Shift: Radical Art in 1970s Britain.* I. B. Tauris, 2001.

Walker, John A. *Arts TV: A History of British Arts Television.* University of Luton Press, 1993.

Wisdom, Norman, with William Hall. *Don't Laugh at Me: An Autobiography.* Century, 1992.

Websites

Danger-man.co.uk written and maintained by Matthew Courtman
Transdiffusion.com and 'Daniel Farson' by Robin Carmody
Jeffkeen.co.uk and 'The Secret World of Dr Gaz - "a comic strip of life" An appreciation of Jeff Keen by his daughter Stella Keen'

Index

All italicised entries are films
unless otherwise stated.

398 *The Bodies Beneath*

STRANGE ATTRACTOR PRESS 2019